GALLIPOLI:
THE MEDICAL WAR

THE AUSTRALIAN ARMY MEDICAL SERVICES IN THE DARDANELLES CAMPAIGN OF 1915

MICHAEL B. TYQUIN

THE MODERN HISTORY SERIES

This series, which focusses on Australian themes, is published in conjunction with the School of History at the University of New South Wales. Suitable manuscripts may be submitted to:

Dr Ann McGrath,
Chair,
Modern History Series Committee
c/o School of History
University of New South Wales
Box 1 PO Kensington NSW 2033

1. *Letters from Irish Australia 1825–1929* Patrick O'Farrell 1984 reprinted in 1989
2. *Divorce in 19th Century New South Wales* Hilary Golder 1985
3. *Beyond Belief: Theosophy in Australia 1879–1939* Jill Roe 1986
4. *The Fenians in Australia: 1865–1880* Keith Amos 1987
5. *Medicine and Madness: A Social History of Insanity in New South Wales 1880–1940* Stephen Garton 1988
6. *Policing in Australia: Historical Perspectives* Mark Finnane (ed) 1987
7. *The Making of the Labor Party in New South Wales 1880–1900* Raymond Markey 1988
8. *The Secret Army and the Premier: Conservative Paramilitary Organisations in New South Wales 1930–2* Andrew Moore 1989
9. *In Women's Hands? A History of Clothing Trades Unionism in Australia* Bradon Ellem 1989
10. *Camilla: C.H. Wedgwood 1901–1955 A Life* David Wetherill and Charlotte Carr-Gregg 1989
11. *The Better Time To Be: Utopian Attitudes to Society Among Sydney Anglicans 1885–1914* William Lawton 1990
12. *Empire and Race: The Maltese in Australia 1881–1949* Barry York 1990
13. *From Minstrel Show to Vaudeville: The Australian Popular Stage 1788–1914* Richard Waterhouse 1990
14. *A Whiff of Heresy: Samuel Angus and the Presbyterian Church in New South Wales* Susan Emilsen 1990
15. *The Parramatta Native Institution and the Black Town: A History* J. Brook and J. Kohen 1991
16. *Gallipoli: The Medical War* Michael B. Tyquin 1993
17. *Australian History in New South Wales 1888 to 1938* Brian H. Fletcher *1993*

GALLIPOLI:
THE MEDICAL WAR

The Australian Army
Medical Services in the
Dardanelles Campaign
of 1915

Michael B. Tyquin

In Memoriam

J.J. O'Keefe A.I.F.
Dr L.L. Robson

Published by
NEW SOUTH WALES UNIVERSITY PRESS
PO Box 1 Kensington NSW Australia

Telephone (02) 398 8900
Fax (02) 398 3408

© M. B. Tyquin

First published 1993

National Library of Australia
Cataloguing-in-Publication entry:

Tyquin, Michael B. (Michael Bernard), 1952–
    Gallipoli: the medical war.

    Bibliography.
    Includes index.
    ISBN 0 86840 189 7.

    1. Australia. Army – Medical care. 2. World War, 1914–1918 –
    Medical care. 3. World War, 1914–1918 – Campaigns – Turkey –
    Gallipoli Peninsula. I. Title.

940.47594

Available in North America through:
ISBS
Portland, OR 97213–3644, USA

Contents

LIST OF MAPS, DIAGRAMS AND TABLES

ABBREVIATIONS

AA & QMG	Assistant Adjutant and Quartermaster–General. Principal staff officer responsible for administration of services, supply etc.
AAG	Assistant Adjutant General. Principal staff officer responsible for the administration of personnel and their welfare in a Division.
AAMC	Australian Army Medical Corps
AANC	Australian Army Nursing Corps
ANZAC	Australian and New Zealand Army Corps
ACCS	Australian Casualty Clearing Station. A 200-bed hospital consisting (in 1915) of eight officers and 77 Other Ranks.
ADMS	Assistant Director of Medical Services. The principal medical officer in a Division.
ADOS	Assistant Director of Ordnance Services. Ordnance covers arms, equipment, clothing etc.
ADS	Advanced Dressing Station. A centre behind the lines to which wounded were sent from the RAPs to have urgent surgical or medical treatment before being directed to a casualty clearing station.
AFA	Australian Field Ambulance★
AG	Adjutant General. Among other matters, responsible for sanitation, provision of medical equipment, casualties and invaliding.
AGH	Australian General Hospital. The largest medical military unit; it consisted of two 520-bed hospitals in the field; of 21 officers, 43 nurses and 143 Other Ranks.
AIF	Australian Imperial Force. The Australian Expeditionary Force.
ALH	Australian Light Horse
AMC	Army Medical Corps
AMF	Australian Military Forces
AQMG	Assistant Quartermaster–General. Responsible for supplies and transport of troops and materiel.
ASC	Army Service Corps
ASH	Australian Stationary Hospital. 200 beds with eight officers and 86 Other Ranks.
BEF	British Expeditionary Force
Btn	Battalion. The main unit of infantry, approx. 550 strong.
CCS	Casualty Clearing Station. 200 beds with eight officers and 77 Other Ranks.
CGS	Chief of the General Staff. He was responsible for working out all the arrangements, and drafting of orders, war organisation, efficiency, intelligence and communications.
C in C	Commander in Chief. General Sir Ian Hamilton, until replaced by Sir Charles Monro in October, 1915.
CO	Commanding Officer
DAAG	Deputy Assistant Adjutant–General

DA & QMG	Deputy Adjutant and Quartermaster–General
DADMS	Deputy Assistant Director of Medical Services
DCS	Divisional Collecting Station. The place where slightly wounded men, able to walk, are collected, treated, fed and rested before evacuation or return to their units.
DDMS	Deputy Director of Medical Services. Filled for a time by Sir Neville Howse VC.
DGMS	Director–General of Medical Services
DMS	Director of Medical Services
DSO	Distinguished Service Order
GHQ	General Headquarters
GOC	General Officer Commanding
GSW	Gunshot Wound
HMS	His Majesty's Ship
HMT	His Majesty's Transport
IGC	Inspector-General of Communications
LHR	Light Horse Regiment
LHFA	(Australian) Light Horse Field Ambulance. The first medical unit behind the regimental aid detachments: six officers and 121 Other Ranks.★
MC	Military Cross
MEF	Mediterranean Expeditionary Force
MO	Medical Officer. At least one in every regiment.
NTO	Naval Transport Officer
OC	Officer Commanding
ORs	Other ranks, i.e. private soldiers
PDMS	Principal Director of Medical Services
PHTO	Principal Hospital Transport Officer
PMLO	Principal Military Landing Officer
PMO	Principal Medical Officer
PBM	Principal Beach Master. A senior naval officer who controls all landing craft on the beach and all personnel and materiel within the naval area, to ensure turn around of all landing craft.
PNTO	Principal Naval Transport Officer, appointed to take charge of all sea transport
QAIMNS	Queen Alexandra's Imperial Military Nursing Service
QMG	Quartermaster-General
RAP	Regimental Aid Post. A front-line medical facility consisting of a doctor, orderlies, stretcher bearers.
RMO	Regimental Medical Officer
SMO	Senior Medical Officer
VC	Victoria Cross

★   I have not followed convention here (i.e. Aust Fld Amb.) for the sake of brevity in footnotes particularly. The same applies for ambulances of the Light Horse.

Preface and Acknowledgements

To those who have heard of this story, be it under the guise of 'the Anzacs', 'Gallipoli', or 'the Dardanelles campaign', images of great sacrifice, incompetence, and wasted lives immediately spring to mind. With the passage of time myths have been created and nurtured, heroes and villains identified and the annual remembrance of fallen soldiers observed. The many official and other histories, memoirs and scholarly articles would lead us to believe that the last scrap of historical significance has been extracted from this episode of Australian history.

In addition to the unsurpassed books of the official Australian war historian C.E.W. Bean, the only other work of note in this field is *The Official History of the Australian Army Medical Services 1914–18* (referred to hereafter as the *Official History*). This was a three-part work written between 1922 and 1943 by Colonel A.G. Butler. It was written to record the problems met with by the medical services of the Australian Imperial Force (AIF) and therefore to serve as a training guide for future generations of medical officers.

In terms of Imperial history a twelve-volume official history of the British medical services was written, but it gave scant recognition to any of the dominions' medical contributions, and suffered from some glaring omissions with respect to the Gallipoli campaign.

Unfortunately these histories did not address all those areas which are of interest to the modern reader generally. They omit the day-to-day trials and problems experienced not only by medical men in the field, but by those soldiers who passed through their hands. For these reasons, together with the peculiarity of the Gallipoli disaster in terms of medical administration, the author was prompted to re-examine the medical aspects of this campaign.

This investigation necessarily recognised the social background against which the men and women of the AAMC (the Australian Army Medical Service was known later as the Royal Australian Army Medical Corps) operated. In addition subsequent research, comparative studies, accessible eye-witness accounts and a re-examination of official enquiries have added several new insights into this aspect of the Gallipoli campaign. Therefore this work forms an analysis and investigation into an area of Australian military and social history largely neglected for almost seventy years.

It may seem that a 'medical' history of Anzac is a specialist field and therefore narrow in what conclusions can be drawn, and to a lesser extent, what interpretations it can make of Australia's overall participation in the campaign. However, a social history of the Army's medical services must incorporate a broad range of issues, which is beyond purely military medicine. Chapters six and seven in particular, deal with some of the more controversial matters of the campaign which are not much in evidence in the accessible literature.

What follows is intended to give the reader an appreciation of the difficulties encountered by a military medical service which, although based closely on the British system, had been consolidated only a decade or so before the outbreak of the First World War. The outline of the actual military history of Gallipoli is deliberately brief and is included only to the extent to which it provides an idea of the problems faced by Australian medical staff.

This work does not pretend to provide anything more than a basic military background necessary to understand the issues being discussed. April, August, and December 1915 have been chosen as significant, because in each of these months particular problems presented themselves to the medical services, which were either not present, or were so to only a small extent, during the rest of the campaign. These problems centre on large numbers of battle casualties, disease, and serious (and sometimes scandalous) defects in the medical evacuation system.

Recent studies, particularly those of J. Laffin and G. Regan, provide greater insights into the military aspects of the campaign as a whole.[1] Therefore the author has confined himself to making observations only where the errors made were particularly relevant to the medical sphere. Underlying the execution of the Dardanelles campaign were factors wholly outside the control of the Australian medical services.

Undoubtedly monumental errors were made at the highest levels of command, with subsequent pressures on the medical services. However, an operation of this type and scale was without parallel in modern military history and mistakes were probably inevitable as they are with any campaign of such complexity. In later years this has been largely ignored with the result that Britain has been cast (certainly by the Australian public) in the role of scapegoat.

There is also what might loosely be termed 'the optimism factor' — the implicit assumption held by many in the armed forces, both in Britain and Australia, that the war would be a short one. Gallipoli was also regarded, at least by the British, as a 'sideshow' to the all important activities on French battlefields. Hence the medical services at Gallipoli in 1915 were accorded a low priority in comparison to their colleagues in France. To Australians at home and the medical and other troops on Gallipoli, this was no consolation for the largely makeshift medical arrangements the latter had to endure there.

Chapters two to five constitute the overall framework with which this book deals. They incorporate much primary material of interest which has never before been published. Chapter three is a detailed and concise investigation of the manner in which Australian casualties and sick were treated during the campaign, both at Anzac, during their evacuation, and in the hospitals to the rear of the fighting zones.

Chapter four, dealing with the transport of wounded, is also of necessity a complex topic covering many areas. In the past this subject has been treated as one of many lesser complications in the overall picture, whereas the analysis here explains the impact that it had for the treatment of Australian Diggers. Some of the more notorious episodes concerning conditions aboard makeshift hospital ships are covered in this chapter. Chapter five looks at the problem and incidence of disease on the Gallipoli peninsula and the ramifications for the medical services, particularly during times of great pressure from battle casualties.

Chapter six brings together a broad range of unrelated issues which at first sight seem purely peripheral, but have until now only been dealt with summarily by historians and other writers. They include the seemingly mundane activities of provisioning troops; the contribution of dental problems to the overall deficiencies in the Diggers' health; psychological problems; and the convoluted area of stores, their provision and transport. The background and recruitment of some members of the medical services are also told, and it is immediately obvious that not all who joined the colours did so without hesitation.

The author seeks to detail political jealousies about which the official histories say little if anything, being as they were so close to events and personalities. It is for this reason that chapter seven, dealing with 'political' and personal rivalries, is a relatively complex one.

Throughout these chapters there is an attempt to explode some of the more popular myths: particularly the stereotypes of the supremely healthy 'bronzed Anzac'; of the British responsibility for the major mistakes made during the campaign; and the impeccable image of Australian medical and nursing officers. By the 1920s some of these 'myths' had not yet progressed into folklore; others had. For by then a stream of books and articles had begun to be published by those who had witnessed events or who had fought at Gallipoli. For this reason some legends are re-examined. The liberty has been taken to designate Privates and NCOs of field ambulances and stretcher bearers as 'medics' — a term not in use during the First World War. This designation will however be more familiar to the modern reader.

The very nature of the Gallipoli campaign and that of the Australian and New Zealand Army Corps (which played a significant part in that campaign), makes it difficult to treat Australian troops in isolation from those of New Zealand and vice versa. I have dealt with the New Zealand medical units and troops in a way which reflects a contemporary feeling at the time (at least after the landing at Anzac Cove) that men from both sides of the Tasman Sea had much in common, at least more so than they shared with British regular, territorial, or other Dominion troops.

Personal diaries and letters, mostly of Australian (some British officers are included) medical personnel: doctors, orderlies, stretcher bearers, and nurses (although diaries of casualties and others are included) form the basis for *Gallipoli: The Medical War*. Australian unit war diaries, the *Official History*, and newspaper articles have also been used extensively. Among the various secondary source materials there is a large number of professional journals written either at the time or shortly after, and these help to provide many different angles to the 'official' view of the medical affairs of the Gallipoli campaign. Contemporary reports are utilised extensively for various chapters.

The most informative of these reports is the official transcript of the so-called 'Dardanelles Commission' which was appointed in August 1916. It is a valuable document in reviewing the activities of the British Army, the Royal Navy, the ANZAC Corps and contemporary politicians, as they relate to (among other things) the medical situation at Gallipoli. The late John Robertson is one of the few Australian scholars to extensively investigate this source.

There is a large number of individuals to whom I owe my thanks for the appearance of this book. The late Dr Lloyd Robson, my (initial) supervisor at the University of Melbourne was a constant source of encouragement and advice throughout my association with him. He also became an invaluable source of moral support as the work took shape. Dr Alan Mayne, who succeeded Dr Robson as my supervisor also provided a number of valuable criticisms. Dr Geoffrey Serle and Dr Bryan Egan also made helpful suggestions at various stages of this work.

I wish to thank those Gallipoli veterans in Victoria who gave me of their time and hospitality in allowing me to interview or correspond with them. These men include Dr Cyril Checchi, the Lambert brothers, Mr Thompson and Mr Meaghan.

I must mention Jan Bassett not only for her suggestions relating to her experience in researching army nurses, but for her encouragement in this project. Others include Lorraine McKnight and her staff at the Australian War Memorial Canberra, Meagan Hammond and the Mason family in Canberra, and Jennifer McGurgan (Gordon Craig Library, Royal Australasian College of Surgeons). Characteristically Mr James Heywood of Melbourne gave freely of his expertise in the maintenance of my microcomputer software.

There is also the staff at the State Library of Victoria, and staff at the Mitchell Library, Sydney; Brenda Heagney, the librarian of the Royal Australian College of Physicians in Sydney; and Mrs L. Hoffman, librarian, AMA (Victorian branch), Parkville. In addition there is the staff at the E. Joske Memorial Library at the University of Melbourne School of Dentistry; Mr Graeme Powell, manuscript librarian at the National Library of Australia; and the staff of the Melbourne University Archives.

In England: Mr C.J. Bruce of the Imperial War Museum for his cooperation and the use of its fine facilities; Mrs Joan Horsley of the National Maritime Museum, Greenwich; and the staff of the Liddell Hart Centre for Military Archives, King's College,

London who were very obliging in providing material and advice. Finally my thanks to Miss Shirley Dixon of the Wellcome Institute of Medicine in London, the staff of the Public Records Office, Kew and to the National Army Museum, London for the use of their facilities.

Michael Tyquin
Melbourne
March 1993

CHAPTER ONE

Introduction

The outstanding features of the Dardanelles campaign were the comparative shortness of its duration, the intensity of the struggle in a confined area, and the exceptionally large numbers of battle and non-battle casualties.[1]

While much will be said in *Gallipoli: The Medical War* about the less savoury and glamorous side of the Anzacs' exploits, and while there was no lack of scandal, gross incompetence, appalling hygiene, high casualty figures and the like, the focus in the introduction is less controversial. This chapter will provide the reader with an appreciation of what went wrong (and just how badly) with the Australian medical services at Gallipoli. Before proceeding however, the opportunity should be taken to obtain a basic grasp of both the structure of the Australian Army Medical Corps (AAMC) and the improvised nature of many of the preparations for the landing at Gallipoli on 25 April 1915.

ORGANISATION

At the commencement of the Gallipoli campaign the Australian Army Medical Corps (AAMC) consisted of a very small permanent army staff whose functions were administration and instruction; a Militia Army Medical Corps; a Volunteer Army Medical Corps; and an Army Nursing Service Reserve. In July 1914 the official strength of the Australian Medical Corps stood at only four officers, including the Director of Medical Services (DMS) Surgeon-General W.D. Williams and 29 Other Ranks in the permanent army establishment, with a further 183 Officers and 1649 Other Ranks serving in the militia. Naturally the Corps was modelled on the British (RAMC) pattern.

The basic medical unit was the Regimental Aid Post (RAP) which accompanied an infantry unit into the fighting. It consisted of the regiment's doctor (RMO), who was assisted by two orderlies, one of whom was trained in looking after surgical and medical equipment and performing the role of assistant to the doctor. The Medical Officer was also responsible for selecting a site to set up his RAP. This could be a tent, a sheltered gully, or other suitable place and it was to this point that the stretcher bearers would bring their wounded.

There were usually 16 (combatant) stretcher bearers in an infantry regiment. They were either infantrymen or bandsmen who, in time of battle, would put aside their arms and don a Red Cross brassard. At the RAP casualties were given such first aid as was possible and 'sorted' according to the severity of their wound/condition. Small wounds were dressed and wherever possible the Digger was returned to the front. Those with severe wounds or illness were evacuated further to the rear to a field ambulance.

A Field Ambulance generally consisted of ten officers and 224 Other Ranks organised in two parts: a 'tent division' (nursing and administration) and a 'bearer division' consisting of three sections (A, B and C), each of which was equipped to hold 50 casualties. This organisational structure differed for Light Horse field ambulances which had six officers and 118 Other Ranks divided into two sections.

Wounded men were moved as infrequently as possible. To this end a casualty was kept on the same stretcher from the time he left the RAP until he was carried to the field ambulance. Bearers were then supposed to be given a stretcher in return from the stock held by a field ambulance. Such was the chaos and demand at Gallipoli that this system quickly broke down resulting in an acute shortage of stretchers for weeks after the landing.

The next unit in the organisational hierarchy was the Casualty Clearing Station (CCS). Such a unit was capable of providing 200 beds and was staffed by eight officers and 77 Other Ranks. As the name suggests, the purpose of a Casualty Clearing Station (at Anzac this was the 1st ACCS) was to clear the field ambulances of their casualties, thus ensuring unimpeded traffic of bearers to and from the lines. Basically it was responsible for the care of wounded of all categories until evacuation was completed behind the lines, or along the 'Lines of Communication' (according to the military term of the day).

'Line of Communication' is an important military concept and it refers to the system of communication by foot, road, sea etc. between an army (at Gallipoli), its advance base (Imbros), intermediate base (Mudros), and the bases at Alexandria, Cairo and Malta. Map 1.1 shows the overall area of operations of the Mediterranean Expeditionary Force (MEF). A second, larger scale map (Map 1.2) towards the end of this chapter provides an idea of the distances of prime concern to the medical services.

A Stationary Hospital was the next largest unit in the medical evacuation chain and it approximates what we would recognise as a civilian hospital. On the island of Lemnos Nos 1, 2, and 3 Australian Stationary Hospitals (ASH), which were employed there at various times, were for the most part tented hospitals. Theoretically they were to be placed at or in front of the advanced base (Alexandria) to receive casualties with minor injuries and illnesses, and who could therefore be nursed and then returned to the front in a relatively short time. One should remember that the *raison d'etre* for any army medical service is to rehabilitate wounded soldiers back to the field as quickly as possible.

The largest unit of the AAMC was the General Hospital. These formations are the equivalent of major city civilian hospitals, with various medical and surgical departments, laboratories etc. They were usually organised on the basis of 520 beds. But in Cairo, where No 1 AGH was established, this hospital grew to accommodate some 3500 beds within months of its establishment in Egypt. A similar growth was experienced by the No 2 AGH which was later set up on the outskirts of Cairo.

This then, was the structure upon which depended the effective, speedy, and hopefully successful treatment of wounded or sick Diggers. But surely this is common knowledge? What of the more contentious issues, the activities which went wrong or were hopelessly inadequate?

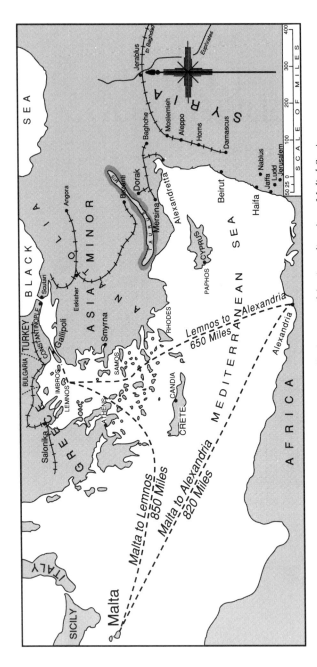

MAP 1.1   Operations of the MEF. *Source:* A.G. Butler: *Official History of the Australian Army Medical Services,* Australian War Memorial, Melbourne, 1930, Volume II, p. 84.

The published history of Australia's official war historian, C.E.W. Bean, and Colonel A.G. Butler's work on the medical services were both official documents and therefore carefully vetted (in Butler's case by Bean). Both writers knew they could only say so much in their written work. On more than one occasion Butler's anger (he was a medical officer at Anzac) at bungling generally and British incompetence in particular, had to be held in check by a firm but sympathetic letter from Bean, who was responsible for editing the *Official History*.

This book will bring these lesser known and (in some cases) forgotten aspects of what was then regarded as a relatively minor operation, into the light of public scrutiny again after all these years. Finally readers can judge for themselves the aptness or otherwise of the training given to AAMC members in 1914–15.

TRAINING

For all ranks in the AAMC training was very basic; and the implications for the medical services' performance at Gallipoli will be dealt with further in later chapters. Suffice it to state here that doctors received little in the way of military skills. In the early part of the war, training in the military application of their art was rudimentary. However, this situation improved as the war progressed. Captain C.L. Chapman of the 5th Australian Field Ambulance (AFA) wrote: 'Colonel told me I am to go with "A" Section and later am to be adjutant...Required to get several books re duties of adjutant, King's regs, transport duties drill (Army Service Manual).'[2]

Another officer, Major L.O. Betts, wrote that he 'was attached to the 9th Light Horse Regiment as Regimental Medical Officer 11.11.1914, having entered on that date with no previous military experience of any kind'.[3] This placed a further burden on those doctors who had been in the militia before the war and who now had to act as instructors in addition to their medical duties. As Captain Chapman's comment above shows, many a young medical officer was thrown in at the 'deep end' when he first entered a regiment.

Dr T. Hurley, a medical officer with the 2nd AFA, wrote this account of the formative days of his unit: 'I was sent...to Broadmeadows Camp, Victoria and found Capt. Shaw had since the day before been preparing a camp site for the 2nd Field Ambulance. Within a day or two the other officers of the unit reported and a commencement was made with the organization of the unit from the recruits allotted to us.'[4]

Medical Officers themselves later realised that inadequate training may have explained some of the errors which had been part of the medical scenario at Gallipoli. Colonel Howse of the AAMC (who was the senior Australian Medical Officer at Gallipoli) received a letter from one of his officers in which the latter berated the lack of adequate training in military medicine at home. The RMO had learned nothing of public health, and 'although most of our [medical] reinforcements had been serving at home or in ships and hospitals on service, not one of them had a word of instruction as to prevention being his chief duty, as to how it should be done or as to the conditions of regimental work'.[5] Prevention was at the core of any medical organisation's functions. If it was still not being properly addressed at home (particularly during the training of Medical Officers), then criticism has to be levelled at the AAMC itself.

Despite obvious deficiencies in training, this was the least of the worries for many of the medical personnel in the AIF, many of whom were looking forward to the adventure of a lifetime. For those who were to serve at Gallipoli, they would later look back on a period of intense work, in primitive conditions, caring for men with ghastly wounds or debilitated by sickness.

HASTE AND IGNORANCE

Critics of the Dardanelles episode point to General Sir Ian Hamilton's decision to set off for battle leaving behind those directly responsible for feeding, supplying and nursing his army to follow as best they could. Undeniably this decision was responsible for many of the subsequent problems encountered by the Australian medical services at Gallipoli, especially problems in April and May. An almost cavalier attitude is discernible in the way Hamilton decided to tackle the immense problem of logistics. Haste, a hallmark of the preparation for the entire Dardanelles campaign, is much in evidence.

On 24 February 1915, Surgeon-General Keogh — the Director-General of the British Army Medical Service — nominated Colonel J. Maher (RAMC) to act as Director of Medical Services (DMS) for the Mediterranean Expeditionary Force, until Surgeon-General Birrell (who had been brought out of retirement) could arrive from Britain. On 15 March Maher arrived at the village of Mudros, on the island of Lemnos, 111 kilometres from Gallipoli (see Map 1.2). His mission was to report on the suitability of Lemnos as a base from a medical and sanitary point of view. He reported that the island was unsuitable

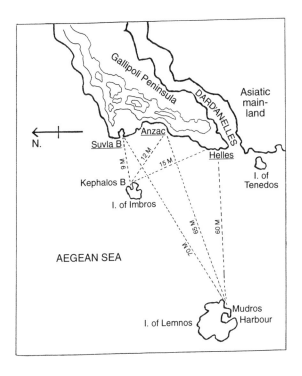

MAP 1.2 Sketch map showing the system of supply in the Dardanelles.
Source: The Army Quarterly, Vol XX, 1930. p 63

on account of insufficiency of water. Subsequently the island was to be used solely as a base for assembling troops immediately prior to the landing and no provision was made for the long term establishment of a medical unit of any considerable size. This, from a medical point of view, was one of the first costly mistakes to be made in the entire campaign.

Sir Ian Hamilton, who had overall command of the MEF, spent several days at Mudros and from there he had initially inspected the Gallipoli peninsula by ship on 18 March. On 22 March he sailed for Egypt to further his plans for the invasion. During all of this time he had no planning assistance, as his administrative staff were still en route from England. Partly on the basis of Maher's report he moved his 'advanced base' from Lemnos back to Alexandria, 1200 kilometres further away from Gallipoli. The Royal Naval Division and the French Division which had been posted to Mudros earlier, were now sent back to Egypt. The Australian (3rd) Brigade, however, remained on transports in Mudros Bay, landing battalions for exercises on shore as the opportunity offered.

This haphazard and often disorganised approach was to continue throughout 1915. Another feature was the paucity of information finding its way to the Australian Government. Official correspondence betrays an increasingly anxious home Government in the second half of 1915. 'It is presumed that every precaution is being taken as regards the purification of water. Are there any other causes to account for the heavy sick rate? There are indications that the men are becoming dispirited. The situation is causing anxiety. Let me know what steps you are taking.'[6] A reply was sent to the Secretary of State suggesting that sickness was due to constant strain, infection by flies, dust etc. There was no mention about the unremitting strain on the men, monotonous rations, or the lack of canteens.

Conversely, the Australian Government (as will be argued later) was totally committed to Britain's war aims, and was not to be diverted from its support to the mother country. In Australia, the records of parliamentary proceedings are almost devoid of any debate over the medical situation in Gallipoli itself or the treatment of wounded either there or in hospital ships. What is recorded in the Commonwealth parliamentary debates instead concentrates mainly on medical conditions in recruit camps in Australia, problems with invaliding wounded back to Australia, and the alleged private sale of Red Cross goods in Cairo.[7]

But not everyone was comfortable with what occurred in the medical sphere of the campaign, either then or after 1915. Even the British official medical history concluded that the medical side of the campaign did not seem to have been thoroughly thought out. It stated that although the treatment of the wounded on the Gallipoli peninsula may have been as satisfactory as circumstances would permit, in the transport of these men to the ships and overseas many of the complaints were justifiable.[8]

John Monash, commanding the 4th Australian Infantry Brigade, was also critical of the medical situation and often wrote bluntly in his letters home about the incidence of sickness and the treatment of casualties: '...it's about time too that somebody asked about the treatment of Australian soldiers in Tommy hospitals, for it's the absolute dizzy limit. Nothing could be better than our Australian or New Zealand or Canadian hospitals, but as to the British hospitals, here, well, the sooner they hang somebody for gross mismanagement the better.'[9]

He quoted Australian medical authorities as saying the rations were poor and insufficient, and was highly critical of the canteen arrangements, such as they were: 'C.O. Field Ambulance, however, says [food] is not on nearly a generous enough scale (as to variety) to ensure rapid physical restoration of the personnel...'[10]

He also felt let down by the Red Cross, a misconception shared by a number of AAMC staff at this time. 'I have talked lengthily about all these matters to health experts...both British and Australian, and I have found none to disagree with me that the interests of the men at the front have been totally neglected, from the point of view of military efficiency by the military authorities, and from the point of view of their personal well-being by the public organisations in Australia.'[11]

Colonel Springthorpe, the irascible senior physician at No 2 AGH in Cairo wrote in his diary 'What to think of our medical Arrangements! Dumbfounded — R.S. & B. [British Surgeon-Generals Ford and Birrell] have rushed the situation regardless of all...apparently careless and insufficient consideration of all below — of comfort, efficiency and all outside the K.R. [King's Regulations] — put energy and brains into it — but poaching on everyone else and glory at all cost.'[12]

Medical preparations had been effectively hamstrung in that neither the RAMC nor the AAMC were privy to the plans for the landing. Information concerning Hamilton's intentions, his objectives and the strategies with which these were to be carried out was never clearly pronounced prior to the Gallipoli operations. Indeed when Hamilton left for Lemnos in April, he did not even indicate where he expected the casualties to go — Egypt, Malta, or England. Nor, at that time, did Hamilton request that hospital accommodation be prepared for any specific number of casualties

This situation was exacerbated by Hamilton's arrogant Chief of the General Staff, General W.P. Braithwaite. This officer was overly protective of his chief but at the same time was unable or unwilling to delegate urgent action upon which the medical services depended for their effective operation.

It would be a daunting prospect even today, to coordinate the medical services for such a large-scale amphibious operation. Those in charge expected it would be a 'short, sharp action', which would take more than adequate ground to ensure the landing of men and materiel. Unfortunately all the ground gained for this purpose (at least at Anzac Cove) turned out to be a narrow pebbly beach, in some places less than ten metres wide.

The Gallipoli landing was originally scheduled for 21 April, but was postponed due to the bad weather. This date explains the alarmed protestations made both by senior medical staff and the

Deputy Adjutant-General (Woodward) who was, under Army Regulations, responsible for the evacuation of wounded. As Birrell's diary notes there were the 'Evacuation Hospital Ship *Sicilia* and 3 transports with personnel and equipment for 29th Division. 4 transports for Australian and New Zealand Army Corps. [Naval hospital ship] *Somali* with Naval Division.'[13]

Bad weather hampered attempts at coordinated training exercises (e.g. boat drill, route marches and stretcher drill ashore and practising the movement of wounded up gangways, by derricks and slings) which could not be carried out with much thoroughness. The situation immediately prior to the landing was therefore made worse by the lack of time (approximately a week) to reorganise units while relying almost entirely on ship-borne communications. On page 78 diagram 4.1 illustrates the system of medical evacuation.

Even before the landing, life was far from comfortable for those Diggers already in hospital on Lemnos. An entry in the war diary of No 1 Australian Stationary Hospital for 9 April 1915 reads: 'Hurricane & rain during night 6 tents blown down. Men up all night shifting patients.'[14] Then on 21 April this tent hospital 'Informed DMS cannot accommodate any more patients'.[15] Only a week earlier it had 183 patients cleared to Alexandria on the *Osmanieh*. However, by this time there were no hospital ships to take the overflow.

On 23 April the storm cleared and the senior Naval commander at the Dardanelles, Vice-Admiral De Robeck, issued orders that the landing was to take place on the 25th. The transport ships began to move out of the harbour, while on board the *Lutzow* a conference was held in which all the senior Australian and New Zealand officers, including those of the medical services, were present. The details of the landing were outlined to them for the first time, together with the military objectives.

Meanwhile instructions were issued to the expectant troops on board the flotilla. Among them were these: 'Three days' rations, some chocolate only to be used as a last resource, take a big drink [of water] before going and take full water-bottles, 200 rounds of ammunition...'[16]

The idyllic setting of clear skies and calm sea disguised the problems that still beset the medical arrangements. Having just started out from Lemnos, one ship had 'been under steam for only about four hours when a case of smallpox was reported on board', and it had to return to Lemnos. It was an inauspicious start for other reasons.

Years before, a paper drawn up by the General Staff in 1906 had concluded that a successful attack directed against the Gallipoli peninsula depended upon the fleet silencing completely any opposition prior to, and during, the landing of troops. In view of the risks involved the General Staff at the time were 'not prepared to recommend its being attempted'.[17] History was to be ignored again and Gallipoli would soon become a household word in every city, town and homestead in Australia.

CHAPTER TWO

Gallipoli — On the Attack

We were aboard the *Seang Chun*...We saw landing parties going ashore on destroyers packed like sardines & in tow of these were barges no less packed. Many of these fellows, before they reached the shore, were shot & tumbled overboard — picked off by snipers...One lot of Ambulancemen were picked off in this way. They were W.A. boys.[1]

T his chapter investigates the way in which the AAMC coped with three different sets of circumstances on Gallipoli: the landing on 25 April, the major offensive of 6 August, and the final withdrawal from the peninsula in mid-December 1915. In the first two cases there was a significant (and to some extent avoidable) repetition of mistakes and errors. In August and certainly in December, the Australian medical services prepared themselves better than their British counterparts. Further, these achievements were made despite continued incompetence in the sphere of strategy and in the administration of supplies — both areas critical to the medical effort but beyond the control of Australian medical officers and units on the peninsula.

Before dawn on 25 April 1915 the first of the Australians landed on a narrow beach on the west coast of the Gallipoli peninsula. For a number of reasons (which are still disputed), they were landed two kilometres further north than they should have been.[2] Instead of facing gently sloping plains, they were confronted with sheer cliffs; almost impenetrable, prickly scrub; and a murderous hail of machine-gun fire and shrapnel from the Turkish positions above. A number lost their lives before they had jumped out of their boats. Others were killed whilst wading ashore. Cries of 'Stretcher bearer!' went up and for a time were unheeded as medics and regimental stretcher bearers were also shot or blown to pieces as they landed. The pebbly beach was described by many contemporaries as being only as wide as a cricket pitch. It was sheltered in parts by a small overhang, about five metres high. It was here that the first wounded were treated, as thousands more troops crammed onto the shore and began to fight their way inland — metre by metre.

THE FIRST FORTY-EIGHT HOURS

The tent subdivisions of the various Ambulances which were still on the transport ships, could only look on as their comrades either fell wounded or made frantic efforts to reach and treat the many casualties who now were visible as daylight broke on the beaches. There were great scenes of heroism and sights of tragic proportions. At 'Hell's Spit' on Anzac Cove one boat could be seen lying aground, packed with dead men, while opposite a concealed machine-gun was a piled heap of 20 men, dead and wounded, some of them half in and half out of the water, exposed to the hot sun. It would be three days before they could be reached.

The diary entry for the 1st Australian Field Ambulance is typical of those medical units which landed on 25 April. 'Anzac 0930...Much heavy fire. Commenced work and continued b/n firing line & Beach until midnight after which the men were divided into Details and thus ensured continuance of work and a slight amount of rest...'[3] Life in the Medical Corps was not necessarily pleasant even during the rare periods of respite: 'Pte. Harris had a gruesome experience today. He was sitting in company with a friend chatting, when a shell came and took his friend's head off, scattering the brains over Harris. Harris got quite a shake.'[4] Despite the death around them, members of the medical services retained their sense of humour: 'Talk about mixed bathing — men & bullets.'[5]

A Regimental Aid Post (RAP) was usually established at the front and stretcher bearers attached themselves to each company. Casualties were dressed and the location of the RAP would be sent back to Assistant Director of Medical Services (ADMS) on the beach and surgical equipment and other stores were then sent up. Abdominal, chest and head cases were carried by stretcher, while other wounded walked or limped to the overcrowded beach helped by other walking wounded. Further along, on the beach, a Casualty Clearing Station was set up and here cases were treated and ticketed. This involved attaching a white label to lightly wounded cases, and a red label to serious cases. Very shortly however, this system had to be abandoned through sheer weight of numbers. After dark, when the majority of troops had been landed, the wounded were placed on board almost anything that could float.

At 4.30 a.m. men of the 3rd Australian Field Ambulance had disembarked from their boats under fire and sustained two casualties immediately. They landed and took shelter under the sand banks at the back of the beach. Virtually trapped, these men could do little more than attend to the ambulance's own wounded, as their position was subjected to heavy sniping. When this eased they set to work improving shelter, making collecting posts and attending to and bringing in wounded from nearby. Officers and sergeants then went out with small squads of medics to scour the country for wounded along the shore and up over the hills as far as possible.

Their work was not made easy by the fact that the landing units were simply scattered groups at this time, thus making a thorough and systematic search for wounded impractical. This was to be a feature of the operations over the next week; it would make recording casualties impossible and locating other members of the same unit a nightmare as recorded in one ambulance's unit diary: '...there was great difficulty in founding systematic work as the valleys in the area were intricate and...tracks were ill-defined & difficult to recognize...& few could give directions to the location where help was required'.[6] Those sections of the AAMC which were not apportioned to the various field ambulances (i.e. battalion and regimental bearers and doctors and their orderlies), were left to work out their own arrangements among themselves and to follow up their Brigades as best they could.

The lack of good maps, and therefore accurate grid references, caused havoc, as wounded could not be found and medical units were not where they were reported to be. Even at this early stage it was obvious, at least to those on shore, that the medical arrangements had gone badly awry. One of the doctors on the scene placed the blame for this squarely on the hapless Birrell, who 'was without foresight and imagination — [with a] stereotyped mind'.[7]

The original medical scheme had assumed that all wounded, prior to leaving the beach, would be sorted out according to severity of wounds. With regard to the classification of wounded ashore Colonel Manders (the New Zealand medical officer in charge of the ANZAC Division) in his orders had detailed an officer for this purpose but he cancelled the order when he ceased to be Deputy Director of Medical Services. The fully equipped hospital ships were for serious cases, the improvised ambulance carriers for less serious cases. On 25 April the only hospital ship off Anzac was the *Gascon*.

Due to the totally unexpected rush of casualties in the first few hours of the landing this ship rapidly filled with wounded. It had not been possible to sort them on shore first so that the *Gascon* received men suffering from serious wounds, as well as those with sprained ankles and cut fingers who would normally have been placed aboard a transport or left on shore in a field hospital. Two transport ships, which had been set aside for lightly wounded cases, the *Clan MacGillivray* and the *Seang Choon*★ (still with their original contingents of troops on board), then took the 'surplus' until they too could take no more. This was one reason for the backlog of wounded on shore.

Private A. Gissing, a medic on board the transport *Seang Bee* wrote of the boats returning which brought back some wounded and patches of blood were seen on the deck in various places. 'Imagine the feelings of the boys whose turn it was to disembark next!' From there on wounded were brought along in a continuous stream. The ship's hospital was filled. 'The mess tables were ripped up from below, blankets spread down and the men were laid here as closely as possible. Before long every available space was covered and we began to refuse men and send them to the hospital ship.'[8]

Numbers aside, the sheer lack of space at Anzac meant that it was impossible to establish any field hospitals, and therefore sorting of any kind was impossible. Simply put, the whole scheme collapsed; although the situation was just as bad at Cape Helles further south where the British 29th Division landed. But there too a contemporary noted that: 'Very many of the casualties took place in the boats before the landing could be affected [*sic*]. These were taken to men-of-war, who passed them on direct to the hospital ship *Sudan* which thereby became over crowded, and

---

★Also spelt 'Chun'

the original plan of sending all cases to Hospital Carriers for differential distribution was upset.'[9]

Gradually over the next 24 hours, members of the field ambulances made contact with their regimental and battalion counterparts. One of the effects of the mix-up of units was that regimental bearers had to carry wounded all the way to the beach, instead of rendering first aid and then removing wounded the relatively short distance from the battle zone to safety behind the firing line, viz. dressing stations and field ambulances. The normal procedure was that the medics of the ambulances would continue carrying a stretcher patient from the ambulance (behind the front line — see diagram 4.1 on page 78) to the rear hospitals. Unfortunately Anzac offered little in the way of normality.

In addition to the field ambulances, the Casualty Clearing Station (1st ACCS) which was among the first medical units to land, had no shelter and no protection from the shrapnel which raked it up and down. It dealt with the wounded who poured down on it in hundreds from the front line and dressing stations in the gullies. This unit (consisting of eight officers and 77 Other Ranks), worked steadily throughout the day and most of the next, treating some 700 casualties. It was also responsible 'for clearing two Divisions with a reduced staff and v. little equipment...'[10] In fact the numbers of wounded forced Colonel Howse's hand, for he began to evacuate by boat at midday on 25 April as soon as he had 'received permission from Beach Master to load wounded at my place on Beach if boats became available'.[11] These 'Beach Masters' were in fact officers from the Royal Navy who acted as traffic controllers with respect to the landing and embarkation of all boats along the Gallipoli beaches.

Even when dug in, these dressing stations and other medical treatment facilities were not immune to fire, particularly from shrapnel. Many casualties were thus wounded again while lying on the beach, as related by Major John Corbin. They 'had to be redressed...several of our men were put out of action by shrapnel bullets, the shelter-shed for wounded was pierced by a huge high explosive shell, which killed a sick man lying on a stretcher, wounded another and so shattered the leg of a member of our unit that it had to be amputated two days later on a hospital ship, and he died.'[12] Almost all medical posts were prone to shot and shrapnel, therefore casualties amongst both patients and staff were not infrequent. Nothing is sacred in war. Lieutenant George Semple Bell, temporarily attached to the 6th Australian Field Ambulance, wrote: 'One of our officers, a Captain Green, was operating on a man when a shrapnel shell from Beachy Bill battery burst overhead...and a pellet went right through his chest and Green fell into the arms of the doctor who was administering the anaesthetic.'[13] It was worse for those beleaguered medics working at the very front lines and 'the work up & down these steep groves was very distressing'.[14]

There was nothing much in military history or tactical textbooks concerning the conduct of operations such as that attempted at Gallipoli. Officers found no solace in the *Manual of Combined Naval and Military Operations* (193). Absence of precedent, and lack of preparation, together with the ubiquitous workings of 'Murphy's Law' combined to dictate the medical response on 25 April. Nor did matters offshore proceed according to plan. Peter Hall, an orderly with No 2 Australian Stationary Hospital, had arrived off Anzac with some of his unit aboard a transport which was totally unprepared for receiving wounded.

The infantry on board had not left his ship and the blankets and other medical stores had not been sterilised, as the sterilising machines had broken down. 'From this time until they arrived off the coast the following morning they brought wounded on board. There were three English doctors and fifteen Medical Corps men (none of whom had been trained for anything but general duties in a hospital) trying to attend 659 wounded men, the majority of them in an awful state. One man begged me to take five sovereigns he had, just to bring the doctor to him for one minute.'[15]

This was by no means an isolated case as Colonel Chas. Ryan, an experienced Australian surgeon, later wrote: '...arrived at Anzac at 6 am on 25 April. Almost at once a boat load of wounded were put on board the *Minnesota*. We had not made any arrangements whatever, as we did not expect to take on any wounded as the *Clan MacGillivray* was taking on wounded. I think there were fifteen to twenty cases came on board but no arrangements were made for their reception.'[16] Even reinforcements did little to ease matters in the first few days after the landing. Private A. Gordon, a medic, noted in his diary that on 27 April he and his section had been transferred to a troopship, where he had to look after 115 men himself, while there were only eight other orderlies to care for a further 550 wounded. He had had no sleep for the three days and nights during which he dressed, washed and fed wounded troops.[17]

The *Seang Bee*, which had filled up with almost 900 wounded by Monday 26 April could not leave the area as her holds were still full of ammunition. The 36 medics on board were drawn from different units and were inexperienced, while of the two doctors 'one was a loafer pure & simple & they both seemed so taken aback by things that they did not attempt to dress wounds till Tuesday...We had over 900 wounded who had to be fed etc & their wants fixed up & we received sixteen loaves of bread per day for their feed...My duties were chiefly concerned with the Dispensary giving hypodermic injections of opium for pain at night. We got through pints of it.'[18]

Medical personnel on other ships told similar stories. One transport was hailed and asked to take 90 wounded on board. It was cold and raining, and these men had been towed in a small boat from ship to ship for hours seeking accommodation. Forty stretcher cases were swung on board by means of cargo nets swung over the side. Several of these casualties died shortly after being taken aboard.[19] Howse experienced this situation first-hand: 'The non-commissioned officer in charge of a boat I put off in late on April 25th, told me that he tried seven transports before he could get wounded taken on, and that they were taken on board one of the transports between five and six o'clock on the Monday morning.'[20]

The Naval Beach Master at Anzac experienced similar difficulties, although he was obviously not to be trifled with. He had occasion to go on board one of the transports lying off Anzac and found that no steps had been taken to embark the wounded. They had been left in the open boats alongside in cold weather for hours because the transport 'was not a hospital ship'. He threatened the ship's captain with immediate arrest, and this apparently had the desired effect.[21]

Toward evening the situation had deteriorated to such an extent that General Birdwood sent a message to Hamilton suggesting a withdrawal. However, the Navy had advised Hamilton that a full-scale evacuation at night would have been impossible, and land commanders were ordered to dig in.

As Howse would later tell the Dardanelles Commission, casualties were put on board ships that night owing to the fear that they should have to evacuate the beach at any moment. Howse believed that there was a question of evacuating the beach on the Sunday night. He also understood that an order was actually issued to the OC of the 1st ACCS some time on Sunday evening that he was to pack up and be ready to embark in two hours. Howse later found after an interview with one of General Birdwood's staff that this was not official, but that the beach would have to be cleared if possible of every wounded man without delay. There was great difficulty naturally under such conditions.[22] It seems that the transport of wounded from the shore to the ships was effectively carried out until 10.00 p.m. on

26 April, when at midnight 'it failed utterly…due entirely to the preparation under way at that time for an evacuation of the position at Anzac'.[23]

Colonel Howse was faced with the certainty that unless special steps were taken, there would be a serious backlog of wounded on the beach which could be kept clear of wounded only by retaining them inland or by removing them quickly offshore. Retention inland was not possible; there was simply no room. Howse therefore concentrated on the embarkation of every wounded man as quickly as possible. It should be noted that Birrell's scheme, which was being operated by GHQ (on board the warship *Queen Elizabeth*), had no provision for what should happen if a retreat was ordered, nor if inland holding facilities were denied, as was now the situation. Howse could not have done otherwise, particularly if a withdrawal was thought imminent. Acting as his own medical embarkation officer, he therefore 'urged on the naval beachmaster that the scope of clearance should be extended, and about noon, after all available troops had landed, obtained permission for clearance from any part of the Beach' — which had already begun anyway.[24]

Much has been said about the management of the flow of casualties from the beaches to ships during the last days of April. While this aspect of the medical arrangements will be analysed in greater detail in chapter four, the background to this episode can be briefly examined at this point. According to Surgeon-General Birrell he gave all the assistance he could while on board the *Arcadian* from 25–28 April. On 25 April he had also tried to communicate with the shore at Anzac and Cape Helles but failed as no messages were allowed to go through. Both Howse and Manders landed with the fighting troops and remained onshore, where, according to Birrell, they were out of touch with the transport ships.[25] However, Birrell himself was just as isolated with what was actually happening both at Anzac and Cape Helles.

Birrell's second-in-command, Lt. Colonel Keble, shared the views of his chief on this point and inferred that Howse, being only a civilian in uniform (and a Colonial at that!), was to blame for any shortcomings at the landing. In other words everyone suffered because of the absence of any *pukka* or 'trained' British medical officer.[26] Keble mentions Colonel Yarr, Howse's opposite number at Cape Helles, where according to Birrell, Keble, and almost every other British authority, the landing had been so much better. But this claim conveniently ignores the fact that at Helles, Yarr too had landed on the beach on the afternoon of 25 April in the same manner as Howse and Manders. Birrell and

Keble thought that some of the confusion might have been avoided if Howse and Manders had remained with the headquarters of their Divisions, leaving their subordinates to land and do the work on the beaches. However, the Dardanelles Commission did not think that this would have materially affected the situation. In its opinion the circumstances made confusion inevitable.

By the end of 25 April three Australian Field Ambulances and the New Zealand Field Ambulance (minus their tent subdivisions) had been landed. These units supplied all the bearer details for carrying casualties down to the beach and in addition, tried to provide accommodation for holding both serious and slight cases on the peninsula. Of the two ADMS, Howse established himself at the southern part of Anzac Cove (near 'MacLagan's Ridge') and Colonel Manders at the northern end (at 'Headquarters Gully'/Ari Burnu — see Map 2.1 on page 29).

FACTORS CONTRIBUTING TO THE CHAOS

LACK OF COMMUNICATIONS

On 26 April Surgeon-General Birrell, the DMS. asked that he or his ADMS. might now join General Headquarters on the *Queen Elizabeth* to supervise evacuation, which was patently not being carried out in accordance with the previously arranged plans. Birrell's request was refused. The next day he left on the *Arcadian* at 5.00 a.m. for the Dardanelles, but was unable to communicate with the shore or other Divisions. Communications, or their absence, were a contributing factor to the less than adequate treatment received by the wounded. The medical services were powerless in this respect.

The communications situation did not improve over the period 25–30 April. On 28 April Birrell was sent this message: '*Lutzow* filling up rapidly. Request name of next hospital ship. Where is the advanced depot of medical stores? Running short of supplies.'[27] The lack of effective wireless communications meant that many orders and instructions, as well as situation reports, had to be given manually and carried by small boats. Fleet Surgeon C. MacMillan later recalled that he couldn't 'quite remember at what hour the cessation of communications took place but, had it not occurred, there would not have been such congestion as there was. We tried all we knew about midnight to get into communications with the flagship but whether our wireless from Gen. Birdwood's Head Qrs got through or not I never knew.'[28]

Colonel Manders made two attempts to get a signal through to Surgeon-General Birrell on the *Arcadian*. His first message (despatched at 2.00 p.m.) reads: 'Wounded arriving rapidly, about five hundred. Probably require another hospital ship. Request ships make nominal roll wounded, impossible here.'[29] To this there was no reply. The DMS was isolated. All signals from the shore were conveyed by the wireless station close to Ari Burnu Point direct to the *Queen Elizabeth*, where Sir Ian Hamilton had part of his headquarters. However Hamilton, in his diary, noted on the 26th that 'Never...has a Commander-in-Chief been so accessible to a message or an appeal from any part of the force. Each theatre has its outfit of signallers, wireless etc., and I can answer in five minutes, or send help...'[30] There was no Deputy Director of Medical Services at Birdwood's Headquarters [in the *Minnewaska*] as no DDMS had been appointed in Colonel Manders' place.

On 26 April Manders tried again and despatched a signal to Birrell from his sector at the north end of Anzac Cove. 'Re previous message, to which ship should further serious and lightly wounded be sent.'[31] The General Staff, who were supposed to be coordinating the evacuation of the wounded, were conspicuous by their absence. At no time did any member of this staff reply to, or act upon, the ADMS's signals from the shore. Due to Birrell's isolation and lack of wireless facilities, no reply was received from this quarter either.

LACK OF HOSPITAL SHIPS

The following is a copy of a signal dated 28 April from Brigadier-General Carruthers (the AA & QMG Australian and New Zealand Army Corps) to General Birdwood, and is quoted in full because of its implications in what follows:

> I yesterday [27 April] organised the hospital transports, put medical officers and equipment on board and despatched them to Alexandria. According to the original medical plan, no ship was supposed to leave the area for forty-eight hours. The following vessels carrying about 2800 wounded have left. *Lutzow, Itonus, Ionian, Clan MacGillivray, Seang Chun*. I have had to disorganise the field ambulances somewhat to get the medical officers and equipment ... The *Hindoo* with stationary hospital equipment has never come at all. I have given all the transports orders to return as soon as possible and have told the medical officers to select and bring back any men slightly wounded who are fit to join the ranks.[32]

According to (then Colonel) Sir CCB. White, Carruthers' position in sending these transport ships away was not that he had any responsibility or authority to do so (as this was Birrell's responsibility). Rather, General Birdwood, the Corps commander was told that there was utter chaos on board the transports. As a result Birdwood immediately ordered Carruthers to put things right. Unfortunately this caused substantial dislocation of Australian medical units designated to accompany the disembarking troops.

The DA & QMG of the ANZAC Corps controlled medical evacuations on the military side, while his naval counterpart was the Senior Naval Medical Officer, Fleet Surgeon C.C. MacMillan. The situation got out of hand partly because of the late arrival on the beaches of the naval beach parties, which landed at 11.00 a.m. on 25 April. However, the fighting had been thick and fast since 5.00 a.m. Naval 'Beach Masters' tended to have a rather limited life span given the exposed nature of their work — and sometimes they were not replaced. There was (what seems to us perhaps) a peculiar delineation of responsibility. The military's responsibilities for casualties ended the moment wounded were placed on board a boat at a pier, and recommenced when those casualties were actually received on board a hospital ship (most of which were the responsibility of the Army, not the Navy). The Royal Navy's responsibility, according to the manuals, began at high watermark on the beaches and finished at a ship's deck.

INSUFFICIENT MEDICAL PERSONNEL

Just prior to midnight on the evening of 25 April the long awaited *Hindoo*, with her precious cargo of medical reinforcements (including two medical supply depots) and stores, arrived off Cape Helles. However she remained there for almost three days as the senior medical and naval staff were unaware of her arrival. She eventually anchored off Gaba Tepe, without unloading, on the evening of 27 April. She had first been delayed by a storm while steaming from Egypt to Lemnos, and had then been 'lost'. Having eventually arrived there overdue, the Navy (unaware of her urgent need by the medical authorities), ordered the *Hindoo* to sail immediately for Cape Helles. Transport ships waiting to take on medical personnel, medicines, and medical equipment in the event of casualties being carried by these ships were left empty-handed — with disastrous results.

The whole medical situation at Anzac between 25 April and 5 May was therefore partly affected by the late arrival of the *Hindoo*. If this ship had arrived earlier, all the transports selected to carry wounded would probably have been adequately catered for in terms of medical staff and equipment. In any event neither

Birrell nor the General Staff oversaw the distribution of such reinforcements as there were (i.e. those of the tent subdivisions of the various ambulances which had been left on board ship after their bearer sections had disembarked). It thus fell to Carruthers to organise something. Indeed he was the only senior administrative officer to possess a copy of Birrell's final draft for evacuation, a singular advantage not then shared by either Howse or Manders.

In any event these officers had no means of contacting Carruthers. Birrell's criticism of the Australians took the following line: 'Any departure from the authorised scheme was due to General Headquarters' orders not being carried out by the ADMS, of Divisions at Anzac, and not working in conjunction with the A.A. & Q.M.G. Branch at Anzac.' This is absurd given the frantic attempts by Manders to reach the *Arcadian* by wireless. Birrell added that GHQ could not be blamed for 'any local confusion that may have arisen at Anzac'.[33] Despite this Carruthers was criticised by Birrell's ADMS, Lt. Colonel Keble, who did not state what Carruthers could have done other than what he did. The problem was belatedly recognised, and partly solved by the appointment of Colonel J. Maher (RAMC) as DDMS Lines of Communication to control evacuation from Anzac.

THE SITUATION UP TO 30 APRIL

On 29 April a British unit — the Field Ambulance of the Royal Marine Light Infantry — landed and assisted in medical work alongside the 1st ACCS, providing the Australians with a much needed break as they had been operating about 20 hours a day since landing. By 30 April the worst was over although the medical services were working with a staff reduced through casualties and secondment to other areas. For example, on 25 April 1915 alone, one field ambulance reported its casualties as two killed, 18 wounded and four missing.[34] Up to that time this unit had cleared more than 3000 wounded: 'all urgent operations were done, including necessary amputations, tying of arteries, several belly cases, depressed, compound fractures of skull, bladder cases and big, compound fractures of the thigh. All these necessitated anaesthetics, which were administered in nearly every instance by non-commissioned officers or by Privates.'[35] Throughout this time it was under the general control of Colonel Howse, as ADMS 1st Australian Division.

Medical personnel from the regimental units as well as the ambulances did not at first liaise with each other; it was entirely haphazard. The cause can be traced to the lack of instructions as to how they were to keep in touch, a technique not practised during their months in Egypt due to lack of appropriate opportunities. After a period of trial and error the Regimental Medical Officers arranged for their bearers to follow infantry companies, and kept for their own use two medics to assist in their RAPs. For the first few days after the landing stretcher bearers worked on their own initiative, some having lost contact with their own units. The 4th Australian Field Ambulance landed on 28 April and replaced a makeshift clearing station on the beach which had been established by the Royal Naval Ambulance at Monash Valley.

Even experienced doctors were shaken by what they saw. To AAMC personnel who had never seen a serious wound before, their job at the landing must have terrified them at first. Private H. Cicognani (a medic) wrote that during the first fortnight abdominal wounds predominated. He also noted that when the men got well entrenched, the number of abdominal wounds lessened, and head injuries became the more frequent: '…a very large number were wounded in the head, probably due to curiosity'.[36]

With reference to the behaviour of Australian troops under fire, and their initial casualty rate, the following tale (doubtless apocryphal, but which is repeated in many different sources), is indicative. Again Private Cicognani was conversing with a Turkish prisoner, who informed him 'that an Englishman would live the longest of all the men at the war. I asked him why. Oh when one shell come Englishman dig in…two shell come Indian dig in…Three shell come Australian jump up & say "Where those bloody shells coming from?" & they get killed.'[37]

In some cases boats were rowed by the same ambulance staff who had found, retrieved and treated casualties on shore (see photographs). After the fire had died down towards evening, they were able to get to the boats and clear the beach. The wounded were put into the boats from which the landing had been made, and which had then been abandoned. Treatment had been basic, but effective. Medics had only simple tools — iodine, field dressings. All splints for broken limbs were improvised, the rifle being much favoured for its availability, rigidity and length, although branches and sticks were also used.

The nature of the terrain was very rugged, but once ambulance bearers worked out routes to the beach, they made straight for the Casualty Clearing Station. Bearer officers, NCOs and their squads spread over the area and responded to the call of 'Stretcher bearer!', a job normally undertaken by bearers of the regiments at the front. A typical method of organising medical units to ensure optimum performance, whilst allowing for rest periods, was that employed by the 3rd Australian Field Ambulance. This system was organised such that four collecting stations were served. One squad was kept in waiting and while returning with a patient, a detail reported and another squad took the place of the squad returning.[38] Two positions were therefore established: (a) forward collecting posts near the head of 'Shrapnel Gully', from where the squads carried through to the beach; and (b) detachments at halting-places halfway down the valley where water was stored, and hot drinks and food prepared.

At the end of the day the medical personnel could take stock. (Between 25 April and 30 April 1915, an average of 460 casualties per day passed through the 1st ACCS.[39]) The medical services had suffered casualties of their own, but there was pride, as reflected in this diary entry by Private A. Gordon: 'Some of the fellows before this [i.e. the landing] had looked upon the A.M.C. men as cold footers — easy jobbers etc., but after that day Stretcher Bearers gained the immense respect of the fighting men who saw that their work was quite as dangerous, if not more so than their own.'[40]

Generally, in the early period of the campaign, the Turks respected the Red Cross, but there were exceptions. 'Turks hidden in secluded spots found our stretcher parties easy marks…Where our boys have suffered mostly was in exposed parts, hill tops etc. where wounded mostly lay & had to be gathered from.'[41] However, the deliberate shooting of wounded was rare, and certainly not a Turkish monopoly, as this excerpt from a letter home by Sgt. C. Laseron relates: 'One chap [a Turk] was only wounded & tried to get away into the bushes but a dozen pellets [i.e. bullets] must have hit him in the following few seconds.'[42] On the other hand there was the Australian 'who captured a Turkish officer, and while escorting the officer to the camp on the beach, he got hit in the leg so that the Turk bound his leg up and then carried his guard into camp.'[43]

Both officers and men of the medical services were equally vulnerable to enemy fire. Entries such as these are very common in medical unit diaries: 'While going out Capt McWhae was hit by a fragment of shrapnel, wounding forehead & right eye, he had to retire to the beach.'[44] 'Pte. Cooper shot through the heart by shrapnel.'[45] The medical casualties soon told. 'I have been detailed off as a stretcher bearer to my Coy B Company as all the old bearers have been killed or wounded.'[46]

Early in the Gallipoli campaign, rumour and folk lore had instilled the average soldier with an abhorrence of being found wounded in 'no man's land'. Lt. Colonel Carbery, the New Zealand medical historian noted 'the gratitude of those taken off from the accursed beach, obsessed by a dread of mutilation by the Turks had they succeeded in driving us back to the boats. Why this wholly unreasonable fear of maltreatment should have existed amongst the wounded is inexplicable, because the Ottoman soldier was always irreproachable in his adherence to the Geneva Convention.'[47]

Later stories circulated on Gallipoli that some Australian corpses had been found castrated or otherwise mutilated are without substantiation and were invariably caused by fauna, machine gun fire, or decomposition of bodies left in the open. A member of the AAMC wrote that 'the great fear of what the Turks might do to them were they taken prisoner, caused men to drag themselves for miles with broken thighs and arms'.[48] In a letter home, dated 10 November 1915, Major (later Lt. Colonel) J. Gordon of the 1st ACCS wrote: 'The Turks have played quite fairly & there is no truth at all in the stories of mutilation etc. They treat the dead & wounded with all respect.'[49]

Surviving Australian veterans are quick to point out that the Turks 'were gentlemen'. Butler too mentions the chivalry of the Turks in reference to an attack on Gabc Tepe on 4 May: 'The Turks did not fire a shot at the wounded men or those assisting them; the more lightly wounded limped down after the stretcher cases. When they had been towed out the enemy's fire broke out again.'[50] Frequently however the Turks had little choice but to fire among the wounded. 'The 9th Battalion who occupy this extreme wing suffered rather badly yesterday as a result of a prolonged attack…what made it doubly bad was the position of the dressing station — it appeared to be entirely in the way of bursting shells, to prove such was the case three stretcher bearers remained intact out of seventeen and a wounded man awaiting treatment there was scattered to fragments.'[51] There is also this eye-witness account from personal experience, by medic James McPhee: 'Carrying a wounded man down to beach a shell sprayed its pellets all around us & our patient was hit again.'[52]

As mentioned above even in field ambulance dressing stations men were not immune from shrapnel. 'The Turk could not be blamed for this as we had, of necessity, to place our hospitals wherever there was room.'[53] This fact accounts for a great many casualties sustained at medical outposts by both wounded and staff. Mistakes were not peculiar to the Turks, and so-called friendly fire also claimed its victims. On the Allied side, the following signal (sent to the Australian Divisional HQ by the Royal Marine Brigade) was received by the Royal Navy at 12.55 p.m. on 27 April: 'An Australian reported...that OUR artillery was shelling Australians immediately on Ch. Bn. left flank from South West. A similar report was received from left of Ch. Bn.'[54]

Cyril Checchi, a young Australian doctor working with the RAMC further south at Cape Helles, also recounted a near miss. 'We had watched the English Fleet the day before bombarding the Turkish positions and one of the shells had landed on the [Turkish] hospital. Just to let us know, they [the Turks] put six shells into our hospital — they did no damage fortunately.' He also related this incident: 'I was giving an anaesthetic in a tent one day, some minor job, and there was one German plane that flew over occasionally and it dropped a series of aerial darts...and one of them came through the roof of the tent..'[55] Pte. Makinson of the 13th Battalion related an incident later in December, when 'the Turks lobbed a few high explosive shells on the field hospital below us, and killed a couple of wounded men (can't blame them much as the hospital is alongside the track our supplies come by).'[56] There was certainly some naivety, as the OC of the 5th AFA for 9 September 1915 recorded that 'General Birdwood informed me not to fly the Union Jack alongside the Red Cross as the enemy took it to represent HQ.'[57]

Certainly the hospital ships were always respected. 'The enemy were scrupulously observant of the rules of the Geneva Convention and never fired on the boats etc., engaged in the transport of the wounded, although the Red Cross Flag was not always conspicuously displayed.'[58] Although there is the incident related by Sister Alice Kitchen, an Australian nurse on the *Gascon* off Gaba Tepe on 7 July: '2 shells nearly fell on the boat full of wounded today, just missed it. The first time the Turks have not played the game properly.'[59] The absence of clearly visible hospital or Red Cross markings on ships carrying wounded was a tragic mistake, and incidents occurred in both April and August. After the War, Howse related that during the April landings it was impossible for the boats carrying the wounded from the shore to differentiate the transports selected as 'ambulance carriers', as they were not marked in any way.[60]

The best known of the daily acts of quiet heroism performed by members of the medical services, is that of 'Simpson' Kirkpatrick and his donkey 'Murphy'. This man was one of a number of medics using donkeys for conveying lightly wounded soldiers between the gullies and the dressing stations. 'Simpson', or Scotty as he was also known to his mates, worked by himself, but actually belonged to 'C' Section, 3rd Field Ambulance. 'No. 202 Pte. "Simpson" has shown initiative in using a donkey from the 26th [April] to carry slightly wounded cases & has kept up his work from early morning till night every day since.'[61] He was killed by a machine-gun bullet in Shrapnel Gully on 19 May.

It was also during this period of operations that one of the most memorable scandals of this campaign arose. It concerned the *Lutzow*, one of the transports designated to take aboard Australian and New Zealand wounded on the first day of the landing. Versions of what actually happened vary from different witnesses and from official reports. It also provides some insight into the commentators themselves. A New Zealand war historian wrote that although 'the *Lutzow* was designated as a hospital ship for 200 serious, and 1000 slightly wounded, there were only two medical men on board: Major Young, a veterinary surgeon, and a medical orderly...Together they would deal with a constant stream of wounded...'[62]

This medical team of two was relieved after almost 80 hours of work. However Surgeon-General Babtie's later comment was that the story 'of an officer of the Veterinary Corps being in command of [a] temporary hospital ship' was 'absurd'.[63]

AN INTERLUDE

After the critical shortage of medical personnel had passed, the 2nd and 3rd Light Horse Field Ambulances were landed on 12 May. However they were sent back to Lemnos on 26 June as part of an attempt to save water on the peninsula. During May the situation improved marginally as the military arrangements settled, 'definite' front lines were established, and numbers of battle casualties decreased. Wells were sunk, medical units dug in, housekeeping became the norm, small piers were built and most importantly medical stores were landed. Then on 13 May all shipping left for Lemnos due to a submarine scare. As will be seen the presence of submarines off the peninsula was to be a serious inconvenience to the Allies, particularly to the medical author-ities who tried to ensure adequate evacuation procedures for the wounded and sick.

Then came a brief lull in the fighting. The dead of both sides lay in festering heaps in front of the trenches for weeks. On 20 May, two Turkish medical officers with Red Crescent (the Islamic equivalent of the Red Cross) flags approached 'Pope's Hill' (see Map 2.2 on page 35), and two Australian medical officers went out to meet them. The enemy desired an armistice to bury their dead and to collect their wounded.

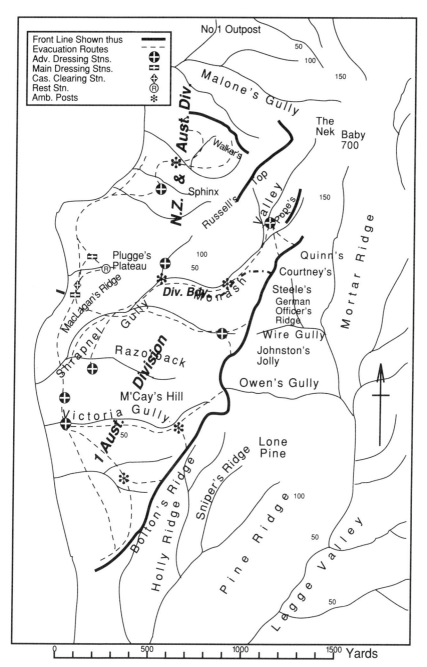

Front Line Shown thus
Evacuation Routes
Adv. Dressing Stns.
Main Dressing Stns.
Cas. Clearing Stn.
Rest Stn.
Amb. Posts

MAP 2.1 Anzac at the middle of May 1915 showing medical positions and routes of evacuation from the front line to the beach. *Note*: Numbers represent contours in metres. *Source*: A.G. Butler, Vol. I, p. 158

The armistice, which was granted on 24 May, had good sanitary reasons to justify it. The corpses were not only 'a nauseating source of discomfort to the defenders', but they were a breeding place for blowflies (Sarcophagides or 'carcass' flies). The truce also provided an opportunity for the Anzacs to exchange their grim army biscuit for Turkish rye bread, and in some cases to glean additional munitions of a more deadly nature. Any Turkish rifles found by the Australians had their bolts removed and were handed to the Turks. However in a diary entry a medic from the 4th Australian Field Ambulance intimates foul play: '...instead of burying the unfortunate dead they [the Turks] were picking up rifles and ammunition so our boys would [not] stand that'.[64]

TABLE: 2.1 CASUALTY FIGURES FOR ANZAC, 25–30.4.1915

	K.in A.	D. of W.	Wounded
Australians	965	161	4 114
New Zealanders	275	78	698

Source: A.G. Butler, Vol. I, p. 178n

Briefly, to show that things were little better in the British sector of the peninsula, something can be said about the attack on the small village of Krithia near the southern tip of the peninsula on 6 May, one in which two ANZAC brigades and their field ambulance participated. Throughout May these attacks and counter-attacks caused heavy casualties, the worst being sustained by the Australian 2nd Brigade (75 percent of its original strength of 3885 men at Anzac) in the Krithia fight.[65]

There were a number of parallels with the Australian and New Zealand experience. First, the British medical officer in charge of this action was told about it only on the afternoon before, and he therefore had little opportunity to coordinate his medical units with those of the ANZAC Corps. Subsequently the officer commanding the 2nd Australian Field Ambulance received no instructions. The DMS — Birrell — again was absent. For the stretcher bearers there was a difficult hand-carry over distances up to five kilometres, often carried out at night.

The same problem with respect to the shortage of stretchers was experienced there. During and after the Krithia operation there was a delay of up to five days before most of the serious casualties were treated. Australian stretcher bearers engaged there lost heavily in casualties.

Otherwise the period between May and August was one punctuated by relatively small-scale fighting, and battle casualty figures were beginning to be overtaken by the number of Diggers

falling sick and succumbing to disease. Captain Davenport of the
5th Australian Field Ambulance noted that by the middle of
August the condition of the men was awful: 'Thin, haggard, weak
as kittens, and covered with suppurating sores. Practically every
man had Dysentery.'[66] The daily sick parade reports were
beginning to record an accelerating incidence of sickness; chiefly
diarrhoea and dysentery. In the case of one battalion on 27
August, 180 men out of a total strength of 220 appeared on sick
parade.[67]

This chronic ill-health due to disease had two immediate
consequences. First, it exacerbated the already reduced manpower of the medical services, themselves just as prone to
shrapnel and sickness as troops of the line. As late as September,
it is possible to find entries such as the following in Howse's
official war diary: 'Today there is a shortage of twenty-two
medical officers in the 1st Australian Division including the 2nd
Light Horse Brigade and Field Ambulance attached to the
Division.'[68] Second, these cases had to be accommodated
somewhere, and there were frequent occasions when either heavy
shelling, submarine activity or storms caused a serious backlog
of casualties at both field ambulances and dressing stations.

QUESTIONS OF ADMINISTRATION

The results of inadequate physical screening of AIF volunteers
was just now beginning to be a thorn in the side of the medical
units, already stretched to cope with the outbreak of influenza,
bronchitis, mumps, measles and venereal disease which had
occurred in the Australian camps in Egypt. A number of troops
who should not have been there because of the negligent manner
in which the appointed (civilian) recruiting doctors carried out
their duties in Australia, made it as far as Egypt undetected. To
some extent Australian doctors had been steamrolled in 'medical
examinations' performed during the initial months of the War
when thousands flocked to join up.

Some idea of the situation can be gained by two pieces of
evidence. The first is a cable sent by the ageing Australian DMS
Surgeon-General W.D. Williams from Cairo on 5 April to the
Defence Department in Melbourne. 'Urge medical board two
medical officers each state to be detailed finally examine every
recruit after passing first medical examination STOP Many men
still arriving should not have been passed STOP Such course will
save Command needless expense landing quite useless men here
and army medical service here endless trouble.'[69]

The second document is a memorandum to the ADMS 1st Australian Division (Howse), concerning three men who had been passed fit by medical officers in various States in Australia and who had been happily packed off to the front:

> The first had a 'congenital deformity' (atrophy) of the phalanges of the 2nd, 3rd, and 4th digits of the right hand, rendering the hand useless for ordinary purposes. The second had a traumatic cataract...[and] can barely distinguish light from darkness. A third had an undescended testicle and was told by Doctor [upon joining up] that he was only fit for A.A.M.C., and that probably his duties would only extend to a hospital ship or general hospital.[70]

All these latter cases refer to reinforcements sent out to the 2nd Light Horse Field Ambulance at Anzac. What possible use they could have been to any unit, let alone to an understaffed medical service, is unclear.

Another problem that concerned the medical services was dental hygiene. Many troops had reached Egypt who should have been classed as unfit on account of their teeth — or lack of them. The problem was made worse by the AAMC not having one dentist on its establishment, although some professional dentists were withdrawn from the ranks to do part-time palliative work.

Major L.O. Betts, the RMO of the 9th Light Horse Regiment wrote that: 'I cannot remember any provisions at all for dental work in Australia, but in Egypt there was a dentist at No. 2 A.G.H. At this period of the war [1915] there was no provision for dental inspections and the standard of dental fitness was very low. There were a fair number of men in the unit who would have been passed "Dentally Unfit" had the standard of dental fitness been the same as in 1916 and after.'[71] Auxiliary services, such as X-ray equipment, bacteriology laboratories etc. were also in very short supply. The situation even in Egypt was little better.

Behind the scenes were the bases at Alexandria and Cairo. The situation in Egypt at this time is discussed at length in Volume I of Butler, where he makes two points relevant to this analysis. The first is that 'the responsibility under the Director-General at the War Office for making provision for the reception and distribution of casualties from Gallipoli fell entirely on the DMS for Egypt, Surgeon-General Ford'. Second, throughout May, the medical situation in Egypt was one dictated entirely by improvisation: 'hand-to-mouth expansion, of ministrations of inadequate staff under unsatisfactory conditions, and of overflow to England and Australia of cases that should have been retained, while invalids who should have been sent home were retained and accumulated'.[72]

To return to the first point, Ford had made neither calculations of casualty figures, nor provision for them prior to the April landing. Instead he was content to wait until whatever casualties there were, landed in Egypt. With 48 hours' notice, the *Gascon* arrived at Alexandria, followed shortly thereafter as we have seen by the five transports (and their 2849 casualties) despatched with no prior notice from Anzac by General Carruthers.

During the preceding few weeks preparations in Egypt had continued at a snail's pace, certainly to the frustration of Colonel Springthorpe, senior physician at the No 1 Australian General Hospital. 'Three Officers, ten nurses, nine orderlies and five General Duty men start to get Ghezireh [hospital] in order (having been told weeks ago 30 percent casualties were expected), what absence of provision and what deplorable neglect on some one's part.'[73] Ford's lack of adequate supervision also meant that these transport ships, once empty of their human cargo, sailed back to Gallipoli without any attempt being made to refurbish them with medical stores, thereby creating a severe drain on the limited medical resources at the front. Until 9 May Australian and New Zealand troops accounted for 75 per cent of the 7884 casualties which arrived in Egypt.[74]

For months after April the medical arrangements at Lemnos continued to take a back seat, which thereby fell victim to a persistent reluctance on the part of the GHQ to upgrade Mudros Harbour there into an advanced expeditionary base. This was despite the fact that the Royal Navy had made the harbour its official administrative base by mid-May. Shortly after, Colonel Maher, the DDMS L of C, moved there from Cape Helles. This was significant because his responsibilities included supervising medical supplies en route to the peninsula, coordinating the temporary hospital ships and fleet sweepers which were then engaged in ferry work from Gallipoli, as well as administering the return of recovered soldiers back to the front.

At Mudros itself no attempts had been made to drill for water on a scale large enough to cater for hospitals of any size. Because of this No 19 British General Hospital arrived on 24 May from England only to be shipped on to Alexandria. Lemnos incidentally was the closest Australian nurses came to serving at the Gallipoli front. In all about 100 nurses served on Lemnos between August 1915 and February 1916. The letters and diaries of Australian nurses on Lemnos later in 1915 contain many references to the shortage of water, even for drinking.

In June, in a belated attempt to still both British and colonial public clamour over what had by then been revealed of the April landings on Gallipoli, the British Army appointed Surgeon-General Babtie as 'Principal Director of Medical Services' (PDMS) to coordinate medical affairs in the Mediterranean. A little later the Royal Navy followed suit, appointing a 'Principal Hospital Transport Officer' (PHTO), Surgeon Vice-Admiral Sir James Porter. The appointment of these officers resulted in some improvements.

Babtie arranged for an increase in the number of hospital ships, more medical staff and an expansion of hospital accommodation on Lemnos. Porter, for his part, was responsible for more efficient medical evacuation by sea. However, Babtie's preparations were substantially incomplete by the time of the August Offensive. This Offensive was to be part of a big 'push' by the Allies to end the stalemate on the peninsula and secure substantial territorial gains there. The medical reinforcements did not land at Mudros Harbour until 7 August. No 3 Australian General Hospital, albeit minus its equipment, was also sent to Mudros, in addition to No 1 and No 3 Canadian Stationary Hospitals (which arrived at Mudros on 16 August). At the beginning of August No 1 and No 2 Australian Stationary Hospitals had been landed, but with their equipment either 'lost' or on other ships still at sea.

However, after the arrival of a competent administrator in the person of Lt. General Altham in Mudros in mid-July, the harbour there began to take on the appearance of a proper base, with piers, roads, and hospital sites being constructed. Roads meant motor ambulances, and the first of the large Australian fleet of motor ambulances in Egypt were sent out, making life much easier for both patients and medical staff. At the same time, part of the medical arrangements for August included greater utilisation of the small island of Imbros, some 19 kilometres from Anzac, and straddling the sea route between Gallipoli and Lemnos.

THE AUGUST OFFENSIVE

While tactical preparations for the August Offensive had been underway since 13 July, senior (RAMC and AAMC) officers were not made privy to the plan until the very eve of the attacks, namely 6 August. With respect to the Anzac sector this plan basically comprised a surprise night attack against the heights of Sari Bair (and its summit — Hill 971). There was to be a feint by the 1st Australian Division at 'Lone Pine', and on 'The Nek' further north, by the New Zealand and Australian Division. (See Map 2.3 on page 40.) Again the system was inundated.

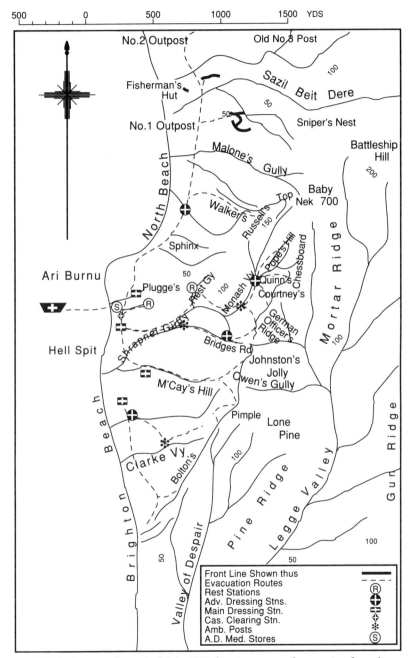

MAP 2.2 Anzac at the end of July 1915 showing routes of evacuation from the front line to the roadstead. *Note*: Numbers represent contours in metres. *Source*: A.G. Butler, Vol. I, p. 210

The following description comes from the diary of Sister Alice Kitchen of No 1 Australian Stationary Hospital: 'Then a large lighter full of wounded came alongside, almost 200 patients on it. Never saw such a lot at once before…They say there are hundreds [of wounded] over there [on the beach] lying about everywhere, waiting to be brought down from the hilly places. The stretcher bearers have lost heavily.'[75] Although this quotation appears to concern events of 25 April, it was in fact written on 10 August. Little had been learned and many of the same mistakes (medical, administrative, and tactical) were to be made again.

At Anzac, in the area occupied by the 1st Australian Division which was expected to bear the heaviest casualties, certain steps had been made by Howse in an effort to avoid a repetition of the April fiasco. Also Colonel Keble, the ADMS, MEF was landed on 5 August to act as Medical Control Officer. Major Corbin of the 1st ACCS was made Medical Embarkation Officer and several RAMC officers were seconded to assist in sorting casualties (lightly wounded were to go to Mudros and severely wounded were to be sent direct to Egypt). Even so, the scale of the attack — and again, its sheer complexity — was to work against these measures.

For the New Zealand and Australian Division's sector Colonel Manders had proposed a detailed plan, using accurate maps copied from Turkish prisoners. He presented these 1/20 000 scale maps (a vast improvement over the 1/40 000 scale map used for the April landing) on the afternoon of 6 August. He had at his disposal the 1st and 3rd Ambulances of the Light Horse, and that of the 4th Australian Field Ambulance. In addition he had his own New Zealand field ambulance and part of the New Zealand mounted field ambulance. There was also an Indian field ambulance, while two British units were to provide casualty clearing facilities.

Although there was no preliminary naval bombardment, as there had been in April, to forewarn the Turks of an imminent attack, other signs must have been noted by the enemy, particularly the hospital ships which had come up and anchored off Anzac preparatory to the offensive. A number of mistakes were repeated with the same disastrous consequences. For instance, in 'the first hurried rush of evacuating wounded most of the available stretchers had already gone away to Mudros, and the Army had few left to bring the hundreds of cases waiting to be brought down to the sea shore'.[76] However, there were other features present during this offensive which had been absent in April. Disease and sickness were two of these factors.

During the proceedings of the Dardanelles Commission, Major Corbin (AAMC) stated that no major improvement had been effected in medical arrangements since the first landing, and the state of affairs was as bad in the operations in August, mainly because there was no means of clearing the beach. However, he did concede some improvement, as one can read in his later testimony: '...we had nothing like the same amount of surgical work in proportion to the number of cases to do. In addition to this, there was infinitely better and more ample hospital ship accommodation [than in April], and so many cases who would have died under other circumstances were rushed on to the hospital ship for operation.'[77]

At the time every Australian and New Zealand medical unit was under-strength and inefficient administrative procedures meant that some hospital ships and carriers were still undermanned. Surgeon-General Babtie himself recognised this. 'There has not been a ship come down or a hospital here in which the staff of M.O.s, nurses and orderlies could not have been doubled, or even trebled with advantage for the few days [i.e. immediately after the August Offensive].'[78] Still, medical officers at the front marshalled their resources as best they could.

On 6 August the RMO of the 14th Battalion had 12 stretcher bearers, a battalion medical corporal orderly, and five other medics — he also had at his disposal a total of six stretchers! The extent of his preparations included sandbags filled with dressings, in addition to a sandbag of dressings wrapped up in each stretcher. He ordered his bearers during the night advance to carry back no wounded, merely bandage them and leave them on the track. They were to 'press on' until the column reached its destination.

By 6.00 a.m. the first of the field ambulances sent an urgent appeal for reinforcements, although in some instances several days passed before additional staff arrived on the peninsula. Every doctor, medic and bearer worked non-stop. In isolated areas at the front in gullies and ravines, wherever wounded had grouped together, lone medical officers did their best. 'At one place in a clump of trees there were thirty or forty brave fellows lying, and one doctor was attending them by the light of a hurricane lamp.'[79]

On 8 August an improvised collecting station formed by elements of the 1st Australian Field Ambulance could only muster one doctor and 35 medics. Together they handled a continuous stream of wounded, and in 24 hours dealt with 1500 wounded. These same bearers had earlier that day also carried and treated the casualties which were the result of an attack on 'Holly Ridge'.

The 1st Light Horse Field Ambulance was following up the troops at the attack on Chailak Dere and evacuated wounded to the beach as it went. Cooperative efforts at forming 'relay posts' from the front to the beach, down through the gullies, soon proved unworkable. A New Zealand ambulance which had formed a dressing station below the Light Horse unit, was shelled and had to move. The casualties were accumulating so fast they could not be evacuated. It was all these units could do to carry out first aid and dress the wounds of the Diggers.

On the following day (9 August), this unit too had to call for reinforcements. A Welsh ambulance unit further down the gully, which had acted as a relay post, could not cope with the rush, and collapsed. This compelled the Light Horse bearers to carry wounded all the way to the beach; at times even the cooks were conscripted to assist in carrying wounded on stretchers. The night attacks and the unfamiliar terrain contributed to a lack of organisation in areas away from the beaches.

The carefully hoarded stocks of medical supplies held by RMOs, dressing stations and field ambulances, began to run low. Unlike the April disaster there were adequate medical stores on depot ships just offshore. The difficulty was getting the appropriate requisition orders to the ships, having these processed, and then finding men to bring stores back to where they were needed. All this took time, another commodity in very short supply to the medical services during this period.

Fortunately during this offensive all units of ambulances were used, including their tent subdivisions. Men from these sections were responsible for dressing wounds, splinting and assisting in operations. Basically then, in August more medical manpower was theoretically available — but this was offset by units now being undermanned. Thus units like the 1st ACCS on the beach were hard pressed. For in addition to caring for wounded from its own area, it received all the British walking wounded from the disastrous Suvla Bay fighting a little further north who had been unable to be evacuated owing to transport difficulties there. In just over two days the clearing station treated approximately 5000 men.

The stress for some became unbearable and they sought to leave the field. Officers did not have to resort to the self-inflicted wounds of the ordinary soldier to escape. At a time when every available man was needed the contempt for the few who fled is evident in a diary entry by the commander of the 4th Australian Field Ambulance, J.L. Beeston: 'The number of officers clearing out is not commendable. One cannot wonder at the men squibbing it, one is more and more surprised at officers in whom we would have placed every confidence before the War and they are so barefaced about it too.'[80]

The lot of the wounded was made worse by the fact that many of them fought wearing only the bare essentials, as a concession to the intense heat of the day. Therefore a badly wounded man who could not walk had to lie (half-naked) all through the nights, which could be bitterly cold. At various stages of the offensive those wounded who did reach the piers when the medical barges came alongside, found that the least wounded were often evacuated first. A senior New Zealand officer noted that the 'lack of facilities for evacuating wounded was as pronounced as at the landing'. He also describes an interesting feature which is not noted by other sources, published or private: 'When a string of Red Cross barges would come in, the walking cases would naturally crowd up to the pier in anticipation of getting off; there was a tendency to leave the helpless men on the beach, but the medical officers and orderlies watched as well as they were able and sent the serious cases to the hospital ships as soon as possible, the less serious ones going to Lemnos by the hospital carrier.'[81]

As if the initial fighting had not been bad enough, soldiers' stories made it seem worse to those not directly involved on the peninsula. These accounts — both accurate reports and furphies — worried the General Staff so much that a memorandum (reproduced on page 43) was circularised two months later warning medical staff not 'to become too seriously impressed by the stories of young officers and men who have come back sick and wounded'. The following entry illustrates the simple manner in which rumours, much beloved of soldiers, was borne.

The diary of Sister Kitchen again, this time on board the hospital ship *Gascon* recounts that 'opinion here varied as to the number of wounded which have been taken off from Gallipoli, but "Chief" thinks 5000 near the mark as he knows the ships receiving and the numbers they are likely to carry. They say Alex and Malta are crowded full & the *Aquitania* here in the Bay [Mudros] with over 3000 on board. Lemnos is supposed to be able to take 11 000 but we "have our doubts". At any rate the equipment of the No. 3 general hospital is floating about in the Mediterranean between Alexandria and Malta although the staff are here...All the patients tell us that there are hundreds and hundreds lying everywhere, many in the broiling sun not even able to get a drink and many here come on board with dressings not done for 4 or 5 days...so many septic wounds, so many limbs likely to be lost.'[82]

Scenes strikingly reminiscent of the original landing were re-enacted in the New Zealand and Australian Division's sector, wherein the objective was the heights of Chunuk Bair. Their

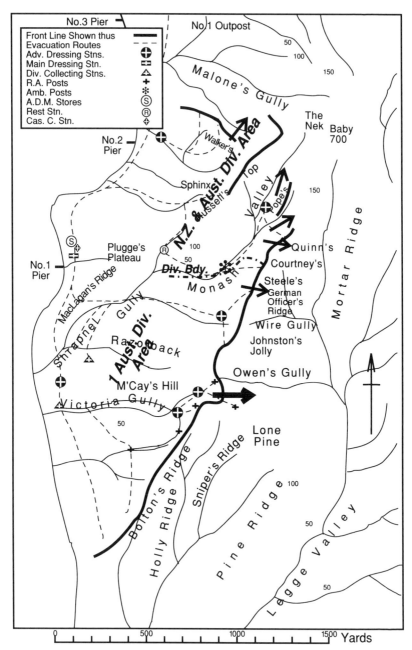

MAP 2.3   The Anzac area showing the routes of evacuation from the Battle of
Lone Pine; also those from Walker's Ridge, Pope's Hill, Quinn's and
Steele's Posts during the feints of 6–7 August 1915. *Note*: Numbers
represent contours in metres. *Source*: A.G. Butler. Vol. I, p. 294

wounded lay and died in the overcrowded CCS on the beach.
Shelling during the day made evacuation impossible and the
crowds of wounded grew. Manders, the New Zealand ADMS,
'who had worked so hard to make sure that this battle would not
see the tragedy of the wounded at the landing repeated...knew all
his medical resources were exhausted'.[83] The next day he was
killed by a bullet.

Strategically, nothing was gained in this sector. On this flank,
Manders' units were later joined by sections of the British 39th
(which employed trained ambulance dogs for seeking out
wounded) and 41st (British) Field Ambulances. Manders' death
may have contributed to problems in the medical arrangements
at Chunuk Bair, which deteriorated more rapidly than those of
the 1st Australian Division further south, where medical
procedures were being overseen by the indefatigable Howse.

Units of this Division were engaged in a massive diversion
along the front line, stretching from 'Quinn's Post' in the north
to 'Lone Pine' in the south (see Map 2.3 on page 40). The affiliated
medical units of the 1st Australian Division under Colonel Howse
consisted of the 2nd and 3rd Field Ambulances. The casualties
were appalling, the attack on and about 'Lone Pine' decimated the
six battalions thrown into this desperate conflict. A similarly
heroic assault on 'The Nek' was just as devastating with only 31
per cent of the 3rd Light Horse Brigade which was engaged (i.e.
the 8th and 10th Light Horse Regiments) returning from this
episode unwounded.

Not only were there insufficient medics, but no special
provision had been made for these operations, as Birrell
apparently was not informed. Originally Howse had been
designated 'Controller' of the beach for the August attack.
However, on the strength of a report he sent to Birrell in which
he expressed his dissatisfaction with the medical arrangements,
he was relieved by Colonel Keble, and subsequently was able to
work with the 1st Australian Division.

The 1st ACCS was faced with the same difficulties as in April
— particularly in a shortage of sea transport.

To summarise then, despite better planning the August
Offensive had much in common with everything that went
wrong in April, although in August there was at least an
awareness of the implications of large numbers of casualties for
the Lines of Communication. Casualties amongst the medical
services alone were of the order of 15 per cent. Despite this, in
its *Final Report* the Dardanelles Commission found (with two
exceptions — notably one an Australian medical officer, the other
a New Zealand medical officer) that 'in the operations in August

there were few complaints of the arrangements for the removal of the wounded from the beaches and their conveyance to the hospital ships, except on the first day of fighting at Anzac'.[84]

What set the August activities apart were the traffic 'jams' caused by large numbers of reinforcements and munitions being forced up one defile (at Aghyl Dere and Chailak Dere on the evening of 8 August), so narrow it necessitated men walking in single file, while large numbers of wounded were trying to get back down via the same route to the beaches and comparative safety. Stretcher bearers had no right of way. Added to this was the blistering heat of the day and the extreme cold of the evenings — many wounded died from exposure where they lay.

The medical arrangements for evacuation were seriously disorganised by the fact that the two British clearing stations which were sent in to help did not arrive on 6 August and could not be found. According to the OC of one of these (the 16th CCS), the captain of the ship with the two units on board was ordered to land them at Anzac if he arrived there before dark. He duly arrived, but as he was unable to contact anyone on the beach at Anzac, he then proceeded to Suvla Bay under contingency orders. Only when they arrived there the Naval Officer in charge of traffic received a cable ordering the two CCSs back to Anzac — thus the delay.

By 8 August the medical services in this theatre were on the brink of exhaustion — on that night over 1000 men lay exposed on the beaches waiting evacuation. On the preceding evening the only hospital ship off Anzac, the *Sicilia*, was already refusing to take on wounded. Some small boats, having been denied accommodation for their wounded, turned back to the shore only to be shelled by the Turks who believed they were carrying troop reinforcements. Tragically, reinforcements in the shape of the tent divisions of the 1st, 2nd, 3rd Light Horse Field Ambulances, the 1st Australian Field Ambulance, and the New Zealand Mounted Ambulance arrived — after the worst was over — on 11 August. Eventually by 14 August, there were sufficient boats to clear the wounded from Gallipoli.

The *Final Report* of the Dardanelles Commission again understates this period in its usual inimitable manner: 'The scheme for the evacuation of the wounded in the August operations was based upon an approximately correct estimate of casualties, and the supply of hospital ships was much larger than at the first landing. On the whole, this scheme worked well, though again there were cases in which the improvised hospital ships were not satisfactory' and the wounded suffered — again. Those preparations made by the AAMC, although adequate in

CONFIDENTIAL.

MEDITERRANEAN EXPEDITIONARY FORCE.

Circular Memorandum to Medical Officers and Nurses on Hospital Ships and Ambulance Carriers.

It has been brought to the notice of Sir Ian Hamilton that, here and there, on Hospital Ships and Ambulance Carriers, Medical Officers and Nurses have allowed themselves to become too seriously impressed by the stories of young officers and men who have come on board sick or wounded. It is natural, under the conditions, that these tales should be over-coloured; it is natural also that contact with so much suffering should incline the listeners to sympathy; but it is certain also that, whether from the standpoint of the individual sick or of the Military operations as a whole, such enervating influences should be resisted.

All grades and degrees of the medical staff must make it a point of professional honour to maintain a hearty tone of optimism calculated to raise rather than to lower the confidence and courage of the fighting men who have been temporarily committed to their charge   "Canst thou not minister to a mind diseas'd?" Thus Macbeth enquires of the physician who, too diffident, replies "Therein the patient must minister to himself." But our hospitals at Mudros have proved to us that those who minister to the body diseased are best qualified at the same time to "Raze out the written troubles of the brain." Let Medical Officers and Nurses on Hospital Ships and Ambulance Carriers see to it then that, under all trials, they surround their sick and wounded with an atmosphere of enthusiasm and of invincible hope.

War Office,
  5th October, 1915.

themselves for dealing with troop operations in its own sector, were seriously offset by the relatively large number of casualties and by lack of communication (and insufficient notice) from Hamilton's GHQ. 'Of 51 867 casualties, sick and wounded, that left the Peninsula between 7 August 1915 and 8 September 1915, 23 686 [45.6 per cent] were from the Anzac front.'[85]

POST-SCRIPT TO THE AUGUST PERIOD

Many people reading of the Gallipoli campaign are apt to neglect the importance the weather played, particularly in the medical war on the peninsula, and of course the disastrous failure of the British attack on Suvla Bay. Its effect on medical accommodation has been noted elsewhere, and its influence on evacuations from Gallipoli will be discussed in chapters three and four. Troops who landed in April were subjected to very hot weather at first, together with the associated medical and sanitary problems the heat inevitably brought with it — particularly flies.

Then, after October, the weather moved to the other extreme and for most Australians it was the first time that they had seen snow. The novelty however soon wore off. An English naval surgeon, T.T. Jeans, painted this picture: 'For a week in November S.W. gales strewed the beaches on the Peninsula with wreckage — tugs, steamboats — and then a blizzard swept down from the N.E. and caused the cruellest suffering to Turks and British alike. On the night of the 28th, when the blizzard was at its worst, the floods of icy water washed away the parapets of many enemy trenches...'[86]

Offshore, after the worst of the fighting was over, the wounded were rather better cared for than the casualties of April, or even at the beginning of August. Lieutenant King-Wilson, a British medical officer on the *Caledonian*, on which about 1000 cases (mainly sick, rather than wounded) were placed, wrote that they 'had practically the same arrangements as on the previous occasion with perhaps a few improvements, but it was not nearly such a rush and the men were not in such frightful condition...The wounded were mostly slightly wounded, and presented no new features, except that they had been better dressed ashore. In fact, when I changed some officers' dressings I was told that that was the third or fourth time they had been dressed in twenty-four hours.'[87]

Soldiers were thus competently cared for when the medical staff at Anzac had time to perform their tasks, and were not overwhelmed by the sudden rushes of huge numbers of casualties from various infantry 'stunts'.

THE FINAL EVACUATION — DECEMBER 1915

Despite a virtual stalemate in the campaign toward the end of 1915, danger was ever-present. This was the view of J.R. Lawson, a medic with the 4th Australian Field Ambulance, who wrote in December of 'Shells flying around put them into D.H.Q. and blew the 16th C.C. Hospital to pieces and blew sick and wounded to pieces while waiting to go on board the hospital boat. It was an awful sight to see.'[88] In other areas there was less to complain about: 'We are getting rather better meals than in earlier months. We have now just got some order about moving. [And then] We have got orders to pack up all personal belongings and be ready to move off at 24 hrs. notice.'[89]

The campaign had been a manifest failure. The fate of the MEF was sealed when Field Marshal Earl Kitchener, Minister of War, visited the Dardanelles on 10 October. He subsequently recommended to the British Cabinet on 22 November that all British and Allied forces on Gallipoli be withdrawn. Hamilton had earlier been relieved of his command on 15 October, once the failure of his August Offensive had been fully assessed by the War Office. On 16 October he was replaced by General Sir Charles Monro. Sir James Porter (who had been organising sea transport and who was now 'redundant'), left for London on 30 October. Plans for a full-scale evacuation were placed in hand almost immediately. Two different plans were originally submitted: (1) A gradual (withdrawal) from position to position; and (2) General Codley's recommendation that every person surplus to the barest minimum necessary to hold the front should be removed direct from the front line and be evacuated direct to the sea in two nights. Fortunately for the medical services the latter plan was the one adopted.

Secrecy was vital and this was 'ensured' by reducing the garrison over the winter months ostensibly for the purpose of allowing rest and recreation for troops who had been on the peninsula since April. The evacuation must rank as one of the most successfully concealed in the history of military operations. Given that camps and hospitals may have harboured Turkish and German spies (often Greek labourers), its success was even more remarkable.[90] It was almost incredible that such a secret should be so successfully kept, given that even medical officers, traditionally 'on the outer', were aware of a proposed December evacuation. The enemy too, was suspicious as one German officer wrote perhaps with hindsight: 'Rumours and suggestions that the enemy were going to evacuate Gallipoli naturally swarmed round us on Gallipoli.'[91]

In *The Summary of Evidence by Major-General G.F. Ellison Regarding the Dardanelles Campaign — July–December, 1915* (Appendix 'M'), Ellison states that among the verbal instructions given him by Kitchener on 12 July 1915, the latter was 'ready to allow large expenditure on secret service. He mentioned £100 000 [a colossal sum in 1915] for any specific object.' It is tempting to speculate that Hamilton's successor may have taken up the gauntlet and 'paid' a Turkish agent or high official to negotiate a bloodless withdrawal from Gallipoli, the prize being an immense quantity of munitions left behind. This was not the first time a 'bribe' had been offered. According to G.H. Cassar, as early as February 1915, the Director of British Intelligence, Admiral Sir Reginald Hall, entrusted two agents to meet a Turkish delegation to negotiate a treaty whereby the Turks would withdraw from the war in exchange for £4 000 000. The representatives from both sides met on 15 March 1915 but failed to reach an agreement.[92]

Two features set the final evacuation apart from the landing eight months earlier: first, the intricate planning involved (see also Appendix IIIB); and second, the almost total lack of optimism concerning its success. General Monro expected fully one-third of his force to be casualties during the withdrawal.

The first real intimation to the Australian medical services that something was afoot came on 19 November, when the British ADMS at Mudros held a conference of the commanding officers of all the medical units on Lemnos. They discussed the 'accommodation of a large number of wounded from Gallipoli in connection, so it is rumoured, with the proposed evacuation of the Peninsula'.[93]

A week later on 26 November, General Birdwood, the GOC ANZAC, officially told the acting DDMS (Howse was in Egypt and did not return until 7 December) that the garrison at Anzac was to be reduced. Lt. Colonel Sutton, acting in Howse's stead suggested a number of medical units to be evacuated. These included the 13th CCS, the 16th CCS (after they had cleared their wounded), and all the field ambulances of the 54th Division, as well as the field ambulance of the 2nd Australian Division. One New Zealand field ambulance and a field ambulance of the Australian Division would be decided upon later. Sutton suggested the immediate evacuation of all sick and other men who could be spared. The 2nd Light Horse Field Ambulance was warned to hold itself in readiness for a transfer to Mudros. Birdwood told Sutton to warn all these units but not to issue any written orders for their removal.[94]

The earliest non-official mention of the evacuation in medical units is found in the diary of Sergeant (later Lieutenant) H.H.V. Woods of the 4th Australian Field Ambulance. His entry for 11 November 1915 simply says 'Rumours of our departure.'[95] There were other signs too: 'First intimation of the evacuation of the Peninsula...We had some indication that the withdrawal was to take place for during the past few weeks no mail would be accepted for the Peninsula.'[96] Such rumours soon became rife, and diary entries thereafter are full of the news. 'The 6th Fld Amb left camp to embark for a destination unknown and I might also state that we are preparing to do the same and there are all sorts of rumours as to our destination.'[97] Speculation was soon followed by action. Private J.R. Lawson, another medic, noted on 16 December that 'We have orders to have everything packed up ready to move at 24 hours notice.'[98]

There is no doubt many were taken by surprise. On 13 December Howse received a curt message from the DDMS L of C Mudros: '*Oxfordshire* arrived with 907 sick, maximum accommodation 660.' Howse replied that he was extremely sorry but that it was absolutely essential to clear the casualties, and he would fully explain later.[99] Others at Mudros seemed equally ignorant. One of the Australian nurses there later remembered only that there had been 'elaborate preparations for the wounded from Gallipoli'[100] reflecting the general expectation of a costly withdrawal.

Secrecy was still paramount, so the outside world, including the senior British medical authorities in Egypt, could not yet be informed. However Howse sent a letter by hand to Surgeon-General Bedford (DMS, MEF) in Cairo, dated 12 December 1915. 'I beg to report that I am detained at Anzac for some days to make arrangements concerning the medical Units which the O.C. considers advisable in view of certain military plans...and trust that you will assist me in every way possible to maintain a good supply of hospital ships so that I will not be compelled to leave at Anzac any sick or wounded in the event of an evacuation.'[101] There had been a conference on the morning of 14 December with the General Staff and other officers, including Howse, and the next day Army Corps Order No 21 was issued, which gave details of evacuation arrangements. The day was spent building up caches of stores, such as food, water, candles, oil, and fuel. Howse instructed the OC of the 1st ACCS to continue taking in these supplies until it and the British CCS had sufficient for a total of 1200 patients for 30 days.

As the campaign drew to a close after eight long months, hospital ships were still in short supply. It makes the following message by Howse somewhat ironic. Howse sent a letter to the DMS, MEF suggesting that 'it is considered undesirable that any unusual no. of hospital ships should show themselves off Anzac until after completion of embarkation of troops.'[102] Although at this time only the *Devanha* — already overcrowded — was standing by off Anzac. However later that month, instead of two or three small hospital ships waiting in Mudros Harbour, the largest liners afloat at the time, the *Britannic, Aquitania* (these two ships alone took almost 6000 wounded and sick in their first trip from Mudros Harbour), *Mauretania* and the *Franconia* had been pressed into service as hospital ships for the evacuation.

While the medical component of the Army was only small compared with the mass of troops and other services, it nonetheless had by this time a relatively large number of units, all of which had to be planned for in the evacuation. Upon his return to Gallipoli Howse issued most of these units with the following instructions on 10 December: 1. Evacuate all patients to 1st ACCS and 13th CCS. 2. Pack all equipment unostentatiously under tents as far as possible. 3. Leave all tents standing. 4. Transport equipment to N. Beach ready for embarkation at 0900 tomorrow. In addition the ADsMS were instructed to detail a few personnel from units remaining to occupy these camps and maintain signs of occupation.[103] By the next day their equipment had been put aboard transports.

On the evening of 11 December instructions were received from the acting ADMS to evacuate all sick and wounded to the 1st ACCS by 08:00 the next morning — excluding infectious cases, men with self-inflicted wounds, and scarlet fever cases. All tents, huts, dug-outs, etc. were to be left standing and a 'busy' appearance to be presented. These orders were followed by more detailed instructions the next day, including orders to convey all alcohol to the CCS. Reports were to be sent immediately to the ADMS concerning action on these instructions, which were to be regarded as very urgent, and to be completed if possible by 15.30. No cases were to be admitted by field ambulances, but were to be passed directly to the 1st ACCS on the beach.

Over the next few days all the valuable medical equipment, such as machinery, surgical instruments and drugs were cleared to the beach under the direct supervision of Howse. Those troops embarking were to carry one day's rations and a full water bottle. Water, food, ordinary dressings, stretchers, and blankets were to be left in all dressing stations. All alcohol had to be taken to the Casualty Clearing Station under supervision and no alcohol was to be left in any dressing station. According to a New Zealand infantryman, not all alcohol reached its official destination. He and his mates drank not a little prior to leaving Gallipoli.[104]

Colonel Howse (recently appointed DDMS ANZAC and DMS AIF) left Anzac on the evening of 18 December. He had arranged for Major Campbell, the O.C. 1st ACCS, to remain as Senior Medical Officer — Anzac, in charge of the Australian Clearing Station and the 13th (British) CCS, with instructions to evacuate or hold these units in accordance with the numbers of casualties reported. The 1st ACCS was to stay until last. This 'rear party' had been chosen because it was the most sheltered and the best equipped. To it, the first medical unit to land, was given the honour of embarking last.

Its members were detailed to care for the wounded should disaster overtake the rearguard. Members were each equipped with a surgical haversack containing field dressings and morphia. The dressing stations were left equipped with the necessary instruments so that if the Turks did appreciate the situation and come over in force, the wounded could be tended by men of their own medical services. It was hoped that the Turks might allow lifeboats from the hospital ships to approach the shore and take away the serious cases.

Major Campbell detailed one of his officers to stay with the last of the rear party, and gave him this letter, addressed to the Principal Medical Officer of the Turkish Army: 'I am leaving Captain Barton of the Australian Army Medical Corps and a small party of A.A.M.C. personnel. I have every confidence that our wounded will be treated with the same care and kindness as we have treated yours, and Captain Barton is only being left that he may be of assistance to you.'[105]

The next day the British CCS left, followed by the 1st ACCS, which boarded the *Dongola* on 20 December 1915 and disembarked at Lemnos, where there was a 'great sight when the rear guard landed here plenty of cheering they got away with only 3 men wounded. They were hit with stray bullets.'[106] The diary of Captain A.S.D. Barton of the 1st ACCS mentions only one casualty, who was hit in the arm by a spent bullet, and who 'was probably the last Anzac casualty'.[107] J.W. Springthorpe, writing after the campaign, differs in his account as to the number and type of the final casualties: 'The doctor of the hospital ship was waiting for the [last] wounded...had three men injured from Suvla — one shot in the foot, one in the side of the face, and one suffering from a fall.'[108]

In a letter dated 25 December 1915 to his mother, Cpl. R. Gardiner (who was Colonel Howse's clerk) wrote that they had received orders to embark on the 15th. They had packed and 'burnt anything likely to be of value to the Turks, got aboard a transport about 11 at night and at daylight next morning we were in Mudros Harbour once again'. He mentioned that the final evacuations were on Sunday 19th and 'right to the last the Turks were apparently in ignorance of the move for the last man walked off without the slightest hindrance'.[109]

There is no doubt that the final evacuation from Gallipoli was a masterly achievement, organised in the minutest detail and planned for almost every contingency. Altogether it was a far cry from the rushed and vague planning which characterised the initial landing in April. The last Australian casualties in hospitals on Lemnos were not evacuated until early January.

The AAMC which was flung in at the April landing had been a victim of a mismanaged, misconceived plan. But the Australian Government and the lack of a coherent command structure within the AAMC itself (particularly during the first part of 1915) also contributed to the Australian medical problems at Gallipoli. During August there was more confidence and coherence within the Australian medical units at Gallipoli, as far as this was possible given the restricted scope of their activities, most of which were directly or indirectly affected by senior British staff.

Close coordination between front-line units and base hospitals in Cairo, and an increasingly efficient use of manpower, became hallmarks of AAMC units and personnel on the peninsula. In both periods these were overshadowed by a vast and sometimes uninterested Imperial military medical bureaucracy, a machine run by Birrell, Ford, Bedford and Babtie in 'splendid isolation'. Theirs was an administration characterised by disconcertingly infrequent fits of ability overshadowed too often by poor administration and lack of forethought.

CHAPTER THREE

Treatment of Sick and Wounded

Our bearers [were] conveying a man on a stretcher when a shell burst near them. One bearer lost his leg...[the other bearer] was seriously hurt, but the patient got up and ran and was not seen afterwards.[1]

The treatment of Australian troops who were wounded or became sick at Gallipoli is one of the most fascinating aspects of the campaign. This chapter deals with the broader medical techniques used at the time. Where explanations of medical terms are not given here, they will be found in Appendix VIII. The way in which AAMC personnel carried out their work, and particularly how they tried to accommodate the unique conditions at Gallipoli, is an important part of its history in that theatre of war.

As we have seen, until the end of August the medical arrangements at Gallipoli were largely makeshift. Factors contributing to this state of affairs were the extremes of weather, the terrain, lack of water, and the distances between front-line medical units and base hospitals (separated by a submarine-infested sea). The implications for surgery and the lack of orderly and regular evacuation from Gallipoli itself, will be readily appreciated. The significance of the gradual increase in disease must also be taken into account.

GETTING THE VICTIM TO MEDICAL AID

Almost throughout the Gallipoli campaign, Australian medical units were badly understaffed, a situation which became worse as disease took a hold on the peninsula. The 3rd Light Horse Field Ambulance opened as a temporary Stationary Hospital at Mudros in June, and literally within minutes 83 patients (all British troops from Cape Helles) arrived at their site. But the ambulance had tents and equipment sufficient for only 50 patients. Efforts to supplement stores were unsuccessful. Two months later the same unit recorded that since its transfer to Gallipoli it had 'treated 884 patients in hospital, sick & wounded but this has been done under much difficulty as neither extra tents nor equipment for so many over our normal capacity could be obtained at first from the ordnance store ship and full feeding equipment was only procured shortly before closing hospital'.[2]

Sometimes a soldier waited for days before receiving care. Endurance, therefore, was an important characteristic of the Diggers, a trait observed along with the Australian 'devil-may-care' attitude. 'One man [who] had both legs & one arm broken, two abdominal wounds, one thru chest & one in the neck — he asked me if I thought his leg was broken.'[3] There is the case of Pte. Clune of the 16th Battalion, who was wounded in both legs. After meeting two of his mates who were also wounded, they hid behind a bush. One volunteered to bandage his leg from which the blood was oozing and the other one loaded his rifle which he had been using as a crutch. He stayed with them all day and 'just sniped Turks in between times'.[4] After dark they were found by some stretcher bearers who brought them down to a dressing station.

FIRST AID TREATMENT

Unfortunately for both the wounded and medical staff on Gallipoli, all transport was by stretcher, foot, and occasionally by mule — none of which improved the condition of the casualty. In many cases they had to face a long wait on the beach and a rough boat ride before being loaded onto a ship. This is not to suggest that the comfort of the wounded was ignored. There were few facilities to ease the wounded man's condition, short of administering morphine. Improvisation was always in evidence, and where a soldier was suffering from fractured bones, limbs were often immobilised whilst he was being carried by stretcher. This was achieved by sandbags and coats. Some stretchers were even fitted with cradles for slinging a leg:

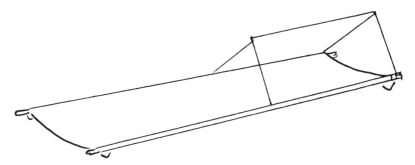

An important consideration in treating sick and wounded soldiers was the pressing need for them to be back in the trenches as soon as possible after recovery. One of the chief functions of the AAMC was to return convalescent troops to the lines. The medical officers on the peninsula therefore played a very important part in determining who would be evacuated and who (sometimes after being held at a medical facility on Gallipoli for several days) could be sent back to man the trenches. Fred Bennett, a medic with the 6th Australian Field Ambulance wrote to his mother: 'When a man is wounded in the firing line a call for a stretcher is passed along until it reaches the dressing station... After I attended him the bearers would take him out of the trenches to the Dr. [at the] dressing station...where he would examine them and see if they were fit to come back into the trenches or not.'[5]

Such was the camaraderie of the troops that men remained for too long in the trenches before reporting sick. It was then too late to do anything other than to evacuate them from Anzac, the one thing these Diggers had tried so long to avoid. After August, disease took over this function from the doctors, necessitating massive reinforcements and ultimately a withdrawal by the MEF from the Dardanelles altogether.

The conditions on Gallipoli dictated throughout the campaign what treatment could or could not be given to soldiers. This was particularly true of surgery, most of which was carried out on hospital ships or in the better equipped hospitals in Mudros, Alexandria or Cairo. Subsequently only life-saving operations were carried out on the peninsula, except when evacuation was impossible either through weight of numbers or storms, and when delayed surgery meant certain death for a casualty.

SOME TOOLS OF THE TRADE

At the front, treatment was of the most basic kind. After reaching a casualty, stretcher bearers were trained to first stop any bleeding, then to take the casualty to safety, after which broken bones would be splinted and the man carried to the next stage in the long chain of evacuation. The standard method used to control bleeding was the application of a small compressed (sterile) bandage, which every soldier carried on his person. This was known as the first field dressing and is described in detail in Appendix VII(a). Unfortunately they were sometimes of indifferent quality as this unit diary indicates: 'I draw your attention to the first field dressings issued to many of the men — made by Elliot Brothers Australia. There is no doubt that they are a disgrace & a definite menace as being grossly inefficient. I herewith send one in the condition as when opened. The rubber tissue is not sealed simply folded — dirt & dust penetrated the dressing.'[6] As we shall see, profiteering by Australian contractors extended to other medical items (see page 137).

Where severe bleeding was involved, resort was made to the tourniquet. This was usually a thin strip of material, string or rubber, placed around a limb and, with the aid of a stick, twisted and locked in position, thereby occluding the flow of blood to the injured part. In the standard military text of the day it was stated that if a tourniquet had been applied on the field, it should always be removed as soon as possible in every case, otherwise gangrene was easily caused.[7] A tourniquet could be easily overlooked, especially in the dark or where hundreds of wounded were crammed together. Therefore at Gallipoli it soon fell into disfavour among medical personnel, the direct pressure method being preferred. Its incorrect application was the subject of a diary entry, wherein the author thought that stretcher bearers should be made thoroughly au fait with pressure points and the use and abuse of the tourniquet. 'A few cases came in today. One was shot through the femoral artery, and was one of the few cases I have seen in which a tourniquet applied by a first aid man was necessary.'[8] In the experience of an Indian field ambulance on Gallipoli, they were considered dangerous, as seldom had a tourniquet been seen 'doing what was expected of it. On the contrary many have been the actual cause of a continuance of bleeding; which often, being largely venous and very profuse, has ceased the moment the tourniquet was removed.'[9]

The tourniquet was also discussed at a meeting of the Anzac Medical Society. This rather unique institution was formed on 7 November 1915 in an effort to keep medical officers at Gallipoli up to date on medical, clinical and surgical developments both there and in the rest of the world. It held four meetings at Anzac, and acted as a forum for discussion, exchange of experiences, dissemination of information, and lectures by distinguished visiting consultants.

The equipment used by medical officers in field and hospital units (the latter supplemented by other stores of instruments) came from panniers or cases carried with the unit. The size of these boxes varied with the type of unit. They contained all the instruments deemed by the army to satisfy the needs of the military surgeon. Generally they sufficed, but some Australian surgeons supplemented their equipment with instruments which they either brought with them or purchased from London. All medical units (including the RAPs) were equipped with medical or surgical panniers (see Appendices VII (b) and (c) for their contents).

Despite the obvious advantages, and indeed the necessity for such an apparatus, X-ray equipment was very rare in the Dardanelles. Fortunately the No 1 ASH had its own machine when it established itself at Mudros, so that at the end of May bullets and shrapnel pieces were able to be removed there in large numbers. Despite two British stationary hospitals, an Indian hospital and a British casualty hospital being set up at Mudros at the same time, none of these units possessed any X-ray apparatus. All their cases therefore had to be sent for X-ray examination to the Australian hospital.

ACCOMMODATION, DAILY ROUTINE AND THE PROBLEM OF STORES

Throughout the Gallipoli campaign facilities at the front were relatively crude. The 2nd Light Horse Field Ambulance accommodated its patients in three large dug-outs cut into the side of a hill. These were roofed with tarpaulins and were capable of holding 20 to 25 patients. A square excavation had been made in which a barely waterproof operating tent was set up. There was also a sandbag hut which could accommodate 15 patients but it was not very successful except for emergencies as the walls were not secure in wet weather and the roof could not be made waterproof. Corrugated iron sheeting for the purpose was at that time unavailable at Gallipoli. There was a large dug-out used as a dispensary and another used as a waiting-room for patients which could provide additional accommodation in an emergency. Ever present were the hazards of shrapnel and stray bullets flying in the immediate vicinity of the hospital tent. One can well imagine the trepidation with which some casualties waited to see the medical officer!

Different units used a variety of schemes to ensure the maximum of efficiency and to conserve manpower. The system employed by the 2nd Light Horse Field Ambulance is examined by means of an illustration of their operation. In its position on Gallipoli, there were four medical officers who operated by night and carried out routine duties by day. Three of these officers took duty in rotation as Orderly Officer, the tour of duty being 24 hours. The Orderly Officer saw and attended to every case admitted during that period.

If on account of the seriousness of the case such as the necessity for an anaesthetic, or because of a number of cases at the same time, he required assistance, he would call the officer who was next on duty. If still further assistance was needed he would call the OC of the Ambulance. Thus the officer who had gone off duty the day before was never likely to be called except in an unusual emergency and could be sure of a good night's sleep. It also meant that the OC was present whenever anything serious occurred.[10]

The following notes are reproduced from the pocket notebook of Captain (later Colonel) A.G. Butler, the regimental medical officer of the 9th Battalion. Although the notes are derived from those covering the month of November, they are representative of the daily routine of a RMO in Gallipoli between the carnage of April and August. Note that 'housekeeping' items such as ongoing training for AAMC personnel were included. As many of the medical staff at this time would have been fresh reinforcements and therefore inexperienced men, such training was very valuable.

Syllabus Training (Entry for 27 November 1915[11])

1. *Stretcher bearers*

(a) Stretcher Drill for the Medical Squad. (2, 3, & 4 bearers): transport single-handed & with two bearers.
(b) Instruction in use of dressings in treatment of wounded. Bleeding & its arrest.
(c) Training in Aid Post routine work. 2 bearers each day actual as dressing orderlies.

2. *Regimental Sanitary detachment*

(a) Lectures on disease (infection), prevention (principles etc.).
(b) The use of disinfectants.
(c) Duties of Reg. Sanitary detachment (i.e inspectors & supervisors).
(d) Practical...in the lines.

To II *Fld Amb*

(i) Cpl ——— (20 weeks at Anzac)	Pains in back & belly pyrexia Jaundice: nausea etc.
(ii) Pte Bourke (30 weeks at Anzac)	Recurrence ulcers of the leg; Difficult to heal. This man was at Anzac from the landing — was fairly well, getting anaemic. May be debility...was on Pot. Sod. for 2 wks. no obvious results.
(iii) Cpl Townsend (22 weeks Anzac)	Pyrexia NYD★ 101° Trouble with teeth Urine Dark; pain in abdomen.
(iv) Pte Elliot (15 weeks Anzac)	Pyrexia NYD & cough Nothing very much Recommend II Fld Amb if possible. No sore throat.
(v) Pte Turner (30 weeks Anzac)	Sore throat & cough.
(vi) Pte Roche (10 weeks & wounded)	Cough — pain in chest. I shall be obliged if he can be taken in II Fld Amb & examined. I can find nothing definitely wrong.

★ 'Not Yet Diagnosed'.

Conditions were almost as primitive at the various Australian hospitals established at Mudros on the island of Lemnos. Because of the dust (particularly in July), Mudros had its limitations: '…it was with the combination of dust and flies that sepsis was fairly rampant, and subsequently operative work became curtailed'.[12] Almost every hospital unit which was landed initially found that their equipment was on another ship or 'lost'.

Major J. Lockhart-Gibson, an Australian opthalmologist — a specialist rare in the Dardanelles — wrote that he had to search for each of his patients as at first they were in different hospitals all over the island.[13] Undaunted by the primitive environment he had a large marquee set up, and still later a group of three marquees, one of which he divided into a consulting room and a waiting room for his numerous ophthalmic outpatients. One of these tents actually boasted an electric lamp — a luxury not to be found even in some of Mudros's hospital operating theatres until months later.

Other Australian doctors, their staff and nurses found the going equally rough. The No 3 AGH on Mudros West had over 800 patients to care for, and in addition several of the hospital's medical staff were sick, including the hospital's surgeon.

What little equipment they had to work with was obtained from the Red Cross store ship. The only food available was the standard Army ration bully beef and biscuits. All patients were nursed on mattresses on the ground — with adverse effects on the staff who had to lift patients from that position as well as having to kneel all the time to nurse them. There was no clean clothing, nor were there sufficient eating utensils. Spoons, cups, knives and forks were all loaned from the personal kit of the medical orderlies, doctors and nurses.

Some Australian nurses (such as Sister I.G. Lovell) in other hospitals there even had to resort to tearing up their underclothes for bandages.[14] In spite of this the senior British medical officers of the MEF were content to state both then and before the Dardanelles Commission, that there was at no time a shortage of medical supplies or stores.

ONGOING TREATMENT

After a soldier had received first aid he would be sent, carried or make his own way, to a RAP, battalion dressing station, or field ambulance. Once there he would be 'classified' according to the nature of his wound or complaint. Typically a NCO would receive orders from an officer as to where the case was to be sent.

A ticket was then made out containing the man's name and regimental number, the nature of his complaint, whether morphia had been administered and in what quantity, and finally his destination. Where large numbers of casualties were involved this system of classification broke down, as in April and August. During these periods lightly wounded men could be sent to hospital ships, where space was at a premium, while the critically injured often ended up on an improvised transport or other vessel designated to carry only lightly wounded cases.

The basic function of the aid posts and field ambulances was to facilitate the early evacuation of all serious casualties, subject always to the availability of boats and good weather. In some instances ships were delayed for reasons other than storms.

In spite of the inevitable deprivations of war, not all individuals suffered. Some British General Officers expected (and received) nothing but the best, no matter who was put out. Incredibly the 'hospital ship *Sicilia* was ordered to Imbros to pick up a sick General Officer and return. She returned at midnight. During that period we were left with no hospital ship to evacuate wounded to. As our position on the beach does not permit of our treating cases by operation and our accommodation for resting cases is v. limited, this entailed extra hardship on the wounded.'[15]

While under their care patients were given food and provided with shelter where possible. Morphine was given for pain, wounds dressed where necessary, and fractures splinted. Wounds were not closed except at the base, where, with the assistance of X-rays, it could be established that no foreign bodies had been left *in situ*.

When a medical unit became big enough to deal with a relatively large number of cases, it had to streamline its limited facilities in the best way possible. The *Royal Army Medical Corps Training Manual* (1911) set out guidelines for sorting casualties and organising the activities of all medical units. These activities included the receiving, recording, and classifying of wounded (both on their arrival and discharge); looking after severe and light cases; and the dying. Places were also selected and marked out for cooking, the reception of arms and accoutrements, latrines, and a mortuary. However not every unit had the luxury of such organisation, as Captain Davenport of the 5th Australian Field Ambulance recalled. His dressing station, so-called, consisted of two wooden boxes for patients to sit on with no overhead covering; it was also completely exposed to rifle fire. 'Dressings were very scarce most of the wounds having to be dressed with the first field dressing. There were no splints of any kind, and the only morphia we had was in the form of pills gr.

1/4 and these appeared to have very little effect in relieving pain...Many of the men with dysentery had not the strength to reach the latrines, and consequently the ground all round was polluted.'[16]

TREATMENT OF WOUNDS

Field ambulances were not supposed to attempt operations at Anzac. Abdominal cases were to be rested, given nothing by mouth and moved only if necessary. Because the only chance of survival this category of patient had lay in speedy evacuation, the prognosis was almost invariably poor. Where a soldier was suffering severe pain he could be given opium. Chest wounds, particularly where bleeding into the pleural cavity of the lungs (haemothorax) was involved, were another category of wound left alone by field units.

However, smaller wounds could be adequately attended to, even in the field. The official army manual pointed out that such wounds, especially when treated with 2 per cent iodine solution 'usually arrive at the base hospitals clean, and covered by a firm dark scab. For extensive and foul wounds a moist dressing is to be preferred...Sutures must not be introduced, since experience has shown that all wounds must be regarded as infected.'[17]

The conditions prevailing at Gallipoli were not conducive to rapid healing; even the smallest cuts and abrasions were likely to become infected. In fact the medical condition was known as Barcoo Rot (or Veldt Sore). Dressings applied to these types of wounds were 'wet' (i.e. packed with gauze saturated in an antiseptic solution). Although it was noted that quick recoveries were not impossible, as one wit put it: 'Our Tent Division says that patients get well quickly after a few shells burst near the [hospital] tents.'[18]

With larger wounds the doctor was required to thoroughly debride (clean) the wound site as the free removal of dead tissue was considered very important. Where large wounds were involved there was often a great deal of pain for a wounded soldier when these wounds were dressed. Where a large area of skin was exposed, the application of a strip of gauze or lint spread with soft boracic ointment or Vaseline was recommended in facilitating the removal of dressings, especially from amputation stumps. An alternative was the use of hydrogen peroxide applied with a spray bottle.

Water — both for drinking and for preparing antiseptics — was always scarce. Sudden severe storms, which often blew down large parts of these tented hospitals, were yet another trial for Australian units looking after wounded on Lemnos: [Mudros, 29 June 1915] 'Wood v. scarce — Water had to be carried 500 yds. Sudden storm this evening blew down large hospital tent and others only saved with difficulty.'[19]

It was the same all over the island. Lance-corporal L.J. Burgess of the 6th Light Horse wrote: 'I am in a Pommie Hospital at Mudros on Lemnos Island & if ever I have an enemy whom I desire something terrible should happen to it would be that he should come to this hospital. There is not even a drop of water to drink & the boys were stretched out on canvas which was all that is between them and the ground, the place is the abode of numberless fleas & other vermin.'[20]

Among the golden rules of medical treatment at the front was not to remove foreign bodies such as bullets from wounds, thereby opening the wound again prior to medical evacuation offshore. It was the procedure to evacuate the casualty to a base hospital with the object *in situ*. However the peculiar circumstances of Gallipoli often worked against such a practice, and many a bullet was removed surgically at Anzac, and certainly on hospital ships.

This incident took place on board the *Seang Choon* and was recorded by Peter Hall of the No 2 ASH: 'There was another chap who had a bullet go in one side of his leg & you could just feel the point of it under the flesh on the other…the doctor in his haste just got hold of a long probe, & putting in the wound got behind the bullet, then with a determined push forced it up through the remaining bit of flesh…he [the casualty] remarked to the doctor "You're making a bit of a welter with that probe aren't you digger?"'[21] Such was the stoicism of some!

Some experienced surgeons who had joined the AIF were appalled at the rapaciousness with which their juniors operated, particularly on board hospital ships. Toward the end of the campaign operations were only rarely performed whilst a casualty was in transit from the front to a base hospital. Due to this eagerness on the part of some medical officers, some casualties died who might otherwise have stood a chance of survival — this was particularly the case with abdominal wounds. Many articles in medical journals of the time stress that with abdominal wounds, surgery was often fatal.

SHOCK

Shock had long been recognised as a potential killer of wounded men. It was treated on Gallipoli in the same manner as was prescribed by any first aid manual of that time — warmth, hot stones, blankets, and occasionally medicinal brandy.

In treating shock, the most widely used drug was morphia. It was usually combined with atropine when used for this purpose. Saline transfusions were not unknown, and these were also given where bleeding had been severe to raise blood pressure by introducing more fluid into the circulation. (Blood transfusions were not done at this period of the war, but were certainly being performed in 1919, donors being given a week's furlough for their pains.[22]) The reason that atropine was given was that in addition to it acting as a cardiac stimulant, it helped prevent the vomiting which sometimes followed when morphia was given alone. (For casualties with serious head, chest or abdominal injuries vomiting had often fatal consequences.)

ANTISEPTICS

What antiseptics were used, and why, is another interesting feature of the technical side of Gallipoli's medical story. There were four 'schools' of thought concerning the best type of antiseptic to use. The alternatives were hydrogen peroxide, iodine, 'Eusol', and various combinations of salt or saline applications. Each method had its proponents, and each was used during the Gallipoli campaign. Where a wound was first examined on the field, hydrogen peroxide solution was often used to irrigate it, not only because of its known bactericidal powers, but for its mechanical action in separating debris from the wound surface.

The other widely used antiseptic was 'Eusol' (an abbreviation for 'Edinburgh University Solution' — a mixture of boric acid and chloride of lime, put into a bottle filled with warm water). Of all the antiseptics used at Gallipoli, iodine was the most popular. There were exceptions however. Captain Story, the RMO of the 13th Battalion, in a lecture to the 'Anzac Medical Society' entitled 'The treatment of wounds prior to evacuation from the point of view of the Medical Officer', regarded iodine as most unsatisfactory.

While there was a wide variety in the initial treatment of wounds, one or a combination of these antiseptics was always used. Some doctors excised the wound to get rid of any soiled and damaged tissue. For the cleaning of serious wounds most doctors also used local anaesthetics (such as eucaine and adrenalin) prior to cleaning and applying an antiseptic. The surrounding skin was cleaned with alcohol and painted with tincture of iodine. Iodine was also swabbed into the wound itself. It was then cleaned with hydrogen peroxide, stitched, and drained where this was necessary.

OTHER CONCERNS

Another concern in treating wounds was tetanus. Various bacilli found in the soil, particularly manured soil, can enter a wound and produce toxins which affect the nerves of the body. If not treated this can be fatal. Tetanus antitoxin was therefore used throughout the Gallipoli campaign as a 'first aid' measure for very soiled wounds, and then, from July, it was given for all types of wounds in a prophylactic dose. The following note appears in the war diary of the 1st ACCS: 'All cases of shell and shrapnel wounds are to be injected with anti-tetanic serum. Up to present we have only done so in foot injury and extensive wounds with earth contamination.'[23] The use of the anti-tetanus serum was one of the success stories of medicine at Gallipoli. However, part of its success was due to the soil types to be found there. In France, where troops were fighting in soil which had been manured for generations, the incidence of tetanus was significantly greater.

Australian troops were also inoculated against the traditional scourge of armies which had decimated previous military forces — cholera. The incentive was the anticipated success of the August offensive: 'At one time, when it was hoped we would get through, preparation was made for a possible out-break of cholera, as it was currently reported that such an eventuality was likely when European troops occupied trenches which had previously been held by Turks. Every man was given an injection of anti-cholera serum...'[24]

FROSTBITE

The famous blizzard of November has been well documented elsewhere by Bean, Butler, and more recent historians. It should be stated that the British in this instance fared worse than the Australians or New Zealanders, due mainly to their greater exposure, deeper trenches, and inadequate winter clothing. The Australian medical services did have their share of frostbite to contend with, but on a much smaller scale than was suffered at either Suvla or Cape Helles. This was because the Australian and Anzac positions were more sheltered and because sentries and front-line troops had just received an issue of waterproof clothing.

Prevention consisted in keeping the feet raised — not an easy thing in some trenches at Gallipoli. Although the effects of the direct application of heat were recognised in more enlightened units, there were problems among some Allied troops. 'About 20 Indians evacuated yesterday with frostbite — mostly Ghurkas...Much frostbite results of ignorance — Ghurkas with limbs numbed, warmed by a fire with disastrous results.'[25] Feet were sometimes bandaged with a covering of wool and pain relieved by aspirin.

However, owing to the cold, water pipes burst and for a time water was restricted to two pints a day. This would continue to be a problem. Lt. Colonel A. Sutton, the ADMS of the 2nd Australian Division, wrote that on 1 December he 'interviewed Brig-Gen White [Birdwood's Chief of Staff] G.S.O. & pointed out that the men could not live on a quart of water [approx. one litre], the normal army issue was a gallon — [4.5 litres — per man per day] it did not meet the physiological requirements. Arranged...engineers to resume pumping when the pipes repaired & was assured of 1/2 ration (4 pints) tomorrow.'[26] One doctor also noted in his unit's diary the 'Serious difficulty in operating in tent owing to frost'.[27]

In 1915 alcohol was also used in the treatment of hypothermia, or exposure. One doctor noted 'Windy weather & much snow. Rum issued — would much prefer hot cocoa for the men.'[28] In a 56 day period this doctor's unit dispensed a total of 14 bottles of brandy, 18 bottles of portwine and 46 bottles of stout.

SURGERY

Then, as now, the decision when to operate was a difficult one. If a soldier could endure evacuation by sea, he stood a better chance from an operation either on board a fully fitted-out hospital ship or in a base hospital. Sometimes however, where the case was critical and the medical officer knew that transport was not forthcoming, he had no choice but to operate. The lack of facilities and the greater chance of infection made the undertaking a difficult one.

Those operations performed on the peninsula by Australian units were invariably performed in or under tents, although the ACCS could, by late October, boast the luxury of a concrete floor and linen sheets on the walls of its operating theatre.[29] The facilities of the 2nd Light Horse Field Ambulance were somewhat primitive, and of course asepsis (i.e a surgical technique which renders sterile the entire space in which an operation is to be performed) was impossible under such conditions.[30] In the centre of their operating tent was the operating table, which was improvised by placing a stretcher on panniers.

For its part the 4th Australian Field Ambulance used pieces of four-by-four timber sunk into the ground, so as to support a stretcher at a convenient height. In this example the stretcher actually formed the operating table.[31] At the head of the operating table was the anaesthetist's table. In one corner of the tent were basins, water and disinfectants for sterilising the hands of the medical team. In another corner was a mechanical steriliser and the means for cleaning the patient's skin and wounds. Towels and dressings were also kept in the tent.

For lighting, two acetylene operating lamps, suspended from the roof, were used. (Most units used a 'Dietz' hurricane lamp as an emergency light source.) One was always kept full and ready to be put in use the minute the other went out! For abdominal work a small acetylene bicycle lamp was used, as this was more portable and could be held relatively closely to the wound site. Outside was a 'Sawyers Stove', which was used to boil water. Towels and swabs were sterilised by keeping them in a solution of 1-40 carbolic acid and simply wringing them out when required.

The rules for surgery were almost universal. Wounds were cleaned as thoroughly as possible, including the use of an anaesthetic if this was necessary. Antiseptic practice dictated that the surrounding tissue be first painted with iodine, after which gross particles of dirt were removed with forceps — the wound was then swabbed out with pure hydrogen peroxide.[32]

All dead skin and damaged tissue was then cut away with scissors and any foreign body which could be reached was removed at this stage. The wound was then irrigated with a mild antiseptic and covered with a moist dressing. Cases requiring major operations such as abdominal section or trephining were evacuated whenever possible.

Every care was taken to avoid infecting wounds, although on Gallipoli this was a difficult task. In 'theatre', be it a tent or a dug-out, surgeons and assistants usually wore white coats. A supply of sterilised towels and dressings was usually on hand (i.e. subject to demand). Boiling water was always used — if water was available for a particular day. Also water shortages did not stop with the arrival of winter. For, apart from storms, the frost froze the tanks and prevented what water was stored on Anzac from being distributed. '...In the operating tent it was a serious obstacle and necessitated a resort to iodine.'[33] Antiseptic lotions such as 'Eusol' were used, and often applied hot. Sterilised towels were then placed around the wound.

Lack of foresight was sometimes evident in treating casualties. An example is the *Gloucester Castle* (in August). It possessed an X-ray machine, but there was no operator who could work it, there was no hydrogen peroxide on board, nor were there any drainage tubes. Drainage was widely used 'to prevent any serious general or local extension of infection which [had] already occurred, and in conjunction with the mechanical methods of cleansing [formed] the essential element in the primary treatment of gunshot wounds'.[34] The ship carried only eight or ten scalpels for operating, a few pairs of pressure forceps, no skull forceps, very little carbolic acid, hardly any catgut for ligaturing vessels and no eye instruments at all. At the time the *Gloucester Castle* was carrying more than 500 badly wounded men.

Generally abdominal wounds fared poorly as many nurses found. 'Had a very busy day, getting in more wounded: a Malay who had abdominal injury and a nice lad from Benalla, the same. The poor things usually die, in spite of operation.'[35]

ANAESTHESIA

The most frequently used anaesthetic was chloroform. However, open ether was the preferred anaesthetic in amputations, as patients suffering from septic infections were considered to be at risk with chloroform, as it had 'ulterior bad effects on the general condition of the patient'.[36] A medical officer of No 2 ASH noted that 'very few amputations were performed unless the limbs were hopelessly shattered'.[37]

For small superficial operations and removal of bullets and shell fragments, local injections of eucaine and adrenalin were sometimes used. In more serious cases, a preliminary injection of morphia and scopolamine was given before the first combination was applied. On Gallipoli itself the exigencies of the situation meant that general anaesthetics such as chloroform and ether were administered by other than trained anaesthetists. Some specialists advised a preliminary injection of morphine and atropine in order to reduce the quantity of the anaesthetic used and thereby minimise any inconvenient after-effects to the casualty.

HEAD INJURIES

Head injuries sometimes had a better chance of recovery than abdominal and chest wounds. The reason given at the time was that the head is 'almost the only part of the body where shell and shrapnel fire [had a] lesser tendency to penetrate the skull [i.e. skeleton]'.[38] Again, operation in the field was undertaken only where this was imperative. The skull was prepared for operation by cleaning the scalp with a solution made up of 1 part petrol, and 3 parts spirit. Strong antiseptic (1 in 500 corrosive sublimate) was used on the brain itself.[39] A number of facial and head injuries came from those soldiers who were engaged in look-out or spotting duties in the trenches. These injuries, together with the loss of eyes, were often the result of the mirror at the top of trench periscopes being smashed by a bullet and fragments entering the eye.[40]

EYES

As we have seen above, the AIF was fortunate to have some of Australia's leading eye specialists working in the AAMC. One of these was J. Lockhart Gibson, who worked out of a few tents at Mudros, having brought with him much of his own personal equipment. He arranged for all eye cases not hopelessly injured to come to 3 AGH from both Gallipoli and all other medical units on Lemnos. Lack of transport often prevented many troops with injured eyes from being landed at Lemnos, and after coming to Lemnos they were taken directly on to Alexandria. The time lag (four days) was sufficient in many cases to ensure the permanent loss of eyes which otherwise could have been saved by Gibson's unit at Mudros, where he had ophthalmological instruments not available even in the base hospitals in Cairo or Malta.

Other men were equally adaptive to the primitive conditions which characterised much of the medical story at Gallipoli. Captain (later Lt. Colonel) Muirhead related how after one trip, he returned to Anzac in May on the *Arcadian* which picked up 500 wounded men. Nothing in the way of wards had been arranged and there was so little equipment aboard that Muirhead, who was doing all the eye work on the *Arcadian*, 'was reduced to removing hopelessly damaged eyes with a pair of old straight scissors'.[41]

Under no circumstances was a foreign body in the eye to be probed under field conditions. Where this was done, it was not performed satisfactorily. Major C. Stephen, of No 1 AGH in

Egypt remarked that 'penetrating wounds of the eye from the glass of the rifle periscope were very frequent and it was sad to remove an eye and find the foreign body that had caused its destruction were eyelashes carried in by a fragment of glass which had been removed satisfactorily at the time'.[42] The lids and parts around the eyes were cleaned with either sterile saline solution or sterilised boric acid lotion to remove discharge or any loose foreign matter. Then some sterilised 1 per cent atropine ointment was inserted between the lids.

EARS

Where the ear drum had been perforated due to an injury, it was simply a case of preventing further injury or infection until the soldier was got to advanced medical care. A light application of 2 per cent iodine solution in spirit was applied to the outer ear canal, care being taken that none of the fluid reached the deeper part of the ear. The outer part of the canal would then be plugged lightly with cotton wool. 'Syringing or the introduction of drops of lotions, particularly hydrogen peroxide, were all considered dangerous.'[43]

CHEST WOUNDS

Chest wounds were interfered with as little as possible. The best treatment was to leave the wound alone, other than cleaning and sealing any open wounds to the lung/s. According to J. Laffin in *Surgeons in the Field*, because of the surgeons' assumption that practice would be similar to that of the Boer War it was considered that the best treatment for chest wounds would be to leave them alone unless a collection of pus should form, in which case a drainage operation would be performed. Laffin states that the belief that operative measures were unnecessary is probably the main reason for the lack of surgical assistance provided for men suffering from chest wounds.[44]

Fatalities in this category died from shock or internal bleeding into the lung. As complete rest formed the regimen for these casualties, all were evacuated to base hospitals as soon as their condition had stabilised. Upon admission to a field ambulance some would have been given morphia and atropine combined, hypodermically, to treat pain and help reduce the symptoms of shock.

ABDOMINAL WOUNDS

Many lives were lost at Gallipoli from abdominal wounds. The surgical solution was in many cases to make a vertical incision above the pubes and insert a large drainage tube. Patients were then kept in the Fowler (or semi-upright) Position and given doses of morphia. When only the small intestine was involved the success rate was good. But often there was massive trauma to the abdominal region. An Australian surgeon noted in his diary that 'the contents of the man's pockets are frequently in abdominal cavity, sometimes clips of cartridges, and once the cap of a shell...'[45]

Lt. Colonel Syme of No 1 AGH, admitted to something of a moral dilemma in military surgery when he wrote that he and his colleagues operated on all the abdominal wounds except those obviously hopeless. 'I am of the opinion that cases of this kind in this war will practically all end fatally if left alone, and a large percentage of the patients die when operated on. If they can be got early, as we did get them, operation gives them a chance.'[46] His view was also reflected by Captain E.J.F. Deakin, who noted that 'cases which were apparently hopeless were not touched, and undoubtedly many whose lives would have been saved in civil practice had to perish because we did not have the time to attend to them'.[47]

The military view is rather that it is not worth wasting time for such chances, and the surgeon is better occupied with other patients more likely to recover. This was the opinion also of a Congress of (German) military surgeons in Brussels in April 1915, at which 1200 military surgeons were assembled. Early operation was advised for skull injuries and for abdominal wounds in which there was danger of internal haemorrhage, or injury to stomach or intestines. It concluded that the earlier the operation in these cases the better was the prognosis.[48]

FRACTURES

The initial treatment for fractures consisted of splinting. At Anzac Colonel Begg NZAMC recommended treating patients with compound fractures on their lower limbs by tying the foot to the handle of the stretcher and then being carried head first down a gully thus getting automatic extension of the injured limb.[49] The other principle was to immobilise the joint, using a custom-made splint of wood or other material, or improvising one, such as a piece of stick or a rifle. Application of the latter was written into military lore with a caution: 'Remove the bolt and see that the rifle or magazine contain no cartridges.'

Fractures of the large bone of the thigh (femur) were of most concern to medical officers. These, and fractures of the knee, were generally placed in a Thomas splint. As one nurse wrote, 'many limbs with shockingly septic compound fractures, which, without them would have been amputated, have, with the aid of a Thomas splint...been dressed with comparative comfort for the patient and ease for the nurse'.[50]

The treatment post-operatively of this type of wound did not differ markedly from that discussed above. Tetanus anti-toxin was injected and the wound site carefully cleaned. An additional problem for the surgeon was whether or not to open up the wound to examine the extent of the fracture and the associated damage. This was particularly relevant where a fracture had been caused by a a gunshot wound. Not a great deal could be done for spinal injuries, many of whom died from complications and the movement necessitated by the many stages of evacuation to a base hospital. Here again, early surgical interference was counselled, and the (theoretical) prominence of X-ray equipment in the treatment of spinal fractures expounded.

AMPUTATIONS

The surgeon often had a difficult decision as to whether a wounded soldier in severe shock would stand an operation to amputate a whole limb. Where an amputation was performed the patient was first given morphine and a saline infusion (or 'drip') was administered via the axilla (armpit), in order to reduce shock. If done according to the military manual, the amputation was by way of a simple circular or flap amputation. In view of experience, primary union was rarely attained, and therefore advised against closing such amputations by sutures.

One of a number of eminent surgeons to visit the Dardanelles was Lt. Colonel A.W. Mayo-Robson, who briefly worked on board the *Sicilia* while off Anzac Cove late in June. He put his vast experience to good use, and among his suggestions were some relating to amputations then being performed on account of gangrene. Mayo-Robson advocated free irrigation and incisions and thorough drainage of wounds (measures which were adopted throughout the area shortly afterwards), with the result that the incidence of gangrene dropped significantly. Many soldiers on the hospital ships who died within 24 hours were such as in ordinary circumstances of warfare would have died on the battlefield.

GAS GANGRENE

The incidence of gas gangrene was never as serious at Gallipoli as it was on the Western Front. It was not frequent at Gallipoli as the necessary anaerobes were not present in the largely uncultivated (and therefore unmanured) soil. However, as most open wounds contain one or more types of bacteria or anaerobic organisms (which can cause gangrene), such bacteria were often present in situations where bandages had been applied too tightly, dressings changed too infrequently, or where wounds had not properly drained.

Gangrene may commence as a local infection with spread of gas through the tissues, and especially the subcutaneous tissue around the wound, or the whole limb can be rapidly infected and may die en masse in a few hours. Treatment consisted of removing as much of the blood clot and dead tissue as possible, providing the wound with free access to the air, and ensuring efficient drainage of the wound. Any wound that showed signs of gaseous cellulitis was freely opened under an anaesthetic, dead skin or muscle completely cut away, and the whole wound cleansed by mopping it out with gauze and an antiseptic such as hydrogen peroxide.

TREATMENT ON HOSPITAL SHIPS

Conditions for the treatment of wounded were better on the hospital ships, although there were of course important exceptions. The diary of the PDMS of the MEF, Surgeon-General Bedford, records an inspection of the hospital ship Neuralia. 'There have been fifty-eight deaths aboard, septic wounds, gangrene etc. since the ship started taking wounded on board at Anzac. Arrangements are to be made to treat septic cases on deck. There are many flies and it is to be arranged that this ship and all others are to be thoroughly disinfected by the Authorities at Alexandria. [Despite this] The sick & wounded were well cared for and treated...'[51]

There were also problems on board ambulance carriers, or black ships which had been converted (in varying degrees) to cater for the sick and wounded. Surgeon-General Bedford provides a good description of both the logistics and haste involved in converting such ships. 'Grantully Castle is being prepared as a hospital ship with accommodation for 450 in cots; seven M.O.s and eight sisters, twenty-nine orderlies...The bunks were too close together for efficient nursing in some cases...The

W.C.s were unsatisfactory, seats nailed down, water leaking in the scuppers...There is a lot to be done tomorrow before the boat can sail to Mudros tomorrow.'[52]

But even in these relative havens of safety there were problems. According to Lt. Colonel G. A. Syme surgeons 'found it difficult to get satisfactory X-ray photographs of the skull, owing to the vibration and movement of the ship'.[53] Nursing patients was also awkward, due to the arrangement of cots and beds which had very little space between them. This also meant that it was almost impossible to apply adequate extension to fractures owing to the arrangements of the cots. On improvised hospital ships there was often a want of appliances and attendants, and continuous irrigation methods were not practicable.

Shortly after the first wounded arrived from Gallipoli in Egypt, local (and influential) observers were scandalised at the condition of many of the troops and the lack of any facilities on these ships. In response to official enquiries from England, the British Commander, Sir John Maxwell, sent a telegram to England, expressing outrage and surprise![54]

During the April landing such surgical resources as there were aboard the ships were to be strained to the limit. On one such ship, immediately after the landing, there had been little time for adequate preparation. The mess tables and benches previously used by the troops were still in position, together with all the litter and debris produced by the hundreds of troops who had just disembarked. Operating facilities were basic. In one corner of a cabin a mess table was set apart for operations. There was a primus stove for sterilising instruments and cotton wool was used for swabs.

On the operating table itself, wounded soldiers, often in dirty and blood-stained clothes (the operation field alone was uncovered and surrounded by wet boiled towels), were anaesthetised by a man who in Civvy Street might have been a commercial traveller, with little experience in anaesthesia. The surgeon's assistant in this instance had been, until the war, a schoolboy about to commence his medical studies.[55]

Later, when the military situation had stabilised, routine again established itself shipboard. The day would begin with ward rounds at 9.00 a.m., followed by operations which often lasted until 1.00 p.m. Such operations would sometimes be performed by the consulting surgeon himself, or, if there were some good surgeons among the medical officers, it was the practice to entrust them with the less serious cases.[56]

Routine was also the order of the day on the hospital transport ships plying between Gallipoli and Lemnos, and

Lemnos and the base hospitals in Egypt. On board, the situation was more orderly than was possible in the field. Private Laidlaw, a medic in the 2nd Australian Field Ambulance and seconded to the *Clacton*, wrote of such a routine.[57] He began his stint of hospital duty at 9.00 a.m. and would work a continuous shift of 24 hours, followed by 12 hours off-duty.

All patients were washed every morning at Reveille. Two orderlies would assist the medical officers at the morning sick parade, which lasted about two hours. Then all the patients in hospital and any outpatients had to be attended. This would usually involve redressing wounds. Foments, making beds and turning patients were also part of the daily regimen. Then there were the patients' meals to be served. Temperatures, pulses, respirations and bowel observations were taken twice per day, morning and evening, as was the dispensing of medicines.

It is not surprising that the conditions generally prevailing at Gallipoli should affect the medical services which were in the thick of it. Peter Hall wrote to his mother from a hospital ship: 'Yet this [good food & beds] does not prevent me from having bad dreams, the appealing cries for "Orderly!" is yet a kind of nightmare with most of us.'[58] Overall, where casualties survived their initial wound, most recovered due to the care which they received on the peninsula. As we have seen such treatment was in some cases rudimentary.

For the period of the campaign (from April to December), the AAMC did render effective treatment in the field. Standards of treatment suffered during periods in which medical resources were over-strained as in late April and early August. The other major external influences on treating casualties were the number of medical personnel available, the supply of drugs and equipment, and the speed with which casualties could be cleared from Gallipoli. The latter two factors, particularly medical evacuation, were largely beyond the control of the AAMC and there were serious breakdowns in both areas.

CHAPTER FOUR

Transport of the Wounded

The whole beach is filled with wounded of all kinds and all descriptions of wounds. It has quite unnerved me for a time. Some of the wounds are so ghastly, whole abdomens blown away and the men still living. They are in such numbers that it is difficult to get along, and there is only one hospital ship in the bay.[1]

INTRODUCTION

Australian medical units at the front managed remarkably well given the circumstances at Gallipoli. However, as such units or their personnel were engaged further afield, that is on hospital ships and transports, they coped less well. This situation continued along the chain of evacuation until Australian base hospitals were reached in Egypt — which were again under the more immediate supervision of Australian, as opposed to Imperial officers. The AAMC therefore worked best when it was in complete control in its own sphere of activity.

What follows is an investigation of the complexities involved in the transport of the wounded all along the Lines of Communication, beginning at the front and finishing at the base hospitals. It also surveys the evacuation work of the various components of the AAMC, and the extent to which the latter's freedom of action was restricted by factors outside its control.

The medical arrangements were in a continual state of reorganisation and were particularly strained in April and August of 1915. A gradual improvement in some aspects of medical evacuation was unfortunately more than offset by the increase of disease and sickness in the AIF. This analysis isolates four phases in the transport (or medical evacuation) of sick and wounded Australians.

To appreciate the difficulties involved in arranging for the transport of wounded and sick troops, an understanding of what is termed 'Lines of Communication' [L. of C.] is critical. In July 1915 (taken here as representative of the entire campaign), these included:

1. The Base at Alexandria (Egypt), distant two to three days' voyage from Mudros, depending on the weather.
2. The intermediate Base at Mudros on the island of Lemnos.
3. The advanced Base at Imbros, where General Headquarters were stationed; and
4. The landing beaches at Cape Helles and Anzac, each of which was under an Advance Base Commandant, with Naval and Military medical, supply, and transport staffs.[2]

The interdependence on the Lines of Communication at each link was such that congestion at one point had serious consequences for the next link. Australian medical units were obliged to work within the constraints of this system and were therefore largely helpless as regards much of the offshore medical transportation.

Only in the area of hospital ships could Australia have played any independent role, but this possibility was relinquished early in 1915 when Australia decided to rely entirely upon Britain rather than fitting out Australian vessels. The unsatisfactory administrative relations between the two countries at the outbreak of the War was the basic cause. There had been no firm agreements or arrangements as to which country should supply certain materiel. Australia therefore left many of the medical and other arrangements for the AIF to Britain — almost by default.

The major faults which lay behind the breakdown in the medical evacuation of casualties from Anzac may be reduced to four. These in turn have much in common with the reasons for the failure of the overall military campaign. First, there was the complexity of a combined amphibious operation, requiring communication facilities which would not become available until decades later. Second, there was a failure by senior British medical officers to plan ahead — based on an incorrect assumption that all hospital and staff reinforcements would be required only on a temporary basis. Such a strategy had an adverse effect on the preparedness of Australian hospitals in Cairo. The third factor was the sheer impossibility of adequately sorting wounded on the beaches before they were placed on hospital and other ships. Finally, there was the poor liaison and communication between the different branches of the MEF and between senior individuals within the various medical services — both British and Australian.This area will be examined in an effort to clarify the problems which confronted the AAMC in this part of its work.

The evacuation of wounded from Gallipoli was carried out for much of the time on a trial and error basis, as desperate attempts were made to adapt to changes in the military scenario. Diagram 4.1 on page 78? illustrates the general evacuation process from Anzac.[3] Of note is the variation in distances between the 'normal' or expected, as laid down by the military textbooks of the day, and what was actually encountered. It also shows the areas of responsibility of the three senior British medical officers in the Dardanelles theatre as a whole.

AT THE FRONT

As troops landed on the beaches at Anzac on 25 April 1915 many were shot even before they left their boats to go ashore. Men trying to disembark were met by a constant and opposing stream of wounded trying to reach the safety of the ships. To compound the chaos there was a shortage of small boats. As fast as stores and men were being landed on the narrow beach, empty space there rapidly filled with the dead and dying. It was only after April, when the army began to consolidate its precarious foothold on the peninsula, that a 'system' of evacuation evolved.

At the first landing not all the field medical units went ashore; the tent divisions of the various ambulances aboard the troopships were obliged to remain on board to tend to the wounded. Apart from small groups of doctors and other AAMC personnel connected with infantry units, only the bearer subdivisions of the ambulances landed. Lack of headway dictated that all heavy equipment, tents and (importantly) transport were left on board the various troopships. Later these subdivisions were brought ashore and set up small field hospitals for the treatment of minor wounds and sickness.

The first link in the evacuation 'chain' was often provided by the casualty's mate. This mutual care was, and continues to be, a feature of warfare. Sergeant C.F. Laseron of the 13th Battalion relates his experiences as a casualty, which, while not typical of all wounded men (he was deliberately shot at by the Turks), nonetheless provides an extreme example of the progress of a casualty from receiving a wound to being evacuated from the Dardanelles.

While attending to a wounded mate, this man was shot in the foot. The impact was such as to throw him down the hillside and into a trench, where he was impaled by two bayonets fixed to some rifles lying against the side of the parapet. His comrades lifted him off and he fainted. After he regained consciousness he spent three hours crawling more than a kilometre (all the way being subjected to sniper fire) to a dressing station. There his wound was dressed and he was placed on a donkey for the trip to the beach, where he joined masses of other wounded, before being sent to Alexandria the next day on the *Galeka*.[4]

A similar story was told by Charles Crome, a Digger, who (half an hour after landing) received a bullet wound in his foot, and another in the shoulder. Nevertheless he fought on until the next day when he was shot in the leg, 'which brought me down'. He then crawled for almost a kilometre and was helped to the beach before being taken on board the *Ionian*.[5]

Usually, however a wounded man would be taken from the field by bearers of his own regiment. Retrieving casualties was far from routine, and there were many feats of heroism and endurance. A wounded man was first taken to the Regimental Aid Post for elementary first aid by the medical officer. These doctors were assisted by their (medical) NCO and one other medic. From the RAP stretcher bearers from the field ambulances carried wounded to dressing posts (i.e. the tent divisions of field ambulances consisting of medical officers, and orderlies). From here another relay carried them to the main dressing station of the ambulance. There the cases were classified as to whether they should be evacuated or retained in the ambulance. If evacuation was necessary they were removed to the Casualty Clearing Station where any urgent surgical procedures were carried out prior to sending the cases off to hospital ships by barges.

Although relatively short distances were involved in evacuating soldiers overland at Gallipoli, the ruggedness of the terrain and the steep slopes often made the journey a hazardous one. An illustration is the path taken by bearers from 'Quinn's Post' to the beach, a distance of about three kilometres. The route was by means of narrow and (in winter) muddy tracks. A comparison of front-line distances and the rear, with respect to France, is shown in Diagram 4.3 on page 87.

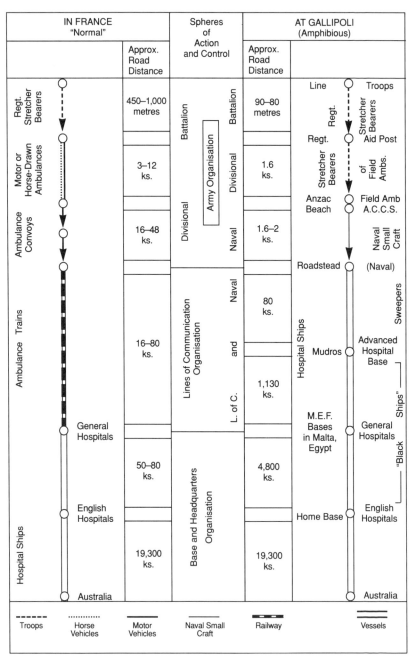

DIAGRAM 4.1 Differences in Evacuation at Gallipoli and the Western Front.
Source: A.G. Butler, Vol. I, p. 208

There were many traps on this track by way of debris and war materiel of all kinds. There were holes dug for water into which bearers walked or stumbled at night and in many places mud and slush was ankle deep. Another element of surprise was signallers' wire. This would often be found at various heights and on the ground — at times tripping or nearly hanging the unwary. In addition there was the constant passing of troops and pack mules which edged the bearers off the path.

At other places the trenches were so narrow that the wounded could only be transported through them in the few 'short' naval stretchers then available, or by draping them in a blanket or waterproof sheet and dragging them along.[6] The commanding officer of another ambulance had also made some innovations: 'Visited Courtney's Ridge today to see the working of the sleigh I designed for the lowering of casualties down a slide, as the transport by hand was too dangerous and very hard for the bearers.'[7]

Two rifles passed through the sleeves of a buttoned overcoat was a popular substitute for scarce stretchers. Shortcuts were taken whenever possible, as James McPhee of the 4th Australian Field Ambulance wrote. 'One of the squad took the feet and another the head of the stretcher and down the slope we slid on backsides for about 30 yards by far the easiest stage of getting down to the bottom of the gully.'[8] Eventually improvements, in the form of wider tracks and the building of sandbag barricades at exposed points, made life a little easier for bearers and their patients.

In normal times the evacuation of soldiers from the front was a relatively efficient procedure. An example is furnished by the observations of one of the many medics who themselves became casualties at Gallipoli. Corporal H. Duncan was 'on parapet duty, when a Turkish shell landed just in front of me blowing the parapet to pieces...I was sent to the battalion aid post, and from there to [the] Casualty Clearing Station. That night I was transferred to [the] hospital ship, and next morning was in bed at [the] field hospital on Lemnos Island.'[9]

Not all were so fortunate, as logistics and bad fortune meant that some wounded would have to remain in 'no man's land'. Immediately after an advance in August, Private Brotchie wrote to his family: 'A few wounded came up, those who were badly wounded were got up except a few who were supposed to have no chance and they had to be left, as the fire was too heavy...'[10]

The evacuations during the period of the August Offensive, although better organised offshore, were little better on land than they had been in April, due to the unexpectedly high number of casualties which again swamped the system. As discussed earlier, by this time senior British medical officers appointed Lt. Colonel A.E.C. Keble (RAMC) to look after Anzac and take control of the evacuation on land at that point. In addition the strength of the Regimental, Battalion and Field Ambulance medical personnel was by August seriously depleted.

Their numbers had been reduced by death, wounds and sickness, and units had received few reinforcements. Typical war diary entries are: 'Pte. Cooper shot through the heart by shrapnel'[11] and 'Large shell fell on one of our men. Killed him (Murphy)'.[12] Despite the rigours of the campaign, most of the medical personnel struggled on, at least until they too succumbed to dysentery and other illnesses. 'The general health and fitness of this unit is satisfactory but I consider that their physical fitness is by no means so good as when we landed [25 April].'[13]

Colonel Begg, a New Zealand doctor, complained that what (insufficient) reinforcements as were available from New Zealand were diverted in Egypt to staff crowded hospitals in Cairo. The NZ Mounted Field Ambulance and the 1st Light Horse Field Ambulance were landed at the beginning of August at the urgent request of the ADMS Col. Manders. 'These units had been broken up and distributed to transports to make up for the lack of hospital ships.'[14] Such a demand had been foreshadowed by events in Egypt early in April, when the officer commanding No 1 AGH at Cairo wrote to Australia's Surgeon-General Williams that all medical reinforcements arriving in Egypt be 'detailed for duty here'.[15] The AAMC both on Gallipoli and at Lemnos was similarly afflicted, despite a total of 590 Australian doctors, nurses and Other Ranks arriving at Egypt in June and July.

There were other problems too. Colonel Rupert Downes, the CO of the 3rd Light Horse Field Ambulance wrote in a letter about the No 1 AGH 'which [had] some 70 medical officers there doing hardly anything & they grab all the reinforcements for mobile units up here which are badly wanted & I think the A.D.M.S. & D.D.M.S. will be having something to say soon'.[16] Matters were made worse for the NZAMC when all medical students serving in its field ambulances were recalled to their universities at the end of July. Australia did not follow suit until after the December evacuation, when all fourth year medical students were returned to Australia to complete their course.

The effective treatment and transportation of wounded was further hampered by the chronic lack of stretchers at Anzac. This was despite 200 additional stretchers being brought ashore by the 1st ACCS and the extra stretchers carried by bearer subdivisions of three field ambulances. The problem was that once loaded stretchers left the beach destined for the transports, they were not returned.

The main cause of the stretcher shortage was that as boats carrying wounded were sent off to the ships, there was no medical officer on board who had the authority to demand the return of stretchers. Although the Royal Navy made a number and more were made on shore 'the lack of stretchers for the first three days considerably delayed the work of moving the serious cases...'[17] There was one instance where two men were sent out with one large barge to bring back stretchers. Neither stretchers nor men returned as they had been seized for duty on some ship lacking medical personnel! However, the shortage of stretchers was partly offset by the Navy offering its store of stretchers. After 26 April engineers also improvised or constructed stretchers at Anzac.

Later in the campaign, staff shortages continued to worsen. In a memorandum to HQ ANZAC Corps, dated 18 October 1915 from the CO 1st Australian Division, Brigadier-General Hobbs referred to the deficiencies in the medical services and pointed out 'that this is considered a most serious matter, for should there be a big action, with the attendant heavy casualties, the A.M.C. Staff would most likely break down under the strain...' A list of shortfalls in personnel was attached. This comprised a total of 24 Medical Officers and 357 Other Ranks.[18] At that time the only expected medical reinforcements for the 1st Australian Division for October and November were 42 Other Ranks and no doctors!

SHORE TO SHIP

The unprecedented degree of naval and military cooperation which the Gallipoli operation called for meant a split in the responsibility for evacuating casualties. Australia's medical services were involved both at the beach and on the various transport ships and ferries, and to a lesser extent to sea transport, the ultimate responsibility for which lay with the senior British service chiefs of both the Army and the Royal Navy. At the beach small boats were loaded under the direction of an officer of the ACCS and the boats' crews, under the command of the Naval Beach Master, off-loaded them at the other end.

Thus executive responsibility for the stage of evacuation between the piers and a ship's deck was strictly naval. However, once at the ship's rail, military units took over for the remaining stages, i.e. sea transport to base hospitals in Egypt and elsewhere.

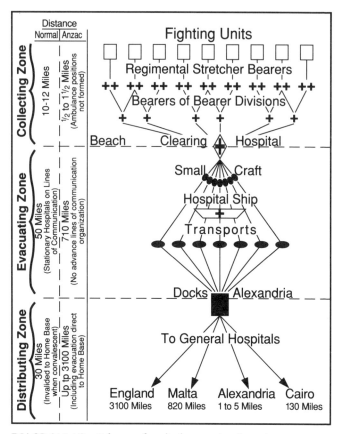

DIAGRAM 4.2   Scheme of medical evacuation from Anzac.
Source: A.G. Butler, Vol. I, p. 116

This shore to ship phase represents the most trouble-prone link in the overall process of removing wounded from Gallipoli. Its complexity, and the ways in which systems evolved to respond to a changing scenario, is illustrated in Diagram 4.3 on page 87.

The whole matter of medical evacuation was plagued by a complete inability on the part of Hamilton's General Staff to plan for realistic casualty figures. An illustration is provided by the initial allocation of six launches, each capable of holding 12 cots — this for 75 000 troops![19] The complexity of the issue is reflected by the evolution of medical evacuation systems (see Diagram 4.3). But more importantly from the point of view of the Australian medical services was what should happen to their wounded after they had been brought from the front to the clearing stations on the beach.

While the AAMC's Colonel Howse was very forthright about his opinion of the arrangements for evacuating wounded, and strongly supported the proposal for a coordinating position to be given to an Australian medical officer, it is curious that he initially refused the position of DDMS for the Australian Army Corps at Gallipoli when it was offered him by Surgeon-General W.G. Birrell, just prior to the April landing. The absence of such an officer had serious repercussions for the AAMC, particularly in April. Birrell, in replying to the evidence of Major (later Lt. Colonel) J. Corbin of the 1st ACCS, at the Dardanelles Commission, states that as the latter should have known the names of the hospital ship and hospital carriers allocated to the Australians for the April landing, he therefore should have been able to redirect wounded coming to him on board those ships.[20] Birrell argued that the 'circumstances prove that the staff of the Anzac Army Corps [namely Manders and Howse] apparently did not pass on the orders they received about the selected ships to the Units concerned'.[21]

This runs counter to Howse's contention that he did not receive any orders (for the 1st Australian Division) from Birrell. The discrepancies may be accounted for by the lack of any means to convey the plans to Howse before the campaign actually commenced (see chapters one and seven).

Captain J.W.B. Bean (brother of the historian), the medical officer for the 3rd Battalion, was wounded shortly after landing in April. His wound was stitched by another doctor, after which he was carried by stretcher to the beach, and he was eventually taken out to the *Seang Choon*. However, the boat on which he was sent from the beach was rowed from one ship to another for a considerable period of time before it could find a transport to take on its cargo of wounded. Once alongside the *Seang Choon*, the walking wounded got aboard. Bean and his fellow wounded were then kept waiting in the boat until he sent a note up to an officer on board. They were then slung up in stretchers and carried below. As no one came to his part of the ship, Bean organised his fellow wounded to help themselves before sending another note for help to one of two British medical officers on board. The reason for the delay? There were 800 wounded on this ship at the time and the medical stores consisted of two surgical panniers.[22]

Major J. Gordon of the 1st ACCS had been told by his CO not to expect any wounded on board his allotted ship, the *Ionian*, which on the afternoon of 25 April had only the stores of this unit together with 15 of its personnel — five of whom were sick. Therefore no attempt had been made to ready this vessel for the reception of wounded. Unfortunately on the same day 450 wounded came alongside, and there was not even the means of getting them on board until the *Ionian* launched its own boats. This could have been remedied had prior warning been given to Gordon and his staff. But as he was told not to do anything at all, he concluded that his men should not be wanted for taking in wounded. The wounded in this case were probably directed to the ship by Gordon's CO (Giblin). He had already landed and knew that this ship at least had medical personnel on board who could do something for the wounded streaming down from the slopes of Gallipoli.

Getting on board a ship did not always mean a casualty's problems were over. The unconventional aspects of the Gallipoli campaign had created other problems. For example the Army stretchers would not fit into the lifts. As Lord Methuen, the military Governor of Malta testily wrote to an admiral in May 1915, 'One can scarcely imagine no one testing this beforehand. What a wholesale slaughter this has been.'[23]

In calmer times (from mid-May to early August) the evacuation of wounded was a relatively ordered procedure. The hospital ships would lower a long wooden box over the side and the stretcher case was placed in it and the whole raised to the deck. Then he was off-loaded into the hands of waiting orderlies and whisked away to wards for diagnosis and washing. Some ships used a steam hoist to effect the rapid loading of patients. One source mentions that the entire process took from only 60 to 90 minutes to perform.

Private L.E. Schaeffer, who served as an orderly with the No 1 AGH and was for a time on the *Karoola*, wrote of the inconveniences of a rough sea which was so bad that by midnight he was 'sprinting in great style as fifty percent of the patients were seasick in addition to their other complaints'.[24]

Even to stand on the beaches at Anzac could mean death, and a number of 'Beach Masters' and other traffic controllers were killed while performing their duties. Their deaths were to have serious consequences for the evacuation of wounded. One of Australia's foremost medical men at Gallipoli, Lt. Colonel Chas. Ryan, was asked straight out by one of the Dardanelles Commissioners who he believed was responsible for the April disaster on the beaches. Ryan replied only that he had also asked the same question of the chief of the British Army medical services, Sir Alfred Keogh, who told him 'that the man in charge [at Anzac Cove] was killed in the first two days, but I said that there ought to have been someone to take his place'.[25] These officers tended to have a short life span. Tragically history was to repeat itself four months later on the same beach.

The inherent deficiencies in the April evacuations were compounded by the inability of Australia's medical units (and indeed the New Zealand and British teams) to sort their wounded. Sheer numbers precluded any but the crudest attempts to classify casualties according to severity of wounds. On 25 April and for the next two days, wounded were pushed pell-mell off the beach on to any craft which would take them. Lt. Colonel Corbin recounted that when he landed in April there were already about 300 wounded on the beach, none of whom could be moved at that time, because all transport was used to bring in troops, ammunition, and supplies.[26]

Small boats and barges were very scarce during the landing itself and for weeks after, and some extraordinary efforts were made to procure anything that could float in an attempt to get the wounded away. In one instance a volunteer party was collected and managed to refloat a large lighter which had run aground early in the day 'laden with kerosene tins full of fresh water & with two others left derelict alongside the pontoon, we were able to ship about 150 stretcher cases & possibly the same number of walking wounded'.[27]

Without question the military situation demanded that the disembarkation of the fighting troops, their ammunition and rations should have first priority and all available craft would be directed to this end. But this 'opened up a problem not only without precedent in modern war, but one which, before the inception of the Dardanelles campaign, had formed no part of the training either of the Staff or the medical services...In these difficult circumstances, Sir Ian Hamilton adhered to the principle that tactical requirements must be pre-eminent.'[28]

Captain Whitelaw of the 7th Battalion landed at Anzac as machine-gun officer and was wounded shortly after at 'Steele's Post' about 6.00 p.m. He eventually received medical attention by a RMO in the vicinity and was assisted to the beach where he arrived at about 7.00 p.m. After waiting a considerable time he was embarked on a large steel lighter, but it was a further three hours before the wounded were towed off to a number of transports which reported they were full or unable to take wounded.

The *Itonus* started to take them on board after a considerable wait. The majority were severely wounded, and it was not until 4.00 a.m. that Whitelaw himself was taken on board, where the medical personnel consisted of a fleet surgeon and a sick bay rating. On the Tuesday morning Colonel Newmarch (OC of the 1st AFA) and two other medical officers came on board with a medical detail but the *Itonus* did not leave for Alexandria until four days later on the night of 29 April. [29]

Newmarch later recollected that the *Itonus* was quite unsuited for its task. There were mules still on the foredeck and the ship had been left dirty, if not filthy after the disembarkation of troops. The latrines were choked, 'the food distinctly bad, and the ventilation very imperfect. The cabins were small and absolutely unfitted for wounded men.'[30]

Much was made both by contemporary observers and later commentators that more could have been done for the wounded if a greater number of *large* ships were available. 'The casualties removed from the *combined* beaches on 7 August amounted to approximately 3 800, 8 August, 4 100; 9 August , 4 200; 10 August, 3 600.'[31]

There was concern over inadequate hospital accommodation. The following letter was written from Babtie (the newly arrived Principal Director of Medical Services for the Levant) to Keogh, dated 7 July 1915:

> ...the large provision of H.S [Hospital Ships] made will not, with the constant influx of new troops, do much more than meet ordinary requirements and ordinary fighting. It will enable us to pour sick and wounded into Egypt at the rate of 10 000 a month. How are they to be got off. The wounded must be cleared, for we cannot keep any but the lighters [*sic*], as we have only accommodation for some 2 500 cases at Mudros and must keep about half of that clear for big battles. You know the conditions of the Peninsula — no hospitals of any sort possible.[32]

It is arguable that bringing up additional ships would not have solved the problem at this time because they could not have been staffed with sufficient medical personnel, and because of the lack of detailed planning in other areas, there was not the requisite medical equipment available.

One example is the inadequate supervision and coordination of supply and storage. At the April landing there was a quantity of heavy motor transport and horses on board the transports. As they could not be used at Gallipoli they were intended to be landed at Alexandria, but 'the motor transport remained on board ship, totally immobilizing the tonnage employed'.[33] Other factors, this time in the shape of the British allies, contributed to the worries of the Australian medical services and did little to ease the suffering of the wounded.

General Maxwell, who ultimately controlled the hospital ships, wrote to Hamilton on 8 May: 'I have arranged very nearly 12 000 beds in Egypt and all wounded are now comfortable and

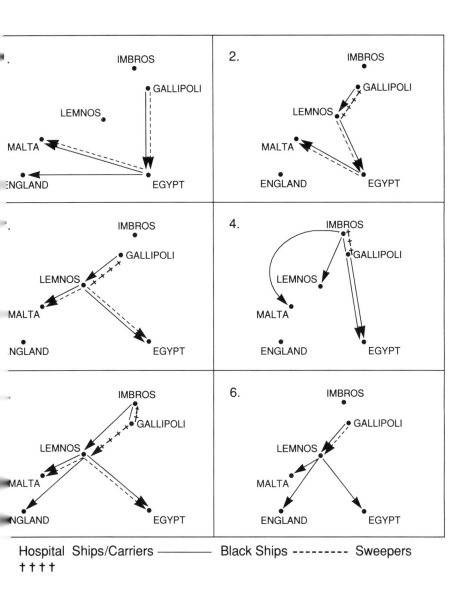

Hospital Ships/Carriers ————— Black Ships --------- Sweepers
† † † †

1. At the landing.
3. During June and July.
5. August Operations.

2. Arrival of submarine menace.
4. August (Porter-Ellison scheme).
6. After October.

RAM 4.3 Developments in the sea transport of casualties from Gallipoli.
        Source: A.G. Butler, Vol. I, p. 378

well cared for. I think we have done you well. For the short journey [48 hours] from [the] Dardanelles to Alexandria it is not necessary to have the fitted hospital ships. These are badly wanted to evacuate to England or we will be overwhelmed...The wounded come from the Dardanelles alright in ordinary transports.'[34]

In many cases the reality was different. 'More wounded arrived today. Beds are placed in every conceivable place. Passages as well as the wards and even the flat roofs had beds on them.'[35] Compare also Maxwell's statement with a ship on which 'benches and tables [were] covered with wounded, some on blankets, others on the bare boards...and all the time a stream of wounded coming down the steps or being lowered down the gangway on slings'.[36] An AAMC private wrote home: 'These fellows lay on the hard floor with bullet & shrapnel wounds, broken legs & arms, & mutilated bodies, mostly without further attention than I or others such as I was able to give them, from Sunday until the following Friday night, when the last of them were disembarked into the hospital trains.'[37]

At the April landing and then again in May, personnel of No 2 Australian Stationary Hospital had been split up and distributed amongst the various transport ships which lay off Anzac. In one instance a unit took on almost 800 wounded in less than 70 hours. All necessary operations were completed by the time it received orders to leave (about 18 hours after the ship had been filled).[38]

Unavoidably, there was a lot of handling and movement of casualties, sometimes several times. It was difficult enough on a ship designed for stretchers, an observation made by Lt. Colonel G. A. Syme, at that time performing surgery on the *Gascon*. 'Very soon a troopship came up & saw she had wounded on board for us; they were carried in stretchers down the gangway of the troopship, put in boats & rowed to us & then carried up the gangway. Then lighters came alongside towed by launches and torpedo boats then wounded could be lifted on board from them by the derricks. They were lowered to the wards by lifts.'[39]

Private A. Gissing, a medic on a different ship wrote that 'the arrangements for wounded on this ship [the *Galeka*] are splendid, a marked contrast to our last. Some of our last wounded are here again. It seems hard that immediately on their return they catch it again.'[40] On the improvised transports, such as the *Clan MacGillivray*, the wounded had to be stoic to the end. There was a ceaseless procession of walking wounded, who managed ladders, and stretcher cases, who were pulled up on board in big boxes by means of the ships' derricks.

Lance-Corporal J.G. Burgess of the 6th Light Horse Field Ambulance, suffering from dysentery, wrote both of his experiences of being evacuated to a hospital ship in July, and of the ministrations of the medical staff. He had first to wait in a field ambulance shelter until a boat was ready to take the day's sick and wounded out to the ship. On the beach he was surrounded by men with blood and bandages on them, who were 'all sitting about…[others]…lay very still on several stretchers. They got aboard the *Rewa* and were taken downstairs where they were given something to eat. Then we were examined and sent to the wards. What struck me though was the kindness of the A.M.C. boys both ashore & on the boat, no woman could have been tenderer than the way they treated us.'[41]

Later evidence, and certainly the published maritime histories, point to the severe shortage of suitable ships, the lead time to refit them, and the fact that the Allies were fighting not only in Gallipoli — a sideshow — but in an increasingly voracious war in France. While more manpower was available in July and August, and certainly the organisation of the hospital ships had improved, there were still not sufficient ships or personnel in the Mediterranean to meet the demand — there was always an imbalance between that and what resources were procurable. Chas. Ryan in evidence before the Dardanelles Commission stated 'I should think there must have been thirty of these large transports lying there. They were simply empty ships, not in any way suitable for a hospital…In some of the ships there was a fair staff of medical officers; in others very few. There were no nurses at all, and we had no modern conveniences for surgical operations.'[42]

The following comment typifies, rightly or wrongly, the view held by a number of medical officers at Gallipoli, including senior British doctors: '…except for the presence of hospital ships I do not consider the methods of evacuating have improved one iota since the time we landed here, 25 April, 1915…'[43]

In August, due mainly to the lack of hospital ships, it was proposed to make Imbros the clearing centre for evacuation by transports carrying casualties from Gallipoli. From here temporary hospital ships would take them on to Mudros, Alexandria or Malta. Although 'beetles' — shallow, steel-hulled craft with a drawbridge, capable of holding 500 men — were to be used for the landing, none were set aside for the evacuation of wounded from the beaches. As in April no craft were allocated for the exclusive use of the medical services.

The Royal Navy's senior medical officer in the Mediterranean, Sir James Porter, officially nominated as Principal Hospital

Transport Officer (PHTO), arrived on the scene shortly before the August operations began. Conscious no doubt of the scandals of April, he was appalled at the inadequacies of the medical evacuation for this second great operation of the campaign. In mid July, Surgeon-General Birrell had written out a proposed scheme for evacuating wounded during the August Offensive. This provided for all available hospital ships (six) to be left off Anzac and Helles, and a further 30 transport ships to be on hand.[44] However this was drastically altered by Porter on 28 July.

Again the General Staff was to interfere in the medical arrangements in the best cavalier style, namely on 13 July when they informed London of the expected number of casualties for the first week in August and stated that possible casualties would involve 'conversion of some thirty transports into temporary hospital ships and the provision of 200 extra medical officers with R.A.M.C. rank & file and nurses in proportion'.[45] The original request by Birrell for many more medical staff, including the use of 1 000 native bearers for stretcher work, had been radically reduced by Hamilton or Braithwaite.[46]

Subsequently plans were changed again as Porter still believed there were too few hospital ships, and on 6 August he drew up what came to be known as the Porter-Ellison Scheme, which provided for eight hospital ships.

The 'Porter-Ellison Scheme' was the brainchild of Surgeon Vice-Admiral Porter. Under this scheme eight hospital ships, in conjunction with a number of trawlers, would maintain a short ferry service to Imbros, transferring cases there to ambulance carriers. Evacuation to the base would be chiefly by black ships and any other available hospital ships. On 6 August eight hospital ships were indeed available at the Dardanelles. However of the 25 transports earmarked by the Admiralty for black ships, only nine had as yet been prepared; a tenth was serving as a depot ship for medical and nursing personnel; 11 others did not arrive at all, and four of those specified were found to be totally unsuitable. To make matters worse 'all these vessels were **debarred** from transmitting by wireless (emphasis added)'.[47]

Lt. General G.F. Ellison was the MEF's Deputy Quarter-Master General and with his assistance Porter planned to prepare every available hospital ship and to ensure that these were on station off Gallipoli in such a way that at least one fully equipped hospital ship would lie off each of the beaches throughout the operations. However, given the lack of time to prepare adequately this evacuation scheme had serious deficiencies — it relied on fair weather and an unlimited supply of hospital carriers (be they hospital ships or converted transport vessels). As usual the scarcity of small craft in the harbours of both Lemnos and Imbros substantially hindered operations.

Porter's scheme therefore foundered on the lack of sufficient transport to carry the wounded from the beaches to the ships, and poor communications. The plan called for all wounded to be taken direct to waiting hospital ships where they would be quickly classified on deck, the serious cases being retained on board and the lightly wounded passed across to trawlers, moored on the opposite side of the ship, for conveyance to 'hospital carriers' in Kephalos, the harbour of Imbros. These ships were not protected by the Geneva Convention and could not lie off Gallipoli as hospital ships did. 'Owing, however, to the requirements of the fighting troops being paramount, there were not enough lighters for the prompt evacuation of all the wounded as they streamed down from the front, and the number of trawlers available for light cases was also far too small.'[48] For the period 7–8 August the weather was rough and delayed the unloading of wounded from ships as well as impeding the passage of ships from Kephalos.

During the August Offensive, three piers were in use on Gallipoli for the evacuation of Australian and New Zealand wounded. From South to North these were No 1 pier (at Anzac Cove), No 2 pier (opposite Russell's Top), and No 3 pier (almost opposite Chailak Dere). No 3 was understaffed and could only be used at full tide. No 2, although a 'safe' pier, was undermanned, while the No 1 pier was reasonably staffed and physically adequate for coping with large numbers of casualties (see Map 2.3 on page 40).

As in April the arrangements on the beach itself were less than satisfactory. One of the Naval Beach Masters at Anzac, Commander Dix, was wounded, and another Royal Navy man (Captain Vyvyan), was appointed to direct operations immediately before the actual offensive began. Vyvyan therefore assumed the overall Naval command on the beach. To replace him on the beach itself was Lt. Commander Caten, who in turn was killed and superseded by Captain Drummond RN who then came ashore and landed right in the middle of evacuating wounded, the details of which he does not appear to have been fully briefed. Thus despite Porter's elaborate preparations, Anzac beach was again the stage for more suffering.

Even when the medical services managed to create some semblance of order in the changing scene at Anzac, they were to be thwarted by the low priority allocated to them by the military in the overall scheme of things. In the Anzac sector during the August fighting, L.W. Jeffries, a New Zealand dental officer (attached to the 4th Australian Field Ambulance), was appointed embarkation officer. He raised a Red Cross flag at the pier there and the evacuation of the wounded proceeded smoothly until a combatant officer insisted on landing stores at the same pier, after which the evacuation of the wounded became a precarious matter as the Turks turned their attention to the pier.[49]

On Lemnos the medical situation actually worsened even while the August offensive was in preparation. As masses of fresh troops and materiel poured into the harbour of Mudros, what organisation was in place for their control teetered on the edge of collapse. Again, there were insufficient small craft for handling stores and men. Three launches for the exclusive use of the medical services at Mudros had been donated by the Red Cross, but these did not arrive at Mudros until late in November. Further, due to the lack of engineering preparation with respect to the construction of piers, all ships had to lie about 500 metres from shore because of their draught. There were still few jetties and almost no port facilities as GHQ had insisted upon sending back to Egypt a contractor who had been sent specially to help construct piers in Mudros Harbour.[50] Even adequate roads were non-existent, to the disgust of the Australian hospital staff there.

For the old hands working on the beach at Anzac, a disturbing aura of *deja vu* must have seemed present. There were the same inadequacies in getting wounded from the beach to the ships. Two horse boats which had been fitted out with awnings specifically for the transport of wounded were commandeered to land troops instead. The commanding officer of the hospital then had to send for the special steam picker (which had been allocated solely for evacuating sick), but it failed to appear. The hospital ship *Sicilia* which came in was rapidly filled to overflowing and reported she would take no more cases. At the same time the *Seang Choon* arrived, but she took only Indian and Turkish wounded; there was no other hospital ship in sight. On 7 August the overworked 1st ACCS evacuated 1 937 cases.

In the August fighting the supply of barges was exhausted. The mounting number of casualties on the beach was exposed to shell fire, and suffered from showers of dropping bullets. Many were killed or wounded again in this way while waiting for evacuation. Colonel C.M. Begg, at that time acting as ADMS of the ANZAC Division urgently briefed Generals Godley and Shaw, who immediately gave him a large number of infantry to assist his overworked medical teams on the beach. Then several barges appeared, and by the night of 12 August, the beach was practically cleared of wounded. There was an adequate reserve of hospital ships. Corbin mentions that after urgent representations to General Birdwood, by 0400 on the 8 August 1915 there were eight hospital ships available. They also sent many small launches and picket boats.[51]

These barges relied on launches to be towed; and the steam pinnaces in turn were prone to breakdown and shelling — and many were holed in this way. But more importantly they had only a limited capacity for water and fuel, both of which had to be replenished at regular intervals, and their absences at times are clearly explained by this need. The supply of small craft therefore varied, depending on the time of day, the severity of shelling (which sometimes meant 'leaving those already on board to take their chance until the shelling eased off'), and the length of time it took to load and unload casualties.

On 7 August the *Delta* and *Dunluce Castle* had picked up wounded according to plan and left Anzac for Imbros. However, instead of releasing their wounded to transport ships at Imbros and returning immediately to their station off Anzac, these hospital ships were sent on to Lemnos. The alteration in the arrangements sprang from adverse tidal conditions, poor weather, and the overcrowding of Imbros's tiny harbour Kephalos — a town almost totally lacking port facilities. From 8 August, Porter's plan was so strained that recourse was made to the earlier practice of using sweepers to carry casualties direct from Anzac to Mudros. At Mudros the only large vessel in the harbour on 13 August was the vast 45 000-ton liner *Aquitania*, which was pressed into immediate service and sent to England (as Egypt and Malta had by then no hospital accommodation left), with only a skeleton nursing staff and a full load of wounded on board.

A less obvious reason for the breakdown is partly contained in Porter's own log, that is 'the failure of the military medical authorities at Mudros [who lived on board the *Aragon*]'.[52] Porter's orders were contained in envelopes addressed to each ship. However, unknown to Porter, Maher (the DDMS) and his staff were stranded on board the *Aragon* due again to lack of small craft, and therefore could not distribute Porter's plans, or indeed even their own orders. Whereas some of the ships earmarked for Anzac (i.e. the *Delta, Sicilia, Dunluce Castle*, and the *Seang Choon*) did obtain their orders direct from Porter's yacht the *Liberty*, 'with the after-coming ships some confusion naturally arose owing to non-receipt of orders. This was remedied as rapidly as possible by verbal explanation and rough notes of the general scheme given by my staff to the ships in question.'[53]

The severity of the fighting in those furious few days in early August is reflected by the casualty figures. At the commencement of the action, there were three hospital ships off Anzac beach —

the *Gascon*, the *Devanha*, and the *Dongola*. By the first evening of the Offensive all were full. It was the same off the beaches at Cape Helles in the south and Suvla Bay in the north. An English consulting surgeon (Mayo-Robson) recalled being told by an officer taking off the wounded in barges, that 1 500 cases were still waiting on one beach. Another officer asked the same surgeon: 'What am I to do; we cannot get any signals through from Anzac...'[54]

Under Porter's scheme these three ships should have proceeded to Mudros immediately. Mayo-Robson had received a typewritten copy of those orders, but through some error they had not been passed on to the captains of the hospital ships. This explains why they remained off Anzac Cove at the August Offensive, even though they were crammed with wounded. Thus the reserve hospital ships would not have come on station, as their officers assumed that all three ships at Anzac still had spare capacity.

Unfortunately little had improved offshore. For Sister G. M. Wilson her experience on Lemnos was a continuation of the bungling and poor coordination which had plagued her unit even before it had left London. She complained that things were so badly organised. Her unit (No 3 AGH) spent three weeks in London 'always packed and ready to leave at an hour's notice'. Eventually four transports brought them to Alexandria. The officers and men had arrived a week earlier 'to find nothing, the boat with their equipment no one has heard of...We are the first women to come so far, except of course the sisters on the hospital ships...there is no water.'[55]

As an aside, another Australian nurse, Sister I. G. Lovell, was seconded to the French transport *Formosa*, which sailed to Suvla Bay for the Offensive. The ship arrived there at 1.00 a.m. and those aboard wondered why no wounded were sent out. It appears that it was still flying the French flag and so the ship was ignored by the evacuating officers on shore.

Eventually someone realised that something was amiss and as soon as the Red Cross ensign was hoisted masses of wounded men were rushed aboard — a full 16 hours after the ship's arrival! 'We were receiving wounded all night and terrible wounds they were — flyblown and septic. All were operated upon admission and the little theatre was kept busy all night — limbs, had they been able to have been treated before & would have been saved, had to be amputated.'[56] These wounded were the first patients of No 3 AGH at Lemnos.

HOSPITAL SHIPS, AMBULANCE CARRIERS AND BLACK SHIPS

The descriptions of the major types of ships used in the Gallipoli campaign for transporting wounded are given here:

HOSPITAL SHIPS were requisitioned liners, extensively adapted for the particular purpose of aiding the sick and wounded. They were in effect floating hospitals and were medically and surgically equipped to deal with all cases of injury and disease; were painted white overall, with a horizontal band of green, about a metre and a half wide, around the hull. At night the hulls were brilliantly illuminated and there were usually long rows of red and green lights along the sides.

HOSPITAL CARRIERS were in effect 'inferior sorts of hospital ships', generally being passenger liners or merchant vessels which had been fitted up as well as time permitted. They carried the distinctive markings of hospital ships and were registered under the Geneva Convention.

AMBULANCE TRANSPORTS [also known as 'black ships'], while equipped to carry and tend the sick and wounded, were also used on return journeys to transport troops and stores. These vessels did not carry the distinguishing marks of hospital ships and claimed no protection under the Geneva Convention. At Anzac these ships could not therefore take on wounded within the firing zone, i.e. close to shore.[57]

The differences are important to an understanding of this important aspect of the medical services' role throughout 1915. This section generally highlights those respects in which the maritime evacuations differed between April and August, and the problems met in both periods. The medical transport arrangements from Gallipoli in April and August were to spark most of the sensational press reports and scandals of 1915.

Hospital ships were actually the province of the Army, not the Navy. Even the military were slow to realise this. 'I told Keogh long ago that it is not fair to have only Naval hospital ships; that we ought to have Army hospital ships...one might have expected more forethought.'[58] To further complicate affairs, the hospital ships received their sailing orders from the Naval medical officer, and details of their destination from the DDMS — an Army medical officer.

In April the only hospital ship in the vicinity of Anzac Beach so marked — i.e. painted white, with a large red cross on her hull, and illuminated at night by a string of green lights — was the *Gascon*. The black ships showed no lights during the night and were therefore completely indistinguishable from other craft. This added to the distress of medical personnel on naval tows trying to find somewhere to deliver their cargoes of wounded, who were usually wet, hungry and seasick in addition to their other woes. Due to shelling during the day, many of these ships had to move further out to sea, that is, away from their pre-arranged sites, thereby making it difficult, if not impossible, for the crews of these small boats to locate them.

At the April landing, in spite of the acute shortage of doctors, almost unbelievably Surgeon-General Birrell refused the offer of the Navy to put its own medical resources at the Army's disposal. Birrell rejected their help because the naval surgeons were obliged to return to their ships each night (as the Fleet itself was on active duty). Vice-Admiral Wemyss who made the suggestion later recalled that he 'was a good deal shocked when my offer was refused'. Wemyss was 'unable to acquiesce in his refusal and went personally to see Sir Ian Hamilton — at that time afloat in the *Arcadian*, to protest against the refusal to make use of available help. My protest had the desired effect; some fourteen naval surgeons were distributed amongst the doctorless ships.'[59] Alas, Wemyss had to intervene again in August.

The names of ships such as the *Galeka*, the *Saturnia* and the *Lutzow* (see page 28) will remain as infamous reminders of the inadequate care, and in some cases preventable, deficiencies in the care of Gallipoli's wounded. The case of the *Galeka* represents the intricacies of the bungled arrangements for the evacuation of wounded troops by sea. Elements of the AAMC were aboard, as part of an amalgam of medical personnel sent to deal with what was often an unknown quantity. While this disaster was not deliberate, those in charge must shoulder some of the blame, either through their inadequate supervision of staff, or a disinclination to take their officers' reports on the ship's condition seriously.

The *Galeka* was a transport ship used at the April landing. In defending its use as a hospital transport, Birrell resorted to the time honoured ploy of blaming the inexperience and youth of the most vocal critics of this ship, and cast further aspersions at their integrity by hinting at hysteria. He reported that the supply of surgical and medical material on board was sufficient for a short voyage. He correctly pointed out that it was not protected by the Geneva Convention, but then blamed the doctors on board, calling them 'impressionable and of an imaginative disposition [and] apt to make statements which they neither can prove nor sometimes recollect clearly a few hours later'. He dismissed their statements and considered that 'the wounded were well looked after and that the S.M.O. and his staff did all they could for their charges under very trying conditions...'[60] What had these impressionable Australian medical officers said?

The senior medical officer on board the *Galeka*, Lt. Colonel Tate-Sutherland (OC 1st Light Horse Field Ambulance), made a statement in which he pointed out that owing to a misunderstanding, food and medical equipment belonging to his unit were left in a barge going ashore, and that this contributed to the situation. A more detailed report by Capt. J.R. Muirhead (Tate-Sutherland's second-in-command), was submitted to Colonel Sexton, ADMS Base MEF on 29 May.

In it he stated that he had been on the temporary hospital ship *Galeka* for at least three days, during which 'wounded patients had to remain in soiled linen, no clean shirts were obtainable to replace blood stained ones'. In spite of an attempt to stop him boarding an ordnance ship in Mudros Bay, he obtained a supply of 300 shirts. Other medical comforts were virtually non-existent on the *Galeka*. 'The ship was ordered as far as I know to return with only four medical men and twenty-five orderlies although we carried over 400 patients.'[61] Ironically, while at Mudros Bay several days earlier the New Zealand Cavalry Ambulance, consisting of four MOs and 73 Other Ranks (who were previously on board), had been ordered to disembark from the same ship.

Until May, Lt. Colonel Keble (Birrell's DMS of L. of C. Mudros) was responsible for inspecting transports, and satisfying himself that they were adequately staffed. After May this responsibility devolved on the L. of C. staff, i.e. Lt. Colonels Maher and Thom. Maher could not be got to give evidence before the Dardanelles Commission as the army would not release him from active duty. His evidence would have been critical in a number of areas, observations about which must remain somewhat inconclusive.

According to the *Final Report* of the Dardanelles Commission the officer responsible for inspecting all (medical) transport ships, Lt. Colonel Keble, was given a light reprimand for not following up a report concerning the conditions on board these vessels (in particular a report on the *Saturnia*, from Major (later Colonel) A.J. Aspinall, which is discussed below). The senior medical officer in charge, Surgeon-General Birrell, when examined before the Commission could only state that 'the first time I knew anything about the shocking conditions was on reading the [news]papers'.[62] It apparently did not occur to him that two doctors may have been insufficient for a ship holding more than 1 000 wounded soldiers.

Just as some semblance of order was being established at Gallipoli a new menace appeared — the submarine. The fleet had received information from Gibraltar on 7 May that a number of German submarines had passed the Straits. On 13 May the battleship *Goliath* was sunk off Gallipoli in full view of the MEF dug in along the peninsula. Then, on 25 May the German submarine *U 51* sank the *Triumph* (off Anzac) and the *Majestic* (off Cape Helles).[63] It made other attempts on the *Vengeance*, the *Lord Nelson*, and three French battleships in the area. These losses signalled a complete change in the system of naval action, anchorage, and supply.

The submarine presence in the Dardanelles theatre therefore adversely affected marine transport for the sick and wounded coming off Gallipoli. The warships which hitherto had provided psychological support to the beleaguered allies pulled back to Mudros Harbour. The unmarked, and therefore vulnerable black ships followed in their wake. From then on these vessels would work mainly after dusk. During daylight black ships had to be loaded up with wounded outside the fire zone. There were immediate implications for the Australian medical units on Gallipoli itself, as there was a corresponding increase in the holding time for casualties in field ambulances and the Casualty Clearing Station.

It was not that strenuous efforts were altogether lacking to rectify matters on board hospital transports. In a letter of 20 June Sir Frederick Treves, Inspector-General, Communications (L. of C. Mudros) recommended to Keogh that no ordinary transports or troopships should be used for evacuating wounded as they were not protected under the Geneva Convention and in many cases had no accommodation for the sick.[64] But it was a case of using what ships were to hand. The alternative was to risk a back-log of casualties at the front. Of necessity the lesser of the two evils was chosen. Evacuation by ship from Gallipoli therefore had to be carried out sometimes in spite of serious shortages of medical staff to look after those on board. This was one aspect of medical evacuation which senior British medical officers underestimated. For them the system always ran smoothly, and when it did not, one could always blame the War.

An insight into life on board an improvised hospital ship in July comes from Sister Woniarski of the No 1 Australian Stationary Hospital. This ship had been hastily fitted out by native labour and among other things it boasted defective plumbing. She wrote that there were awful swarms of flies which made life hard for the patients on board. Someone forgot to put a pharmacist on board and even the most basic surgical appliances were in short supply.

The ship's galley was the only place where instruments could be sterilised, as each ward had only one 'Primus' stove for this purpose and most were out of order. There were only six nurses on board so that each nurse worked from 16 to 18 hours a shift. She added that the 'loss of thirty-nine cases before we reached port was partly due to the severity of their wounds, but also to the intense heat below decks'.[65]

Surgeon-General Babtie, in a letter to Hamilton from Alexandria dated 27 July, had warned him of the likely problems concerning the wounded during the offensive, and requested more transport and the closest coordination between the Army and Navy. He also pointed out that the total number of beds available in both Egypt and Malta was not likely to exceed 12 000 or 13 000.[66] Babtie had done his research but his plans depended on the successful outcome of Hamilton's proposed strategy.

Even in August the shortage of qualified medical staff to man various ships, to nurse both Australian and British units was appalling. So bad was the shortage that a 'Very Urgent' signal was received by the OC No 2 ASH, which read: 'A number of Class B. *convalescents* are required to proceed to England as *nursing attendants*' (emphasis added). 'B Class' convalescents were those soldiers 'fit for service on the lines of communication', but not ready to return to their units.

Private Silas, a medic from Perth who was evacuated from Anzac in May, volunteered despite having a fever, for orderly work aboard the *Galeka* as the ship was so short-staffed. In spite of his condition his shift was from 6.00 a.m. to 11.00 p.m. each day.[67] 'Please let me know…how many men you have suitable for this duty, who are not likely to be fit for the field for at least a month.'[68] The realities had at last hit home, a belated development from the almost irresponsible optimism of earlier days, days when Keble could say of nurses '…at present and possibly for some very considerable time, if ever, we have no use for them closer than Alexandria…'[69] Certainly in April, even when the number of doctors on board was theoretically sufficient, they were not of much practical use. The *Dunluce Castle* had 700 cases on board, and while there were four doctors on board, all of them were general practitioners — none were surgeons.[70]

On those seemingly rare occasions when reports of obvious administrative blunders did find their way to higher quarters, the results could be interesting. To illustrate this point, there is the case of the *Saturnia*. The first alarm came with the following signal to the Chief of the General Staff, as recorded by Lt. Colonel C.F. Aspinall (one of Hamilton's staff officers):

> Yesterday afternoon it was reported by the R.C. Chaplain that there were 800 sick and wounded on the *Saturnia* and only two doctors to look after them. Admiral Wemyss accordingly ordered each man of war in harbour to send a surgeon on board. Almost immediately (30 August) the Deputy Adjutant General of the M.E.F. received this telegram: 'The D.M.S. told me that the casualties on 28th amounted to 1842. There were three hospital ships at Helles on 28th. Perhaps therefore you would enquire why 1600 wounded were evacuated on fleet sweepers etc., and why they had to be accommodated on an ammunition ship [the *Saturnia*] in Mudros.' (sgd) J.W. [Braithwaite] C.G.S.[71]

On the same day, Surgeon-General Birrell informed Braithwaite that the figure of 1600 was incorrect and further stated that the accommodation on board was adequate. This was despite the fact that the *Saturnia* was a supply ship and filled to the gunwales with ammunition at the time.

Those who were actually on board the *Saturnia* also differed with the official version of the situation on board. On 28 August Captain Fraser of the 2nd LHFA was ordered with 12 men of his unit to proceed to the *Saturnia*. He was told to prepare the ship to receive about 600 to 700 wounded. At 7.00 a.m. the next morning 570 British wounded from Cape Helles were dumped on board from the *Prince Abbas*.

Another medical officer, Major Purchase, a New Zealander, estimated the figure at closer to 1100. He surmised that the wounded were sent to this vessel in consequence of the mistaken transmission of a signal.[72] His story although graphic, is almost typical of many shipboard medical scenes in those days. While he was on the upper deck he dressed 'a man who had about the largest wound I have ever seen, his whole back being laid open, and he was simply crawling with maggots'. Admiral Wemyss later came on board and was so shocked that he asked Purchase how he could help. Purchase replied that he could do with some help. Shortly thereafter the surgeons began to arrive. It appears that Wemyss had signalled for every available naval surgeon to turn up.[73]

The irony of this example was that at this time the *Saturnia* was less than one kilometre from the HQ ship *Aragon*. The wounded were eventually transhipped to the *Nile* and the *Minnewaska* before being sent on to Base hospitals. Many civilian eyewitnesses in Egypt particularly were shocked to see flyblown wounds. However, 'when the wound was washed and cleaned, there was very little inflammation and the general condition of the patient was much better than some of the patients who had received treatment…*en route*.'[74]

Stories had been filtering back to Australia for some time concerning the treatment of its wounded. No doubt many of these reports were highly colourful and even apocryphal, but eventually public opinion became outraged. On 13 August Hamilton received a cable from the War Office which quoted a telegram received from the Governor-General of Australia, stating that very bad accounts had been received there from private sources of the lack of medical attendance on hospital transport between the Dardanelles and Alexandria. This came as a surprise to Hamilton, as he had apparently been informed locally that 'ample personnel had been sent to Egypt to supply nurses & doctors for all transports, and that no ship carrying wounded had been sent away without sufficient personnel'.[75]

TRANSPORT TO BASE HOSPITALS

This section deals with the penultimate link in the medical evacuation chain and concerns developments which occurred mainly in Egypt. No 1 Australian General Hospital had been in Egypt since January, and it became the bulwark for the Australian medical services in that country, both while the AIF was in training there, and well into 1916.

The registrar of this hospital later wrote that the rapid expansion of No 1 Australian General Hospital was undertaken entirely by a staff originally intended to care for the standard 520-bed establishment. Not until mid-June did medical rein-forcements arrive, and the hospital received only a portion of those.[76]

Most of the accommodation was of an improvised nature. Hotels (some luxury class) predominated, although troops were nursed in a boarded-over skating rink and a joinery and for a time were placed outdoors due to lack of accommodation.

An idea of the growth of the No 1 AGH in Cairo is indicated here:

	BEDS
Heliopolis Palace Hotel	1 000
Luna Park	1 650
Atelier	450
Sporting Club	1 250
Choubra Infectious Hospital	250
Abbassia Infectious Hospital	1 250
Venereal Diseases, Abbassia	2 000
Al Hayat, Helouan (Convalescent)	1 250

Ras el Tin (Convalescent)	500
Montazah Palace (Convalescent)	500
Grand Hotel, Helouan	500
	10 600

As early as March 1915, Surgeon-General Williams (AAMC) had cabled to Australia the news that No 1 AGH had expanded with annexes to 2000 beds.[77] He pleaded for the immediate addition of 20 medical officers, 25 NCOs, and 230 nurses and Other Ranks. The solution proposed by the Defence Department in Melbourne was to use reinforcements which were already en route to Egypt.

This episode illustrates that the Australian Government had no real idea as to what were appropriate (medical) staffing numbers for the AIF. Colonel J.B. McLean, the CO of the No 1 AGH wrote after the war that: 'We were warned weeks and weeks beforehand to expect a tremendous casualty list, but there were neither hospital ships, medical men, orderlies [sic] or nurses to cope with it, and the same condition of affairs existed not only in the ships, but at Alexandria and Cairo...'[78] Matters were not helped by the fact that when the first wounded arrived the No 2 AGH was in the process of moving from Mena House to Ghezireh Palace (both in Cairo).

Before a system was established in Egypt for dealing with incoming casualties, things were rather chaotic. It was a rude awakening for Australian staff (which numbered at this time 28 officers, 92 nurses and 216 Other Ranks) at No 1 AGH. On 29 April without notice or warning of any description, train loads of wounded began to arrive in large numbers. On 30 April and 1 May no less than 1352 cases were admitted. Due to the chaos previously described, the hospitals were filled with slightly injured soldiers. Pte. B.W. Rainsford, a medic serving in Cairo, wrote that of the casualties who arrived from the front on 30 April 1915 'nearly all [had] minor wounds'.[79]

The system, or lack of it, was completely beyond the control of the AAMC and there were other participants who could only look on and wring their hands at the stupidity of it all. The military governor of Malta (850 kilometres from Lemnos, where several hospitals had been prepared) wrote to Hamilton to let him know of 'the arrangements I made when first I heard of your Expedition, for one could see the loss of life there must be...Why not send your wounded straight here? There seems no sense for instance, in sending in the *Caledonian* 800 [wounded], to take out 100 at Alexandria, and to send the rest on here. I have some splendid military and civil surgeons available...Keogh and R.F. [Surgeon-General R.W. Ford D.M.S. Egypt] are playing up alright...'[80]

The OC of the 1st Australian Field Ambulance (Colonel B.J. Newmarch) wrote that during the period 25 April to 9 June about 4000 sick and wounded passed through his hands. In that time he saw only one ship that was properly equipped and in any way fit for hospital transport. 'All reports [were] handed to the A.D.M.S. Alexandria. From the way he conducted affairs I should think they [his reports] were all gone [i.e. lost or destroyed]. He had a holy contempt for Australians and I returned his insolence with interest added.'[81]

Another AAMC officer had a similar experience of British red tape but with a different outcome. Lt. Colonel Muirhead had journeyed across from Gallipoli on board a ship with men coming round from anaesthetics and those with broken jaws being forced to eat bully beef and hard biscuits. On landing at Alexandria he was told that Lady Carnarvon (who was informally attached to the British Red Cross at Alexandria) wished to see him. She asked about Red Cross stores aboard the transport ship (Red Cross stores often supplemented inadequate army issues on these ships) from which Muirhead's patients were disembarking. He told her that there had been no Red Cross stores on board. Wasting no time this formidable woman went into action.

The next morning Muirhead was told to report to the ADMS who — in a fury — told him that Lady Carnarvon had made a terrible row at Headquarters, subsequent to what she had learnt from Muirhead the previous day.

Other civilian volunteers who had assisted on the wharves at Alexandria also asked questions and had written home about the 'scandalous' conditions. The following is typical of the official reaction. In a letter to Birrell dated 17 May 1915, Cairo, Ford wrote: '...a wire came from England, some busy body I suppose, not knowing the extraordinary difficulties, asking silly questions about wounded on transports, when obviously you had to pack them off practically from the battlefield. They arrived *well dressed* [Ford's emphasis].'[82]

Muirhead was then asked to asked to write the ADMS a full report of what was said. This he did, omitting the fact that from Mudros to Alexandria there was not a single bedpan on the ship. On reading the report the British officer was astounded and asked his second-in-command how it was that he and other officers had hitherto been reporting 'that the ships are all right?'[83] According to Muirhead relations with the ADMS improved dramatically and that subsequently ships leaving Alexandria were better staffed and provisioned.

Diagram 4.4. on page 105 showing the docks at Alexandria in Egypt, will assist the reader in an appreciation of some of the difficulties involved in evacuating sick and wounded to the Base hospitals here. The diagram shows the distribution systems in Egypt itself as these affected the Australian medical services.

Once at the wharves of Alexandria these wounded men were transferred by motor or horse waggon direct to hospital trains or to local hospitals. 'During the first ten days of the crisis (after 25 April 1915) approximately 16 000 wounded men entered Egypt, of whom the greater number were sent to Cairo, and during those ten days an acute competition ensued between the supply of beds and the influx of patients.'[84] Diagram 4.5 on page 107 is based on a sketch by Sergeant Kenny of the 3rd AFA and it shows how he understood the evacuation system to work. There were scenes of much activity in Cairo at these times. Sister C. McNaughton wrote in her diary that 'the night we arrived [at the Ghezireh Palace Hotel on 13 August] eight hundred patients came from G. [Gallipoli] and most of them were seriously wounded...so we just got here in time. They were coming in from eleven pm til three am, just one continual humm of motor ambulances. Some have died but they all got the best of care and very bad cases a special nurse.'[85]

Alexandria and Cairo were not alone in receiving little, if any, advance warning of the arrival of casualties. Even in July, medical authorities on Malta were expressing frustration at the poor coordination of the whole evacuation procedure. Malta had a number of excellent hospitals, and a large number of military barracks, which, owing to troops being on active service, had been converted to hospitals. 'My transport and medical people are rather put to it by my not knowing till ten thirty pm last night that the *Somali* would be coming in at seven am today...possibly your staff officers could let us know a little sooner.'[87]

By late July the authorities were at last alive to the realities of a lengthy and complex campaign. Surgeon-General Babtie, in contrast to Ford's 'wait and see' policy, realised the need to increase the hospital accommodation in Egypt and Malta.

Surgeon-General Ford appears to have followed a plan akin to modern-day crisis management whereby each problem was met as it came along, forward planning being used hardly at all. In a letter to General McGregor, HQ, Cairo, dated 22 April 1915, Ford shows this unpreparedness. 'The hospital ships on arrival at Alexandria will come under the orders of the G.O.C. in Chief, Egypt, and the disposal of all sick and wounded on board will be

1. "The Cotton Wharf"

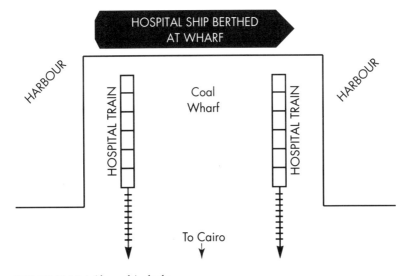

HARBOUR

HOSPITAL SHIP BERTHED AT WHARF

HORSE AMBULANCES
□ □ □ □ □ □ □

MOTOR AMBULANCES
△ △ △ △ △ △ △

COTTON SHEDS

HORSE AMBULANCES
□ □ □ □ □ □ □

Stretcher cases waiting here or inside cotton shed

HOSPITAL TRAIN on this line

2. "Coal Wharf"

HOSPITAL SHIP BERTHED AT WHARF

HARBOUR

HARBOUR

HOSPITAL TRAIN

Coal Wharf

HOSPITAL TRAIN

To Cairo

DIAGRAM 4.4 Alexandria docks.
Source: After a sketch by Sgt O.P. Kenny 3rd A.F.A., A.W.M. 41/3/9.10.

carried out with the knowledge and approval of the D.M.S. in Egypt. Sick and wounded arriving from overseas may have to be accommodated in various hospitals in Egypt and even Civil hospitals as well if necessary, and this can only be done through a centralised authority...'[88]

He had been told of Hamilton's (reduced) casualty estimate of 20 000 for the forthcoming August offensive. On 21 July Babtie wired to the Director General, Army Medical Service in London (Sir Alfred Keogh), his summation of the situation as to hospital accommodation. There were then about 18 000 beds in Egypt, of which 10 000 were occupied, Malta was preparing 10 000 beds, of which 5 600 were then occupied. As we have seen, the actual casualties from the August fighting totalled almost 30 000 men. By September the entire hospital and evacuation system for the Gallipoli campaign had collapsed.

After a conference of senior Navy and Army medical and logistics officers the Inspector-General of Communications for the MEF (General Altham) wrote to Keogh. He pointed out that even assuming no further military operations at Gallipoli and no reinforcements for the MEF and assuming also that the normal rate of sick and wounded did not exceed 800 a day, evacuation could just be carried out if the Admiralty added the huge liner *Mauretania* (with accommodation for nearly 2000 patients) to the existing fleet of hospital ships (this was not done until late November).[89] The alarm bells were sounding louder than ever, and as usual the response was slow.

Then on 13 August General Altham was officially informed by Surgeon-General Babtie that no further medical accommodation was available in either Egypt or Malta. Lemnos had already reached its limit of 4 000 casualties. Despite considerable expansion, all accommodation was again declared full on 4 October, due to the influx of sick, as opposed to wounded, soldiers. The only solution was to load up large ocean liners and transport patients direct to England. This method of evacuation was then employed intermittently from August until the final withdrawal from Gallipoli in December.

Despite all the evidence to the contrary, Surgeon-General Ford, when asked at the Dardanelles Commission whether he was at any time short of hospital accommodation, vehemently denied it. 'No, I think in Egypt we were rather ahead of events, because we built up with anticipation of a large number of wounded — we did not know how many because unfortunately there was no interchange of opinion between the M.E.F. and the Headquarters in Egypt.'[90]

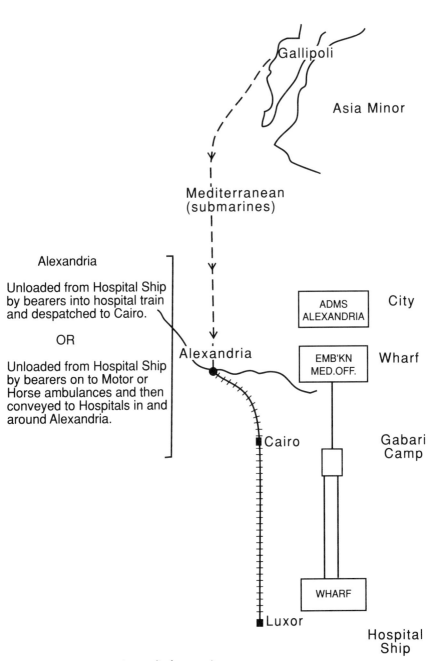

DIAGRAM 4.5   Egyptian medical evacuation routes.

However, in an early report from Col. Maher, the Deputy Director of Medical Services (L. of C. to the DMS, MEF), dated 29 July, the following statement appears: '...the hospitals in Egypt are reported as congested and there are only 600 vacant beds at Malta.' Maher went on to say that accommodation for 4000 beds had been applied for at Mudros and the site selected, and admitted that 'until the huts are erected and personnel and equipment provided the accommodation for the sick at Mudros will be a source of grave anxiety.'[92] The increase in overall casualty numbers from Gallipoli, due to disease and sickness generally was such that in October there were no hospital beds available anywhere in the Mediterranean.

For most of the Gallipoli campaign evacuating from the front, particularly to the base hospitals, became something of a vicious circle. The more casualties sustained on the peninsula, the more hospital ships were required to move them. But these same hospital ships were required to empty the base hospitals to England and Australia as the hospital population in Egypt and Malta swelled in proportion to the increase in the number of casualties.

Australian medical units were dependent on Britain, not only for sea transport but even for ambulance trains in Egypt. They were also subject to the whims of Surgeon-General Ford and operated less efficiently than could otherwise have been the case — that is to say if they had been supervised directly and comprehensively by Australian headquarters medical staff. This conclusion still recognises the inefficiencies within the AAMC itself. But certainly in the provision of medical transportation, Australian medical personnel could only play a small role in caring for their countrymen. The relative helplessness of the medical services was to be exacerbated when the entire Expeditionary Force was afflicted with that other horror of war: disease.

CHAPTER FIVE

Disease

...a flood of sick which far surpassed all expectations and brought about an acute cry for reinforcements at the front and a renewed crisis on the lines of communication and at the bases...the causes of disease had gone too long undiscovered and unchecked, and the newly-arrived divisions went down before them even more quickly than the old [*sic*] ones.[1]

Disease is nurtured in those surroundings where sanitation is not, or cannot, be implemented and supervised. This in turn ensures the rise of disease carriers and at Gallipoli this was principally the fly. Once disease gained a foothold, it had to be identified, its victims treated and survivors protected from further ravages. Finally the cost of disease to the military and to the Gallipoli campaign itself has to be considered — a factor largely ignored when we think of Gallipoli and what it meant for Australia. In all these aspects the activities and influence of the Australian medical services played a crucial part.

After the Crimean War, military medicine advanced considerably in the understanding of diseases and their causes. This knowledge, however, was still confined to medical textbooks. Some of the more enlightened staff officers and those who had served in the Boer War (for example Colonel Neville Howse) did appreciate the ramifications of poor hygiene and the importance of keeping disease at bay. For others (of whom Hamilton was one) who had served in South Africa the lessons appear to have been ignored. To a considerable extent the enlightened appear to have won the day. (See Appendix IV, Table 3, for comparative figures between South Africa and Gallipoli.) At the top levels of the MEF there was still insufficient awareness of the most effective preventative measures. Only after various disabling diseases had made huge inroads into the ranks, thereby directly threatening the entire expedition itself, did GHQ heed the earlier advice of its medical establishment.

In the Dardanelles theatre no section of the AAMC was spared, for disease meant both manpower wastage and a substantially increased workload for the medical staff who remained, even after the fighting had devolved to siege warfare and casualties from battles declined. By September the overburdened hospitals at Lemnos were swamped with Diggers for whom debilitating disease was the last straw.

To add to the troubles of the AAMC in Egypt, fresh troops arriving from Australia brought with them a host of diseases — some of them infectious. Due to inadequate sanitation, accommodation and inoculation in training camps in Australia, a number of men left for Egypt carrying influenza, mumps and measles. Venereal disease was still high on the list of diseases amongst Australian reinforcements, and it constituted a significant 'nuisance factor' for the AAMC, not only because it had to provide treatment, but it had to find accommodation and nursing staff to care for this category of patient. The incidence of venereal disease among the AIF simply reflects the male civilian population, for in post-Federation Australia, VD was much higher than the modern Australian might care to know.

Colonel Howse, the ADMS 1st Australian Division at this time, did not make himself popular with some medical units due to an uncharacteristic display of lack of foresight in the area of epidemiological and other research facilities. Colonel J.W. Springthorpe of No 2 Australian General Hospital wrote of an inspection of the hospital at the converted Mena House hotel: 'Inspected by Gen. Ford — Howse says "don't want Bacteriology and X-Ray Outfit." He may not but we do — (illustrating his frame of mind toward the Scientific side of our world — still characteristic when he later became Director of Medical Services).'[2]

SANITATION

Although the least glamorous, one of the vital functions of any medical service is to superintend and advise on sanitary measures. Its importance had long been recognised by the Army. The Manual of Elementary Military Hygiene (1912) stated that in the South African War (the Empire's most recent comparable campaign with respect to Gallipoli), for every man admitted to hospital on account of wounds, 17 had been admitted because of disease. The AAMC found that undue responsibility was placed on it for the propagation of sanitary measures at Anzac which more correctly belonged to Divisions, Brigades and individual regiments. Engineers were also used heavily, particularly in the construction of permanent latrines and drains and this to some extent moved the onus further away from those combatant units whose responsibility field sanitation really was. One doctor wrote that he had 'inspected the ANZAC area with O.C. 21st Sanitary Section and found that many units were failing to keep their areas free from refuse'.[3]

There was apathy among the Diggers despite the ranks thinning out as a direct result of poor hygiene. Combatant officers later realised that it was in the best interests of their units to police the various sanitary regulations which had been circulated as part of routine orders virtually since the first landing.

However, comprehensive sanitary measures at Gallipoli were relegated to the lowest priority until almost too late. Birrell's successor, Surgeon-General Bedford, who arrived in September 1915, wrote home to his chief that an official sanitation officer (Lt. Colonel Aldridge) had been sent out and appointed ADMS (Sanitary) at GHQ in July. Despite this Birrell had not considered that he was required and he sent Aldridge away. This officer then remained in limbo for more than five weeks before being used in his professional capacity. Bedford added 'I have no doubt that during that time the sanitary supervision of the Force did get somewhat out of hand.'[4]

The ferocity of the first attacks, together with the terrain at Anzac, worked against the early organisation of sanitation until several days into May. Curiously enough in the last days of April, after the landing, an officer of the Military Police was appointed to oversee/control sanitation. However, this short period was enough to establish breeding grounds for insects. Fortunately there were neither mosquitoes nor scabies on Gallipoli. However flies, and later, lice, more than compensated for their absence. They were to be the bane of medical staff, and the cause of much sickness and discomfort. Insects featured prominently in soldiers' letters and diaries. 'In the insect line we could count quite a tidy little collection...We had flies by the hundred billion. They were everywhere, from the heaps of dead to the cooks' pots. Put jam on a biscuit and it was always a sprint between you and the flies, the event usually ending in a dead heat.'[5]

Once the initial April landings were over, men were picked from infantry units to look after the cleanliness of their own lines. A medical *Sanitary Report* concerning Anzac Cove (dated 28 May) noted beach pollution, most of which came from the two Divisional supply depots where there was unavoidable spillage of foodstuffs and grain, which in turn attracted and bred flies. At that time refuse was put into tubs near the beach and dumped at sea.

Despite the pleas of medical officers, rubbish was not burnt until late in the campaign because it was argued that smoke attracted enemy fire. However, in the immediate HQ vicinity at Anzac Cove, incinerators were operational by the end of May. This area was also privileged because on 4 May Howse actually got together a 'sanitation company' of about 30 men, obtained from various units behind the lines. This was organised in three sections of eight or nine men under NCOs, each operating in part of this Division's operational area, digging the necessary latrines, and cleaning the ground, especially near the wells. However (unlike Cape Helles), there was no 'professional' sanitary unit operating at Anzac until 13 August.

With the growth in the fly population at the end of May, there was a corresponding increase in diarrhoea (often incorrectly diagnosed as dysentery). But there was at that time no medical officer able to isolate the cause. With the warmer weather and in an attempt to head off an increase in illness, the AAMC kept basic sanitary regulations before the troops via frequent memoranda.

It was not long before the fly menace and other health hazards began to attract attention from senior army officers. In a memorandum of 14 May from the General Staff of the ANZAC Army Corps HQ to the DA & QMG, it was noted that Diggers were using the springs for washing, and were washing in buckets, close to the water and fouling it. Latrines had not been filled in. Apart from the stench, flies were gathering in numbers of tins with meat etc. in them, thus breeding further.[6]

As Corporal Kitson wrote: 'Flies soon became our worst enemy, starting about the middle of May and becoming unbearable about the middle of June, bringing in their train dysentery and enteric fever. The dysentery became very prevalent

THE GASTRO-INTESTINAL GROUP OF INFECTIOUS (TRANSMISSIBLE) DISEASES
ANALYSED INTO INDIVIDUAL DISEASE ENTITIES

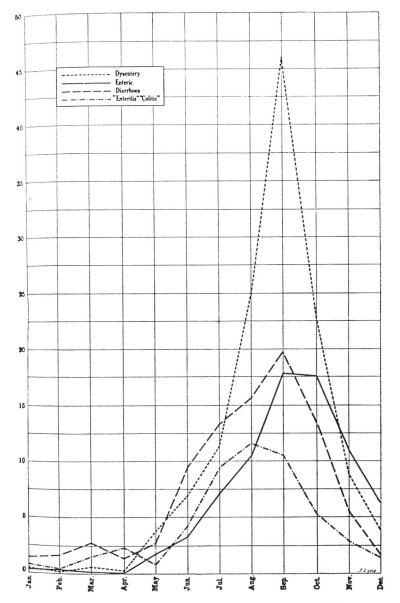

The clinical diagnosis was controlled by laboratory investigation in probably not more
than 25–30 per cent.

Source: Butler, Vol. I, p. 347. Note also that in all arms throughout June and July the
wastage from sickness was in excess of the replacements by reinforcements and
recovered casualties.

about the middle of June and swelled the sick parade enormously, sometimes the number of [men at] sick parades totalled 200.'[7]

Operations frequently had to be curtailed because of the combination of dust and flies. Such sickness was also an important factor in the military situation as the period of convalescence required for dysentery victims was usually three months.

The other factor to be considered was the large number of inaccessible corpses which lay between the trenches, although a short armistice negotiated in May with the Turks permitted the burial of many bodies, and this no doubt checked the fly menace for a time. Latrines continued to constitute a major health hazard. 'Closed latrines are scattered everywhere and for those in use there is no means of protecting them from flies...'[8] The shortage of suitable materials such as wood and tin was such that this problem was not adequately tackled until the campaign was almost over. The first improvised fly-proof latrines 'were made by a Pioneer sergeant just before the Lone Pine battle, and were constructed from the timber of a boat or boats that had been broken up...'[9]

The only bright spot in an otherwise dismal unhygienic environment was the proximity of accessible, if dangerous, beaches for bathing. Given the shortage of water, this was the only means by which Diggers could wash. In addition, swimming provided a much-needed break and exercise for the men. Despite constant casualties from Turkish shooting and shrapnel, the Australian and New Zealand commanders did nothing to stop this activity probably because such a directive would have been impractical to police.

'From a hygienic point of view, the sea was the salvation of the men. Everyone near the beach bathed twice a day even at the risk of "stopping one", while the men from the hills came down whenever reliefs took over.'[10] However, senior British medical authorities were unimpressed, Birrell being moved to write 'A good deal of diarrhoea among Australians — possibly due to sea bathing.'[11] Although it must be said that at this time causes for this alarming increase in diarrhoea were based on guesswork. In one field ambulance diary this conjecture was recorded: 'possibly due to the wholemeal biscuits & large supply of onions & limited vegetables...'[12]

On Lemnos it was some time before the island's sanitation was anything more than rudimentary, despite being the base for a number of sizeable military hospitals. The lack of pre-planning, shortages of building and engineering materials, and the ubiquitous lack of small boats to move such materials to shore were to blame. When matters did improve, the hospitals still used very basic measures to prevent infection and to avoid disease running amok, as had happened at Gallipoli. 'We had a large incinerator, which burnt up all the refuse of the camp. In the infectious wards, chloride of lime, when we could get it, was sprinkled on the ground, and when we could not get this, cresol solution was sprinkled about two or three times a day...'[13]

Lack of space and continued fighting worked against the early establishment of a comprehensive and satisfactory sanitary system at Anzac. Nor, at the time, were the vitamin deficiencies (particularly B and C) of the Army diet sufficiently addressed. The results were to be costly. The increased workload for a progressively decimated medical service would also become an important consideration in the eventual decision to abandon Gallipoli.

DISEASES

There was a great amount of sickness at Gallipoli from June 1915 and the diseases which concerned the AAMC most were dysentery, typhoid (and paratyphoid A and B), jaundice, and influenza. The changing seasons played an important part in the relative prominence of each of these. At the time many sick troops were not correctly diagnosed, and the massive numbers suffering from debilitating diarrhoea did in fact have dysentery. Mercifully the historic killer of armies — cholera — did not break out, mainly due to a comprehensive inoculation program; nor did Trench Fever (common on the Western Front) occur at Gallipoli.[14] The demands of the military ensured that the AAMC was basically in a no-win situation. Commanders were becoming increasingly impatient at convalescent troops being retained in hospitals on Lemnos and in Egypt. Thus, as the campaign progressed, and more and more soldiers became ill, the pressure for retaining unfit Diggers at the front also mounted. Naturally, retaining such cases at the front for military reasons increased the spread of infection.

In order to better appreciate how badly the AIF was mauled by disease, mention should be made of Colonel Sir J. Purves-Stewart, Consulting Physician to the MEF. Immediately upon his arrival at the island of Imbros on 8 September this officer, an experienced Harley Street man, made enquiries as to the ratio of sickness amongst the various forces then operating on the Gallipoli peninsula. After studying sick returns, he concluded that the proportion of sick was markedly different amongst the three forces. This was a fact not hitherto deduced by medical officers on the peninsula.

Purves-Stewart brought a fresh perspective to things and drew a new and somewhat startling conclusion. This concerned the question of the physical condition of the troops that had not reported as sick but who were still in the firing trenches — as front-line troops. Stewart had made a three day study of troops at Gallipoli and he knew that some of them (such as those at Anzac Cove) had been under continuous shellfire for over four and a half months. Unlike the Western front there had been no rotation of regiments to the rear.

Troops at Anzac were therefore presenting an abnormally high percentage of sick, three or four times as many as troops at Cape Helles. The increase in dysentery and other intestinal diseases (which then formed the bulk of sickness), together with the prevention and treatment of these diseases was also the subject of special study by a Commission on Epidemic Diseases. There is also reference to a Cholera Committee, formed (as Admiral De Robeck wrote in a letter to a colleague) 'to take precautions in case there should be any outbreak and considering the crowded state of the peninsula we should be very lucky if we escape without trouble'.[15]

TABLE 5.1: PERCENTAGE OF SICK EVACUATED

	WEEK ENDING AUG. 28	WEEK ENDING SEPT. 5
Helles (about 30 000 troops)	4.4%	5.1%
Suvla (about 26 000 troops)	1.9%	1.7%
Anzac (about 30 000 troops)	**6.6%**	**7.5%**

These percentages refer only to troops who were on **active** duty, not those 'off sick'.

Table 5.1 clearly shows the difference in health between soldiers at Anzac and troops in other parts on Gallipoli. Stewart wrote that the 'contrast between the old and the fresh troops was striking. The older troops were emaciated in 77% of cases...64% of these men were suffering from indolent ulcers of the skin, chiefly of the hands and shins...A large proportion, 78% had occasional diarrhoeal attacks...Most striking of all was the rapidity and feebleness of the heart's action. The medical name at that time for this condition was Disordered Action of the Heart, or effort syndrome, which was held to be 'nothing more than a manifestation of anxiety neurosis'[16] — tachycardia being observed in 50% of the old troops...74% of these troops suffered from shortness of breath.'[17]

In reply to this report, which Purves-Stewart submitted to Hamilton on 18 September, the latter wrote in October that the conditions of health which were 'the result of the exceptional exigencies of this campaign, have not been unnoticed; and steps are being taken — so far as circumstances permit — to improve the general health by giving men, in turn, rest and change from the peninsula. The matter of canteens has received full consideration (a full five months after landing!)...'[18]

The difference in the health of soldiers at Anzac and those living elsewhere on the peninsula appears to be attributable to three main factors. First, the poor rations and their lack of variety must have served to lower the men's resistance to infection. Second was the absence of any respite from a front-line environment. This may have made Diggers prone to illnesses which might not have presented if troops had been able to exercise and enjoy some recreation. A third element may have been the more intensive battle fatigue suffered by those at Anzac, although British troops at Helles were also subject to a similar environment, shelling etc.

To appreciate how this situation arose, let us return to the beginning of the campaign. The fly menace has already been noted. Flies were the chief means of spreading both bacillary dysentery and amoebic dysentery (which had been brought from Egypt), the difference being that symptoms of the former develop more quickly and are more severe. Jaundice also started to occur in August and by October had replaced dysentery in significance. It reached epidemic proportions towards the end of the campaign. While fly breeding went largely unchecked, dysentery (which at Gallipoli, with the exception of amoebic dysentery, was not waterborne) and infectious intestinal diseases generally became rife. On Lemnos, Sister B.E. Henson wrote in one of her letters home that 'Quite a number of our officers have been invalided to England...Dysentery is the chief trouble...either it or the anti-toxin wins in two or 3 [sic] days. At present I am in a dysentery ward and we have only lost one case.'[19]

The situation was no better in British units. 'From August 31st until September 17th I was down with dysentery, like many others. Royal Army Medical Corps personnel could not get away from the Peninsula with this complaint unless they were almost "packing up" owing to the shortage of men and the absence of reinforcements.'[20] In 1915 there was much confusion in discerning one from the other. As Bean wrote, 'Had it been possible to diagnose the diseases as they appeared, much more might have been done to prevent them.'

In September orders were given to treat every case with emetine; but at that date No 4 Advanced Depot of Medical Stores at Anzac possessed neither emetine nor needles for its injection.

When Bean wrote after the war '…what proportion of the cases during those months was dysentery and what proportion diarrhoea the cause remained a matter of opinion.'[21] But earlier, in July, the writing had been clearly on the wall, according to Lt. Colonel B.J. Newmarsh: 'The health of the men is not so good as formerly — dysentery is becoming very acute and cases of extreme collapse are occurring.'[22]

Typhus and cholera (which did not occur at Gallipoli) were diseases common in the Turkish part of the Mediterranean. Typhus is an infectious disease carried by the body louse, of which there was no shortage in the cramped conditions of the trenches at Anzac. Paratyphoid was another problem.

According to one medical authority, paratyphoid fever (so called because the symptoms were less severe than ordinary typhoid) was more prevalent in Gallipoli and Lemnos, where it was ten times as common as typhoid fever itself. For the MEF as a whole he quotes 5700 cases of enteric fever which occurred among the 96 683 medical casualties of the 300 000 men who fought at Gallipoli up to the middle of December 1915. Of those about 93 per cent were paratyphoid and only 7 per cent were typhoid fever. Paratyphoid B was the prevalent type up to the end of October, when paratyphoid A became more common, almost replacing paratyphoid B by December.[23] The AAMC was impotent in the face of the unknown, and the sense of helplessness can be gauged from the unit diary of the 7th Field Ambulance in November: 'B. Section have been most unfortunate — Many of their men seem to be suffering from Typhoid or paratyphoid. No info. can be gained as to where they have contracted it.'[24]

The problem common to all of the intestinal diseases at Gallipoli was diarrhoea. As a medic, James McPhee could with authority write 'With the cold it's an experience for the unfortunates with bowel complaints to have to go down at night from the dug-outs to the low ground, and sit on an ice cold latrine pole: the close "psst" at intervals of a stray bullet makes company welcome, and visits as brief as possible.'[25] Butler wrote a number of maxims in his own diary at Anzac, one of which was 'Most uncomfortable situation: To suffer from diarrhoea when the latrines are under shrapnel fire.'[26]

For a while, men thus stricken were evacuated as they were of no use in the trenches. But as casualties mounted and reinforcements were similarly afflicted, more and more casualties were kept at Anzac, often in special dug-outs at the various dressing stations. There they were rested and placed on a 'soft' diet, when suitable food supplies could be obtained. Each medical officer did what he could in the circumstances.

Cairo: a horse drawn ambulance bringing the sick into the former luxury hotel,
Mena House, occupied by No. 2 A.G.H.
(Reproduced with permission of AWM, Canberra)

Cairo: another view of No. 2 A.G.H. taken in October, 1915.
(Reproduced with permission of AWM, Canberra)

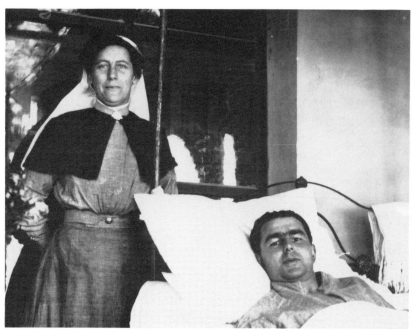

Carer and casualty: Sister Foster of No. 2 A.G.H.

A fleet of Australian ambulances in Cairo. *(Photograph taken by Sgt. R.M. Whitelaw and reproduced with permission of his daughter, Mrs B. Fitzgerald, Ballarat)*

Stretcher bearers training in Egypt with a simulated casualty.
(Reproduced with permission of Australian War Memorial, Canberra)

Cooks of the 1st Australian Field Ambulance (situated above 'Brighton Beach')
giving out a light diet to walking sick.
(Reproduced with permission of AWM, Canberra)

Wounded about to be loaded aboard an 'ambulance carrier'.
(Reproduced with permission of AWM, Canberra)

Inset: The 1st Australian Field Ambulance in whaleboats being towed ashore by a
steam pinnace at 8am on 25 April, 1915.
(Reproduced with permission of AWM, Canberra)

Congestion on Anzac Beach, 3rd May 1915. The 3rd Field Ambulance were situated
in the shelf of the cliff on the right. *(Reproduced with permission of AWM, Canberra)*

John 'Simpson' Kirkpatrick and his donkey 'Murphy'.
(Reproduced with permission of AWM, Canberra)

The hospital ship, Souden, on station off Anzac on 25 April 1915.
(Reproduced with permission AWM, Canberra)

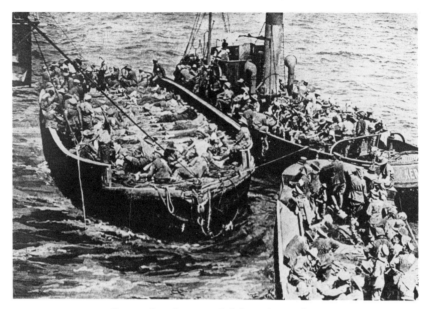

Evacuating the wounded from Anzac Cove.
(Reproduced with permission of AWM, Canberra)

Members of the 2nd Field Ambulance manning the oars in Lemnos Harbour.
(Reproduced with permission of AWM, Canberra)

Sister Emily Hoadley, No. 3 Australian General Hospital, at Lemnos.
(Reproduced with permission of AWM, Canberra)

Convalescing on Lemnos.
(Reproduced with permission of Imperial War Museum, London)

Ambulances and hospital ship at Alexandria. *(Taken in 1915 by Sister C. McNaughton, No. 2 A.G.H., in the possession of her daughter, Mrs P. Barnes, Werribee)*

A hospital train taking patients from the No. 2 A.S.H. at Tel-El-Kebir to the No. 1 A.G.H. in Cairo. *(Reproduced with permission of AWM, Canberra)*

Group of senior NCOs of the 2nd Australian Field Ambulance, probably taken on Lemnos prior to 25 April 1915 (note Red Cross brassards).
(Reproduced with permission of Dr D.L. Baylon, Cairns)

Below Left: Colonel (later Major General Sir) Neville Howse, Assistant Director of Medical Services to the 1st Australian Division at Anzac: he later became Australia's senior army medical officer. *(Reproduced with permission of AWM, Canberra)*

Below Right: Captain (later Colonel) A.G. Butler, R.M.O. 9th Battalion and author of the Official History of the Australian Medical Services 1914–1918. *(Reproduced with permission of AWM, Canberra)*

Above Left: Lt. General Sir Alfred Keogh, Director General of Army Medical Services, R.A.M.C. Britain's senior medical officer. *(Reproduced with permission of R.A.M.C. Historical Museum, Aldershot)*

Above Right: Surgeon Vice Admiral Sir A.W. May, Director General of the Royal Navy's Medical Department. *(Reproduced with permission of AWM, Canberra)*

Below Left: Colonel (later Major General) R.H.J. Fetherston, Acting Director of Medical Services, Australia. *(Reproduced with permission of AWM, Canberra)*

Below Right: Surgeon Vice Admiral Sir James Porter, R.N. Principal Hospital Transport Officer. *(Reproduced with permission of AWM, Canberra)*

Dug-outs of the 2nd and 3rd Australian Field Ambulances at Anzac Cove. Note telephone wires. *(Reproduced with permission of AWM, Canberra)*

Dressing station in a dug-out near 'Quinn's Post' with doctors and medics waiting for patients and casualties. *(Reproduced with permission of AWM, Canberra)*

The 5th Australian Field Ambulance in 'Rest Gully' at Anzac.
(Reproduced with permission of AWM, Canberra)

Inset: First aid in the field.
(Reproduced with permission of Imperial War Museum, London)

Looking down on Watson's Pier. Shells bursting on Army Corps headquarters.
1st Australian Clearing Station is situated on extreme left of photograph.
(Reproduced with permission of AWM, Canberra)

A.G. Butler, as the RMO of the 9th Battalion opted for a system whereby a medic had a special dug-out and did nothing but prepare invalid foods — sago, rice, cornflour, porridge etc. to which milk was added. Any Digger with diarrhoea was given a slip marked 'light duties' and the number of days 'sick leave'. It was then signed and dated by Butler. The patient was given an issue of hot, nicely prepared invalid diet.[27] Sometimes these steps were palliative only and while the symptom may have been addressed, the cause remained. Unfortunately the period of invalidism on account of typhoid fever was about six months, and such a long period of convalescence had serious consequences for the fighting effort.

Some soldiers had been inoculated for cholera en route for Egypt aboard troopships, and not a few received a second dose.[28] The War Office records indicate that on 17 June the ADMS Base MEF wired for cholera drugs and apparatus in view of a possible outbreak of that disease and these were despatched with surprising efficiency on 20 June.[29] On 5 July Birrell wrote: 'Cholera inoculation to commence. Optional unless a case reported at Constantinople, when to be compulsory. This compulsory inoculation however vetoed by C. in C.'[30] Hamilton and his minders had intervened yet again!

Nonetheless the AIF for its part undertook an inoculation program. In a letter to his mother, Corporal Gardiner, Howse's clerk, wrote 'All the troops are being inoculated against cholera which is prevalent on the peninsula during the summer months. I was done this morning. What with vaccinations for small pox, and inoculations against typhoid and cholera, one does get a mixture of germs in him.'[31] By 16 July Howse could record that 4000 Australian troops had been vaccinated.[32] Whilst outbreaks of cholera were reported in Turkey, there were no cases in Gallipoli in 1915. This in itself was no small achievement for the medical services.

Midway through the campaign, fatigue and poor diet caught up with the 'original' Diggers who fell easy prey to sickness. A New Zealand staff officer later recalled the month of September at Gallipoli: 'The troops, weakened by continuous hardships and malnutrition, were an easy prey to dysentery and similar ailments. The dressing stations were also kept busy by men troubled with septic sores. Scratched by the prickly scrub, or with meat or jam tins, the wounds were healed with great difficulty...'[33]

The war diaries of the various medical units chronicle not only the prominence of disease, but the increase in different types of sickness, which in turn was a function both of the length of

time men had stayed at Anzac (during which their health
deteriorated), as well as changes in the weather. In the month of
July one unit alone presented an average of 67 men a day at its sick
parades.[34]

After August a number of respiratory diseases, loosely
grouped under influenza, was added to dysenteric diarrhoea.
Then in September which was the peak month for infectious
diseases, PUO or pyrexia (fever) of unknown origin became the
prevailing sickness, while the typhoids were still worrying
medical authorities. There is this entry for an ambulance unit
diary: 'Since Sept 5th number of typhoid cases = forty-four. This
represents roughly twelve percent of 1st L.H. Fld Amb. These
figures show the great incidence of Typhoid amongst medical
personnel engaged in nursing these cases.'[35] In October another
ambulance had admitted: 'Diarrhoea — one hundred and
twenty-eight, Influenza — one hundred and ten, Dysentery —
one hundred and eight, Enteric Fever — forty-nine, Tonsillitis —
forty-five, Rheumatism — thirty-three, Pleurisy — thirteen,
Diphtheria — twenty-two, Pneumonia — nineteen, Gonorrhea
— thirteen.'[36]

The picture being painted in official diaries was bleak. In this
report the 5th Australian Field Ambulance indicated its activities
for the month of October. 'No of wounded seventy-three, No of
sick 857. Returned to unit 331, Evacuated 532, Remaining
sixty-seven.' Between August and November (inclusive) the 6th
Australian Field Ambulance treated 896 wounded, 2108 sick; of
all these 1857 were evacuated and 909 men were returned to their
units.[37] The implications for combatant units at Anzac are clear,
as a further report, this time by the 3rd Australian Field
Ambulance attests '...for the month of Nov. Admit: fourteen
wounded, 348 sick; evacuated: ten wounded, 174 sick.'[38] With the
coming of cold weather in December the 'Prevailing disease
during past week — Influenza, Jaundice, Trench Foot.'[39]

Apart from Diggers presenting to medical units either sick
or wounded, there were also accident victims, and these added to
the burden of the medical service. Some were quite serious, as
noted by Sister A. Kitchen, serving on board the *Gascon*. 'Last
night we got in another man with his R. [right] hand blown off
with a hand grenade: things they make themselves out of jam tins
and all sorts of things like that. They occasionally go off too soon
and then there is tragedy; or in throwing it, hit the back of the
trench.'[40] Another incident which occurred on board ship was
noted by Captain (later Major) Barton thus: 'Chaps all fooling
round with rifles...when one chap fired his and bullet went thro'
a cabin across passage thro' another wall and blew the top of a

chap's head off as he was asleep in his cabin. Only found five hours later when called for duty.'[41]

IMPLICATIONS — MILITARY AND MEDICAL

Graph 5.1 on page 113 indicates not only the growing incidence of sickness at Anzac, but the rapidity with which it overtook the AIF's battle casualties.

From July onward, a series of medical reports issuing from commanders and medical committees were unanimous in their recognition of a decimated soldiery, and signalled ominous portents for the next few months, particularly the winter. Many troops had been on continuous active duty since 25 April, fought numerous engagements, and were constantly subjected to the physical and psychological stress of combat. There had been no relief in terms of rest, change of diet or routine, and reinforcements had been few. To these factors was added 'the intensely weakening effect of the prevailing epidemic of acute diarrhoea, a large proportion of the division was suffering from mental and physical exhaustion...and were in need of a complete change.'[42]

The following is a diary extract, dated 16 September, written by an infantryman, Sergeant Lawrence: 'the men have steadily gone from bad to worse. Every day now sees four to seven from our company go to hospital. Myself, I am feeling as well as it is possible to feel under these conditions, very weak in the stomach...I have, in common with the others, had several attacks of diarrhoea or dysentery...it leaves one terribly weak.[43]

The medical services, themselves struggling in the face of declining staff numbers, were hard pressed to cope, which in turn increased the pressure to evacuate offshore where the sick men could be properly looked after in hospitals, and above all, isolated, in cases of infectious disease.

As the men of both Divisions collectively underwent a metamorphosis from the sturdy, bronzed physiques of legend to staggering, emaciated men barely able in some cases to hold a rifle, it became obvious to their commanders that immediate measures could no longer be postponed. Medical personnel worked amidst pathetic scenes, such as that described in his diary by Private V. Worland in September: 'Men of 1st Infantry fainting etc. while waiting to be examined.'[44]

Surgeon-General Bedford also noted in his diary the poor health of the troops at Anzac and recommended that the 1st Australian Division be moved to a rest camp. As a result a

Commission was formed to visit Anzac and it subsequently recommended a more varied diet, improved sanitation, protection of water wells, but no rest camp. But the poor conditions continued to take their toll on the AAMC. In September alone, the 2nd Australian Field Ambulance 'lost' 41 of its men, '40 being evacuated sick, [although]...twenty-four men rejoined the unit...five of whom were reinforcements'.[45] In the following month this unit had 52 of its members evacuated sick.

Those worst afflicted — the rank and file in the front lines — left vivid accounts of their own observations. By August the men were in a bad state. 'Before the [Lone] Pine affair they were bad enough but the last few days here have completely broken them up. It is piteous, really to see them. Great hulking fellows or at least the remains of them crawling about doubled up with internal pain due to dysentery, lying down utterly exhausted every hundred yards they go, others masses of septic sores.'[46] The toll was heavy and the tactical implications were serious. A member of the 4th Light Horse Regiment wrote that 'Of the original squadron that left Victoria 150 strong we have two officers and sixty-nine men left and only half of them are fit for duty now.'[47]

If the Turks had made a determined push at this stage, it is questionable whether the Anzac position would have held. By the time the August Offensive was over General HQ was acutely aware of the position.

On 23 August Hamilton cabled to the War Office that 'the average net wastage from sickness and war is twenty-four percent of the fighting strength per month'.[48] The previous day Bedford for a second time recommended that the 1st Australian Division be moved to a rest camp, but this was stalled through lack of reinforcements to relieve units designated for rest periods on Mudros. Imbros had already been used as a rest camp in July; the average stay of Diggers at that time was four days. By September however the period had been extended to four weeks.

From 7 September wider relief was possible due to the arrival of brigades from the Australian 2nd Division, and the 1st, 2nd and 4th Brigades left for a well earned rest at a new camp established at Sarpi, West Mudros. On 20 September Colonel Monash (then commanding the 4th Brigade) wrote home from there: 'Since last writing the declining health of the troops became daily more acute, and so at last the higher command, from sheer force of circumstances, was compelled to consent to a withdrawal of five of the brigades which have done the lion's share of the fighting up to now.'[49]

The spectacle of these wretched men arriving on Lemnos was a memorable one for many of the hospital staff working there. Some of the men marching past these units on the way to camp simply collapsed by the roadside. Sister H. Selwyn-Smith recalled 'We had been at Lemnos about two months when the men began arriving off the peninsula for a rest. I shall never forget seeing the first lot march or rather stagger past. Most of them looked haggard and ill, numbers dropped out on the way to be admitted into the hospitals that day or the next probably.'[50]

Not a few men thought themselves well out of it, as Sergeant D.J. Partridge wrote: 'We are over for a few days spell, what's left of us and I don't mind betting you that it's a treat to be out of that hole of a place.'[51] The Australian staff had other worries.

C.E.W. Bean has written that there was a 'justifiable fear that if once an officer or man became parted from his unit at the front, however short the separation intended, none could foretell when he would return to it. This greatly increased the desire of all responsible commanders to keep their sick at Anzac, and that of many of the sick themselves to stay there [from a sense of duty to their mates]'.[52]

The return of troops to their units was not helped by poor staff work in the AAMC itself. Many a soldier was evacuated in 'quiet times' without proper documentation. This led to confusion and was responsible for many casualties being lost to their units for those same long periods when their units could not obtain replacements. The following is fairly typical of the 'internal' complaints received by medical units: 'D.D.M.S. written to report that wounded and sick coming ashore are not provided with nominal rolls or any notification of Hospital they are detailed to.'[53]

This situation represented a painful dilemma for the medical services. Should seriously ill soldiers, especially those suffering from infectious diseases be treated (and retained) at the front, or should they be sent to proper medical care, but in the process possibly be lost to the 'system' for weeks or even months?

The long periods of time spent by sick or wounded troops convalescing in Egypt, Malta or England was a sore point with many AIF officers. The chronic lack of seaborne transport prevented the speedy return of convalescents. In the case of Monash, upon arriving at Mudros with his troops for a rest, he selected various officers and sent them 'to Alexandria, to round up convalescents and reinforcements'.[54]

AAMC units based on Lemnos did not escape disease either and it made life all the more difficult for those left to treat and nurse the massive influx of sick from Gallipoli. Until mid-November almost 60 per cent of the male staff in No 3 Australian General Hospital, which was the most recent arrival of the three Australian hospitals on the island (31 July), had themselves been hospitalised and many were subsequently invalided back to Australia. Female nurses weren't as badly affected, possibly due to their greater diligence in personal and camp hygiene than their male colleagues. This fact did not pass unnoticed by the Australian nurses on Lemnos, as Sister E. Davies proudly remarked: 'I have heard some statistics of the percentage of members sick in the Unit. Sisters five percent, Medical Officers thirty percent, Orderlies seventy percent, so women are hardiest after all, you know what men are for throwing in their alley (as boys say).'[55]

The Australian hospital units in Cairo were equally prone to sickness and other occupational 'hazards' as were their counter-parts on the peninsula — more so when they were nursing men with infectious diseases. A large percentage of doctors, hospital nursing and orderly staff could be off-duty all the time. As one of their number wrote: 'The persistently hot climate, combined with overwork, the inability to take adequate exercise, and the added risk of disease inseparable from hospital life, have all tended to bring this result about.'[56] But as the Gallipoli campaign dragged on other factors combined to add to their woes.

CHAPTER SIX

Other Causes of Concern for the AAMC

The conditions at Gallipoli precluded in a great measure the relief to unbearable tension afforded to 'weaker vessels' by wine, women and AWL...This had two results. First a large evacuation from psychophysical and psycho-somatic breakdown, 'debility', indigestion, and functional disorders. Second, repeated short epidemics of self-inflicted wounds. [1]

This chapter provides an insight into problems (while less significant than disease) which nonetheless, together contributed to the difficulties of the Australian medical services in carrying out their duties at Gallipoli. The lack of water (crucial to medical procedures) and the inadequate diet which eventually helped contribute to gastrointestinal disease and debilitating diarrhoea proved a continuous source of anxiety to medical personnel. Dental problems also sapped the strength of some of the fighting men on the peninsula, while medical units faced constant problems with respect to the supply and distribution of medical and surgical supplies and equipment. The medical services were also blamed for keeping convalescents away from the trenches for too long, a criticism which while partly justified was yet another factor largely beyond the control of the AAMC. Psychological problems also had to be dealt with by medical staff.

WATER

The scarcity of water on Gallipoli was to be a major problem for most of the campaign. It was indirectly responsible for a number of health problems and was a contributing factor in several military failures — the Suvla Bay (north of Anzac Cove) attack in August being the most noteworthy. There was almost never sufficient water available for Diggers to drink; and from their meagre ration they were expected to cook their food and wash and, according to one writer, 'when operations were on, even in the intensest [sic] heat the average ration of water for all purposes was, perhaps, at most, a pint and a half, sometimes only a pint'.[2]

These shortages are illustrated by the following signal to the Fourth Battalion (from its Adjutant): 'Owing to the stress of circumstances the supply of water to troops in the trenches has become a very serious matter. Tomorrow the maximum amount of water which will be available per company [approximately 200 men] for all purposes will be eight tins [145.4 litres] …sufficient to make one lot of tea of about 1/2 pint per man.'[3] Water was essential for the proper functioning of medical units, as it was required for sterilising instruments, mixing solutions, irrigating wounds, and for other cleaning purposes. But as one doctor later admitted it was so 'short at periods…we had to dress the men's wounds with salt water'.[4] After the onset of disease in July, units sometimes found it difficult to muster sufficient men fit enough to go down to the beach and undertake the long haul back to the trenches with their tins of water.

Although there were a number of potable wells on Gallipoli, these could never supply the needs of such a large body of troops; in fact there had been earlier scenes of thirsty men cutting canvas hoses which brought water from flat-bottomed boats to troughs on the beaches. Therefore, during the period from the April landings until almost the December evacuation, all troops on Gallipoli had to rely on water coming from as far afield as England and Egypt. A large new oil tanker was brought up to Imbros full of water from Port Said. This vessel was then fed by the constant coming and going of smaller tankers between Mudros and the waterworks in Egypt. Even transports on arrival from England emptied their surplus water into this tanker before returning home. The precariousness of the supply lines has already been noted, susceptible as they were to submarines, mines, storms, delays and mismanagement. The supply of water was to become an added headache for the military and medical authorities concerned with the Lines of Communication.

During the first days of the initial landing, troops and their beasts of burden inadvertently polluted the few streams on Anzac, subsequently rendering them useless. But fortunately there were no contamination problems either of water in the tankers or water coming from the wells at Anzac — both sources were well guarded by armed troops. This was just as well because for a long time there were no purification chemicals available in this theatre of war.

Despite the best efforts of both the Royal Navy and the army to improve the water supply, there were always problems. In May, Vice-Admiral De Robeck, the Navy commander for the Dardanelles, noted the plight of troops north of Gaba Tepe whose 'chief anxiety is water' and he requested as many 300-ton iron tanks as possible which were to be dug in under the cliffs. He noted that the water arrangements up to then were 'not very satisfactory'.[5] However, as often as not these tanks were holed as soon as they were landed. A similar fate overtook some large water condensers at Anzac Cove which were soon found by Turkish shells. The amphibious nature of the Gallipoli campaign caught the Army unawares, as traditionally armies relied on rivers and established wells. Simply, the MEF had no provision for storing water.

The scarcity of water was directly related to the quality of care which could be provided by the medical units. If chemicals could not be diluted, 'soft' rations made up or instruments sterilised, then fewer troops could be treated on Gallipoli. Therefore sick (as opposed to slightly wounded) troops especially were transferred from Anzac to Lemnos or Egypt, where water was relatively more abundant.

RATIONS

For the Gallipoli campaign as a whole it may be said that rations were usually of sufficient quantity and quality. However, some of the allies fared better than the AIF. There were the French, who had better food and cooking methods. Many of the British troops had access to a greater supply and variety of rations. For the Australians the same unvaried issue being consumed over several months made the onset of health problems almost inevitable. At the commencement of the campaign, the ration was adequate for fit troops, for whom the food was a change from their shipboard rations. The weather was mild and sanitary problems had not yet arisen.

Most Diggers were content with their food at this time, as Major Richards of the 1st ACCS noted: 'We get fresh meat now occasionally. Beside the ordinary "bullybeef" we get — corned mutton, fresh beef (tinned), onions, potatoes, compressed vegetables etc. — all in abundance.'[6] However after May, when a military stalemate set in, the weather became hotter and the transport of supplies became more precarious, soldiers soon became tired of the monotonous salt bully beef and hard biscuit. In July and August particularly, 'cases of gastritis, enteritis and entero-colitis were the chief source of medical anxiety…Herein were the hospitals greatly handicapped through lack of fresh foodstuffs, for in nearly all cases tinned food and condensed milk (in a good many cases of questionable quantity) were what was supplied.'[7]

Most men cooked for themselves as the nature of the terrain and the type of fighting precluded organised mess arrangements. This factor was to contribute to the spread of gastrointestinal infection, due to both the lack of water for washing utensils and to the fly menace. The regimental and unit cooks usually only provided tea. It was a moot point as to whether the 'tea' was the genuine thing, if Private T.W. Liddell is to be believed. 'The tea is invariably a liquid and to serve its purpose as a beverage. Sometimes it isn't saturated with sugar, or spoilt with excess of milk; often too it makes one think of flood waters; never however do the flies refuse to bathe in it if left uncovered for a few seconds.'[8]

The theory was that water rations could be better supervised by cooks. They were often the only men with (official) access to what firewood was available. Supervision of hygiene was difficult, as was proper storage of foodstuffs, which easily became contaminated by flies and dust or went bad in the heat. The latter was a common problem with fresh meat, which was often good Australian frozen beef, but by the time it had been carried up the slopes, it was usually flyblown when it reached the trenches.

The following is a report from Surgeon-General Birrell, written to Hamilton after Gallipoli, presumably for the latter's use during his questioning by the Dardanelles Commission. Birrell's report is not only a generalisation, it is an indictment of the poor medical reporting system, by which field conditions were relayed back to the medical military authorities for action. To illustrate this point, extracts from Birrell's report have been contrasted with diary excerpts of actual experiences in the field. He wrote to Hamilton that:

'...fresh meat was issued three or four times a week.'
['The 5th A.F.A. had been at Anzac for almost a month before it saw fresh meat...'[9]]
'Potatoes and onions formed part of the ration and Lime Juice was also a daily issue.'
['Lime juice issued made us all very sick; kept in zinc tins for some time & [was] a mild form of poisoning.'[10]]
'Units were allowed to draw equivalents as rice or oatmeal of part of the meat ration.'
['We would also like a change of food, rice for instance is unknown.'[11]]
'...fresh bread was supplied on most days.'
['We were issued with bread for the first time.'[12]]
'The troops at no time were on short rations.'
['We were allowed less than a pint of water per man a day.'[13]].[14]

In fact the *standard* army issue was eight times that amount, i.e. one gallon (or 4.5 litres) per man per day. However, those responsible for this situation ate well, and they rarely went ashore to see things for themselves.

There is an oft-quoted anecdote noted by the Australian war historian C.E.W. Bean concerning the *Aragon* on which the GHQ had its mess:

> ...the rebuffs frequently received by officers or men from Anzac and Helles, in visiting on business the somewhat glittering company on the L. of C. H.Q. ship *Aragon*, created much bitterness both in the British and overseas fighting forces. For example, Col. P.C. Fenwick, a medical staff officer of the N.Z. & A. Div., who visited the ship in the endeavour to obtain for his men a supply of disinfectants and other materials, has recorded that the medical authority whom he found on board first informed him that he did not, officially, know him, and secondly, that it was not his (the authority's) province to supply them. Fenwick wrote in his diary that, while waiting on the ship, he 'heard one officer breathe a sigh of thankfulness. "That's good news", he said. I asked what. "Twenty cases of soda-water have come safely for the top-dogs."

Such incidents, of daily occurrence, contributed sensibly to the disillusionment of the troops.[15]

A comparison with how other troops fared at Gallipoli is helpful in assessing the situation in which the AAMC worked. The Turks appeared to exist on relatively stoic fare, but were inured to it. There is a description of some Turks taken prisoner in June. Private G. Gower, a stretcher bearer with the 15th

Battalion wrote that they 'were in an awful state. Old clothes, no water in their bottles, and they were only issued with 1 biscuit and 1 small onion to last them 24 hours.'[16]

On the other hand the French allies who were in a better site and possessed a well organised commissariat, were considerably better off overall than either the Diggers or the British. A French doctor wrote home to his wife that he lacked 'nothing. Corned beef abounds, also bread. There are potatoes, cold meat — mutton and beef — chocolate, rum...'[17] Birrell also wrote that 'the French got a daily ration of red wine, and I think that after most of the officers of our mess gave up their ration of lime juice and drank red wine, obtained from the French Headquarters Mess, their health improved'.[18] Another Englishman at Gallipoli wrote 'On the whole, the French retained health and vigour best, their ration being less monotonous, and themselves more fastidious in cookery.'[19]

The fact that the French were better provided for throughout the campaign calls into question many of the 'excuses' put up at the time as to why the AIF generally could not be similarly supplied, particularly with water, vegetables and fresh bread.

Alcohol occasionally made its way into the lines — usually rum. Sometimes there were implications for individual members of the AAMC, in this instance a particular stretcher bearer by the name of Brean: '...when the cry was raised for stretcher bearers one day Brean simply removed his pipe and casually enquired "Where?" Some rum had got about secretively. Brean was called upon to carry a chap who had collapsed up to the doctor and when he got him there the doc found out that all that was wrong with him was an overdose of rum. Brean was a much disgusted man.'[20]

Stories of poor provisioning, the non-appearance of foodstuffs from Australia, and the lack of canteen facilities — in conjunction with the increase in sickness amongst Australian troops — gave rise to much criticism at home. Bread occasionally received by Australian troops, but it was often mouldy and made with dirty flour; and it was the subject of a number of medical reports. But apart from providing variety to the diet, fresh bread, as noted by a medical officer would 'be a Godsend for men with broken teeth & dentures of whom there are many'.[21]

Eventually pressure began to be exerted through official channels. Late in August Hamilton received a telegram from the Secretary of State, in which Hamilton was asked to report about rations generally, their variety and whether canteen stores sent in July and August had been received. He was also asked to explain 'the cause of debility of such an excessive number of men among the Australians'.[22] By this time too, other organisations, notably the YMCA, the Australian Comforts' Fund and to a lesser extent, the (Australian) Red Cross, started to establish themselves and they provided material support to the casualties and patients of the AAMC. The Australian Comforts Fund, founded in August 1914, was responsible for looking after the needs of 'all men under Military O.C.', whereas the Red Cross cared 'for all men under Medical O.C.'[23]

For some the standard ration could be supplemented by less orthodox means, as Private V. Laidlaw related: '…we were very lucky today, in getting fresh fish, these fish are got by bombs, the concussion temporarily stuns them and you just wade into the sea and pick them up'.[24] It was becoming obvious to medical officers that a considerable amount of sickness was due to both the monotony and lack of vitamins in the diet. Strenuous attempts were made to have a canteen sent to Anzac. 'Canteen arrangements are in train to bring canteen ship here but nothing definite yet. Urged necessity for prompt action of army.'[25] There was ample precedent for such an establishment as Sir Ian Hamilton noted in his diary. He had endeavoured to secure a canteen as early as May, when he 'cabled the Q.M.G. begging him either to let me run a canteen on the lines of the South Africa Field Force, myself; or to run it from home himself.'[26]

In August the first ships carrying large supplies of canteen stores began to arrive, but it was never enough. Hamilton noted that it was 'a mere flea bite of £10 000 worth'.[27] Major-General W.R. Birdwood had written to Hamilton telling him that the AAMC's doctors ascribed much sickness to the monotony of the diet. Bean and every other Australian at Anzac made the same observation. Even when the opportunity was taken up by the men the returns were often meagre. An obviously peevish Private F.H. Smith of the 2nd Australian Field Ambulance recorded that he 'went down to canteen on beach to draw our share. Got very little. Scored [a] bottle of pickles and one of sauce.'[28]

It's not generally recognised that Australian medical units on Lemnos had to pay exorbitant prices to supplement the ration issue. The commanding officer of the 5th Australian Field Ambulance wrote that he had '110 patients in hospital — Have reported to the A.D.M.S. that eggs have not been procurable since Oct. 7th…It seems strange that although eggs are not procurable as a medical comfort, the men of my unit were able to purchase them at [a very expensive] 2/- per doz.' Diggers going across to Lemnos were 'loaded with commissions and made the Greek traders rich by buying tinned figs, pineapples, and milk at fabulous prices…'[29] Those coming from a bread basket such as

Australia were scandalised. 'The prices charged for things are enormous, it is a wonder the gov't does not do something to regulate the prices.'[30] Both the Australian and the British governments were slow to move, despite pleas from the medical authorities.

In September, Colonel Howse had disputed official British reports which stated that supplies of rations to Australian troops were adequate. He cited a number of supply returns which indicated severe inadequacies in the supply of fresh bread, vegetables and frozen meat. He also scotched a further criticism which stemmed from a British supply depot concerning the assumption that the abnormal amount of jam and molasses consumed by Australians must have contributed to the increase of diarrhoea. 'As no molasses has been issued to the 1st Aust. Div. it cannot have been a factor and I do not believe that well made jam could account for such a type of Dysenteric Diarrhoea that exists at Anzac.'[31]

The Deputy Adjutant-General for the MEF, Major-General Woodward, was later quizzed on this point by the Dardanelles Commission. One of its members told him that Birrell had stated casualties' rations were supplemented by lighter foods such as arrowroot, rice, tapioca, condensed milk; and that rations could be changed to rice or oatmeal from bully beef and biscuit. Woodward's reply was that as far as he was concerned vast supplies had been sent to Anzac and more medical comforts than to any other part of the occupying force. In other words the Australians had the best of everything.[32]

When questioned before the same Commission, Godley (who commanded the New Zealand and Australian Division) stated that it was entirely possible that his men were unaware of the opportunity for substituting other foods for bully beef and biscuit, due to his Division's QMG staff not publishing the fact in routine orders to commanding officers and company officers. Godley also agreed that this amounted to a neglect of duty on the part of his own Quartermaster-General's staff.[33]

Whilst on an inspection tour of the area the Director General of Medical Services of the AAMC, Colonel R.H.J. Fetherston, cabled home in November: 'Gladly welcome any supplies from Australia AAA Include every form of food used in Hospitals and amounts required very large as 9000 beds in Egypt and about 5000 Dardanelles under Australia commands...greatest want of our troops...is...invalid foods such as oatmeal, Arrowroot and milk and meat extracts also all forms of dry canteen stores AAA'.[34]

And yet in October the commander of the 2nd Australian Division wrote to the Australian Governor-General comparing the Australian position with that of their British neighbours, who 'had a canteen, we had none. Meat and fresh bread were much oftener issued [at Cape Helles]. Firewood was supplied and water was plentiful. In all these our men were worse off.'[35]

The YMCA, working from Egypt, set up a store on Imbros and ran a daily shuttle service to Anzac with large consignments of cakes, buns, different kinds of fresh fruit and vegetables. Their difficulty was trying to meet demand. This organisation also established a bakery on Imbros. After they had been there for two weeks they crossed over to Gallipoli, and a few days later (in September) set up a YMCA 'building' in Reserve Gully. Of the other two organisations (neither of which had any 'official' function), both the Australian Red Cross and the Australian Comforts' Fund had insufficient manpower to ensure adequate distribution of goods once they arrived at Alexandria from Australia.

Consequently very little reached sick and wounded Australians actually on the Gallipoli peninsula. The lack of (Australian) Red Cross provisions was also notable in Egypt. Sister May Tilton wrote that she was 'allowed to make up seven-pound parcels for Gallipoli, and this kept me busy for many days. All my money was spent supplying their needs. There were no Red Cross supplies at No.I [A.G.H.] except home-made jams sent from Australia.'[36]

C.E.W. Bean was more critical and wrote that '...although very large sums had been raised by the Red Cross in Australia and were at this time being spent in Egypt, very little reached the sick at the front...Indeed it is doubtful if the majority, either of the men or of the medical officers who clung to duty at Anzac, realised at this time that such a fund existed.'[37]

DENTAL PROBLEMS

Dental problems were a major source of difficulty for the AAMC and the AIF and yet are rarely mentioned in the Gallipoli literature as being a source of serious concern. Men without teeth could not live on the rations provided, and they were sometimes ill with diseases hastened by inadequate dental hygiene. Such men necessarily commanded valuable medical time and facilities. Militarily they were unfit, and wastage from this cause was later to be both a cause and effect of the rate of reinforcements.

This particular problem was, however, of Australia's own making. Initially, lack of interest, rigid establishment codes, and later a want of equipment, all caused this glaring shortcoming in the medical services. Before the Gallipoli campaign began Australian dentists tried to make the Army aware of the problem, but to no avail. There was simply no provision in the Army for dental treatment and dentists who tried to enlist as such were refused because they were not provided for in the (British) War establishment — to which the Australian military forces subscribed.

While an AAMC Dental Reserve was formed in January 1915, the first appointments under the new establishment were not made until March, but they did not become active at Anzac until late in 1915. Before the AIF left Australian shores, General Bridges had asked the Defence Department to reconsider its refusal to send a dental team with the troops. After all, New Zealand had included dental officers in its contingent (although they were not given any instruments). 'I believe', Bridges wrote in one of his despatches, 'that the service of a dentist in the field would make for efficiency and economy as an alternative to the transfer of men to the base for treatment'.[38] This observation was also the nub of the medical services problem. As will be explained below they were often directly blamed for contributing to the drain of available manpower at Anzac. Army commanders were exasperated at losing their fighting men because they were sent away on account of teeth problems.

In June Surgeon-General Babtie, the Principal Director of Medical Services, wrote to his chief in London about the problem. He noted correctly that the Diggers had very bad teeth (as did most of the Australian population at that time) and that many British also required dental treatment, as they had 'plates which get broken, wilfully or accidentally. If we can contrive to mend these...either on the peninsula or at Imbros, we will stop a lot of invaliding and sending men to Egypt.' Babtie's report was no doubt spurred by an entry he made in his official diary a week earlier: 'Dental — No arrangements at present. Men sent with broken plates to Alexandria. This is to stop!'[39] He recommended that supplying dentists was the only way to stop serious wastage. Howse had already approached him to supply 20 dentists for the Australians, but Babtie was content to start with 20 for the entire MEF.[40]

Later in that month Colonel Howse tried again to resolve what was by now becoming an alarming problem, as many RMOs were reporting that men with serious dental problems were beginning to suffer from persistent dyspepsia and diarrhoea.

They recovered whilst they were on an 'invalid diet', but as Howse pointed out, on return to ordinary rations these soldiers again ended up on the sick list and were subsequently evacuated from Anzac. His idea was that properly equipped dentists and dental assistants should be appointed and concentrate initially on urgent work.[41]

At first, lack of suitable dental equipment hampered what little could be done at Anzac. One doctor serving with the No 1 Australian Stationary Hospital 'brought with [him] from Melbourne a dentist…[who] in three months…mended hundreds of broken plates, besides attending to all sorts of cases; in fact, he was invaluable…We ran out of dental requirements, and, up to the time I left, we never could get any, although we indented for them time and again.'[42]

A.G. Butler was another frustrated doctor in this respect and he wrote home at the time 'I wish to goodness we had some dentists, if there was a dentist to each Bn. as well as a M.O. it would make an immense difference in the comfort of a lot of men.'[43] In August dental work began in earnest at Lemnos with the landing of No 3 Australian General Hospital. Butler calculated that between September and December this unit alone treated 1 387 soldiers for pressing dental problems. For the same period the number for the entire AIF was 9 229. As late as September senior officers were still being rebuffed in their endeavours to obtain dentists. Despite this the CO of the 3rd Australian Field Ambulance received the following wire from the DMS: 'Your suggestion re appointment of Dental Officer not approved.'[44] Although by then at least two dentists were available on Lemnos, they were 'absolutely unable to cope with the work required'.

The dental situation as an administrative problem was largely self-inflicted. In Cairo the CO of No 2 Australian General Hospital grumbled that there were 'Two qualified dentists with dental mechanic, now at work and always busy…and yet Fetherston [the acting Director of Medical Services in Australia] declined them ("No place on the establishment — hence no place in the War") at the start when I offered him fifty — and there have been both difficulty and delay since in getting O/Cs to transfer any who enlisted as Privates.'[45]

Despite relatively large numbers of medical officers and staff working in Egypt the dental situation there was still poor. The local civilian dentists had been overwhelmed with Army patients. Not a few men obtained emergency treatment from mates who had been dentists in Civvy Street, others simply suffered in silence or were sent from Alexandria to Egypt or Malta and not infrequently returned to Anzac having had no treatment whatever. 'There is considerable difficulty experienced now amongst our men of getting any dental attention ashore and especially where a man is wearing plates and breaks them.'[46]

Eventually — on 6 July — the Australian Government at last authorised 'the appointment of fourteen dental officers, twelve mechanics and thirteen Privates for service in the A.I.F. overseas'.[47] Such reinforcements took time to materialise where they were needed most and appointments were made up from dentists in Australia and those serving abroad in various convalescent and medical units. But the supply of dental equipment was to continue to be a problem.

However the AAMC — ever resourceful — did its best to adapt. Some ambulances and other medical units had a dentist and/or a dental mechanic within their ranks, working as medics. These were soon hard at work dealing with troops of their own Brigades. 'Urgent medical treatment could be arranged for at the C.C.S. where a general duty sergeant, who was in civil life a dentist, had obtained a partial equipment and did excellent work.'[48] One of these was a Sydney dentist, G. Douglas, who had enlisted as a Private in the 1st Australian Field Ambulance and who had also taken with him his own equipment (later augmented from Red Cross stores).[49] As he was not officially on Establishment, there was no Table of Equipment for him to use. (This was an army list of requisite equipment to be used, carried, and stocked by military personnel.)

Therefore during this period the Army store depots carried no dental equipment at all. The New Zealand Field Ambulance had a dentist attached to it supplied with gear from Egypt. He worked out of a small dug-out beside a dressing station. Along with two mechanics he kept the teeth of the whole division in repair, as 'the biscuit was so hard that artificial, or sometimes even natural, teeth were liable to injury.'[50]

THE PROBLEM OF SUPPLY AND STORES

The medical services relied totally on adequate supplies of medical and surgical equipment, drugs and dressings. If these were not forthcoming, or this supply was interrupted, the AAMC was effectively neutralised — improvisation had its limits. This is why the problem of stores and supply is important in understanding the activities of the AAMC especially at Anzac. Diagram 6.1 on page 138? indicates the differences between the supply system as it operated in France and Gallipoli.

At first everything — medical stores, even food — was scarce. Recalling the first few days after the landing, Major Corbin wrote: 'We had tea constantly and had biscuits, but practically nothing else for the first few days.'[51] On ship as on shore, according to Private A.D. Gordon, 'Over two days now on board this packet [A.10 Troopship], and still no provisions made for the A.M.C. men to get any tucker.'[52]

But once the initial landing was over, there was a very measured increase in the number of boats available for bringing in stores. Thus the situation did improve gradually as this description (by Colonel J.J. Beeston) of Anzac Cove in May testifies. 'The beach is a mass of supplies of all kinds...The rations are all of the best...and the men are not stinted as to quantity. The biscuits though are very hard on the teeth.'[53] He also had this colourful description of the iron ration: 'One particular kind of biscuit known as "forty-niners", had forty-nine holes in it, was believed to take forty-nine years to bake, and needed forty-nine chews to the bite.'[54] The availability of such rations at Anzac itself however, was a function of the distribution system, i.e. how far away one was from the makeshift wharves on the beaches.

The provision of Army supplies was relatively precarious throughout 1915. Hamilton's staff at first did not accord it a very high priority. But Ordnance (or Supply) was one of those branches of the Army on which the AAMC relied absolutely to carry out its functions. Despite the multifarious responsibilities of the Deputy Director of Medical Services, the total staff of that officer consisted of one staff sergeant.[55] Private G. Walsh of the Army Service Corps wrote what was probably an accurate reflection of the AAMC's attitude to his own Corps: 'I cannot say who they have on their blacklist. Probably it is the Turks and the Ordnance Department.'[56]

Quantity was not the only problem. Quality, particularly of Australian-made medical supplies, was often less than satisfactory, with Army standards being openly ignored. Profiteering by contractors in Australia was also common. To illustrate this point, there was an enquiry held under the War Precautions Act 1914–1916, as to the purchase of medical and surgical stores and pharmaceutical goods for the Australian defence forces. In one case the difference in the individual price of hypodermic syringes between two military suppliers was 7.6d.! As this particular report stated, military standing orders for purchasing medical equipment 'appear to have been almost if not entirely disregarded...'[57] So much for universal and selfless patriotism on the home front!

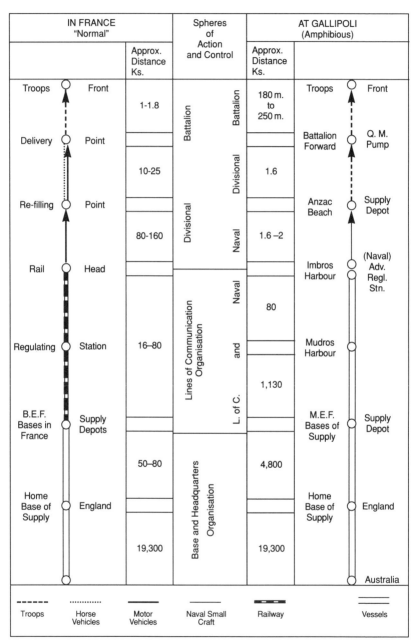

DIAGRAM 6.1   Differences in Supply System at Gallipoli and in France.
Source: Adapted from A.G. Butler, Vol. I, p. 208

Vast quantities of stores were involved at a time when shipping was in short supply and the sealanes were becoming increasingly dangerous. During questioning by the Dardanelles Commission, Sir Alfred Keogh provided a number of cogent statistics. These relate directly to the Gallipoli campaign and are relevant because the AAMC (by arrangement) necessarily drew heavily on British medical stores throughout 1915.[58]

At the commencement of the fighting in 1915 Britain sent out to the Dardanelles two base depots and two advanced depots of medical stores with 4 000 cases of medical stores weighing over 180 tonnes. In addition to these depots there were Army medical stores in Egypt and Malta. Nearly 800 indents were received from the medical store depots for medical stores and equipment required to replenish regimental and medical units. These comprised 42 000 cases and bales (almost 5 900 tonnes) shipped in 140 consignments.

The problems in the area of supply of medical and other stocks were compounded by the fact that the responsibility for supply was shared between four separate organisations. The AAMC supplied and distributed drugs, dressings and instruments within its own Corps; the Army Service Corps looked after food and 'medical comforts'; while the Army Ordnance department supplied stretchers, tents, beds, blankets and hospital equipment. There were other considerations — the ubiquitous red tape; at other times the strict supervision of an ADMS with an eye to economy was in evidence, viz. 'There seems no doubt as to my complaints re deficient medical comforts, all the same the A.D.M.S. has struck off my list arrowroot and cornflour.'[59]

Again both the AAMC and British medical authorities made matters worse for themselves. At the beginning of 1915 Williams (the Director of Medical Services for Australia), who was in Egypt, received from the British DMS, MEF a list of Red Cross medical and surgical stores considered sufficient for 30 000 men which he subsequently forwarded to Australia ('to be supplied if possible'). The magnitude and vagueness of the demand made action in Australia impossible, and the fact that the articles listed under 'Red Cross' would normally be supplied by the military increased the confusion as to the position of the Red Cross and other voluntary organisations.

Finally there was the (British) Red Cross, which was often used by the AAMC as a source both of equipment and medical comforts (e.g. pyjamas, toothbrushes etc.). Australian Red Cross stores were not properly distributed and thence rarely seen on Gallipoli. A problem in any one of these four organisations had direct repercussions for Australian field units on Gallipoli which, because of the geography of the place, and the reliance on men and mules for conveying stores, could only stock so much materiel at a time.

For this reason too a competent quartermaster was central to the efficient functioning of any medical unit: 'The duties of the quartermaster are particularly onerous during active operations owing to rations and supplies being required urgently in all directions. Requisitions come in from scattered regimental officers for blankets, splints, dressings and medical comforts and on the speedy fulfilment of their demands depends the expeditious and comfortable removal of casualties from forward areas.'[60]

The AIF at Gallipoli was dependent on British supply units which worked on a system by which each Corps had its own depot on the peninsula. The problem therefore was not always one of insufficient sources of supply, but rather the ubiquitous problem of finding enough small boats to transfer stores from ships to the peninsula. There were several British medical supply depots on both Lemnos and Gallipoli.

One of the results of the ill-defined sharing of responsibilities between the Imperial and Australian governments was the stock of medical equipment, medicine and drugs. Prior to leaving for Gallipoli, the AAMC drew its requirements from the 1st ACCS as Australia did not supply its own medical stores depots, and (as noted above) relied almost entirely on British depots for its medical needs throughout the Gallipoli campaign. Well before the April landing Surgeon-General Williams had been presented with £10 000 by the Australian Red Cross to be outlaid at his discretion. The first stores bought from this fund arrived in Egypt in mid-March 1915. Most of them went to the dispensary of No 1 Australian General Hospital in Cairo which had become, de facto, the main medical store for AAMC units in Egypt. Despite its best efforts the (Australian) Red Cross could only supplement to a small extent the huge demands made by the Diggers at Anzac and Egypt.

As the British Red Cross took the responsibility for all Red Cross work on the Lines of Communication, the Australian branch's activities were centred in Egypt. There were (British Red Cross) stores at Alexandria and, in May, at Mudros which were eventually drawn upon by the AAMC. The Australian Red Cross established a depot of its own on the island in October. An attempt had been made to set up a Red Cross depot on Gallipoli 'but it was blown away on the first day we put it there'.[61] As it was not found practicable to maintain permanent Red Cross depots on the peninsula, a regular system of delivery from

Mudros was organised. The stores were sent in charge of a responsible Red Cross representative who either stayed on the peninsula while the stores were being distributed, or handed them over to the medical officer in charge.[62] These stores consisted of items as varied as blankets, lemons, chocolate, syringes and formaldehyde.

Other supplies were of a less orthodox nature and the following question put to a medical officer at the Dardanelles Commission would be amusing if the context had not been so serious. The transcript read:

> **Q.** With regard to flies, could not mosquito netting or something of that description have been ordered from England to have prevented much of that nuisance? — **A.** Late in July there was some netting arrived, but it was not mosquito netting, it was ordinary inch mesh fish net...The theory was that a fly would think it was a spider's web and would not go through, but the theory would not work out. — **Q.** What brilliant genius sent that out? — **A.** I do not know who was responsible for that but it was very useful for fishing.[63]

One of the most significant contributions to the Gallipoli effort by the Red Cross was the provision of a picket boat and two Red Cross motor launches and crews, which were used not only for distributing Red Cross stores, but for transporting senior medical staff around Mudros Harbour to oversee transport and hospital carriers — a singular inadequacy up to this time.[64]

In view of the medical transport system the British Red Cross was also 'able to provide for the most pressing needs of the Hospital Ships proceeding with sick and wounded to Alexandria and Malta'.[65] This was one of the sore points between the Australian medical services and the Australian Red Cross, namely the lack of medical comforts such as pyjamas supplied by that organisation on those ships bringing thousands of wounded from Gallipoli to Australia.

One of the many side effects of the haste with which the whole campaign was undertaken was the loading of the MEF's stores, of which medical supplies and equipment were only a part. Unsuccessful efforts were made to prevent the despatch of stores before they could be properly sorted out at the dockside. As one commentator wrote tongue-in-cheek: 'It only remains to be said that, three months after the opening of the campaign, the medical stores arriving in Mudros from England were still being found at the bottom of the holds of the store-ships. However they were to reach the Peninsula in time for the evacuation.'[66]

In view of the difficulty of discharging stores quickly at

Mudros, the British Transport Department strongly urged that transports be sent direct from England to Alexandria where the stores should be landed, sorted, and forwarded in smaller vessels to Mudros as and when required. The Transport Department's suggestion, however, was not adopted, 'mainly through reluctance to expose the cargoes to a double submarine risk'.[67] This proposed solution may not have worked in any case. The essence of the supply problem was recognised, at least by some, in the lack of adequate small seagoing craft. It was observed that the Principal Naval Transport Officer for example, had 'at his disposal barely enough craft for the daily requirements of the Peninsula and islands'.[68]

There were other, perhaps less obvious dangers. The following confidential report sent to the British Prime Minister from Gallipoli speaks for itself: 'should mention that the…routes they [transports] are to follow are laid down by the French naval Commander-in-Chief, and, in passing, I would suggest that collisions might be less frequent if different routes could be laid down for outward and homeward-bound vessels.'[69]

Other senior officers were equally critical of the handling of stores, especially at Lemnos. On his arrival at Mudros the Chief Engineer of the ANZAC Corps found that some vessels had been in the harbour for up to four weeks without any attempt being made to unload them. Due to the way in which they had been loaded it was almost impossible to get at the goods required in their holds without unloading what was on top. As there was no space on deck and no harbour facilities at that time the difficulties can be appreciated. The Chief Engineer, ANZAC Corps (General de Lotbiniere) later recommended that in future engagements, civilian contractors should be employed instead of the Royal Navy. For instance, on one transport 'there were eighty tons of fresh beef and the captain, wanting the space, and not being able to get rid of it at Anzac, threw it overboard'.[70]

Australian hospitals setting up on Lemnos found that even basic hospital equipment was often unavailable for several weeks. Sister L.E. Young of the No 3 Australian General Hospital recounted her experience in August 1915 of the arrival at night of troops from Anzac. The patients were placed on the ground 'with a tarpaulin and blanket under them, another over them and not a stitch of clothing on them after cutting off their uniform'. She went on to describe washing the men in bed pans prior to theatre, because these were the only containers holding water that could be procured or borrowed at that time.[71]

On the peninsula itself, the drain on medical stores as a result of the unexpectedly heavy casualties resulting from the August

Offensive was compounded by the increasing incidence of sickness at Anzac. The AAMC reported to the supply authorities that great difficulties still existed in obtaining an adequate supply of medical comforts and drugs. Of major concern was the shortage of farinaceous foods to combat diarrhoea. Stocks were now running dangerously low. Colonel Sutton, Howse's second-in-command reported 'Supplies Depot has given me a return of Arrowroot, Cornflour and Bovril on hand for this Division. The stock on hand is sufficient for one Fld. Amb. for one day...Diarrhoea is so prevalent that these are absolutely essential if we are to maintain the strength of fighting units.'[72]

The recently arrived DMS, MEF (Surgeon-General Bedford, who had replaced Birrell in September) soon realised the extent of the problem and took some practical steps to improve matters. He wrote to Sir Alfred Keogh (the British Director of Medical Services) that medical stores depots were insufficient to cope with demand — particularly for Epsom salts and castor oil for treating diarrhoea. He had therefore cabled to England for more. Significantly he noted that this should have been done earlier, as 'the proportion of depots to Divisions was far below that laid down by Army Regulations'.[73] Later in that month Bedford again wrote to Keogh, this time to reassure him that the medical stores situation was in hand. He emphasised the unprecedented demand on stocks as no one could have foreseen the vast demand, and that a 30-day reserve supply of drugs and material was being organised for all three zones on Gallipoli 'to ensure against any interruption of supply, either from the weather or other causes'.[74]

An idea of how such quantities were so rapidly used may be gauged by this diary entry by Private A. Taylor: '...most of the time I was bad with dysentery but the Doctor fixed me up he gave me half a pint of Castor Oil in one dose...'[75]

Australia and the AAMC must share some of the blame in the shortfalls in medical and related stores during the campaign. Supply was further confused by uncertainty regarding the responsibility of Australia for providing them to Diggers at Anzac. This situation was complicated by the ambiguous and often undirected role of voluntary supply organisations, particularly the (Australian) Red Cross.

'The contrast between the local Hospital started by the British Red Cross...and these auxiliary hospitals on No. 1 [Australian] General Hospital, A.I.F. in the way of environment, food and comforts could scarcely be exaggerated. They are as commendable and satisfactory as ours are unsatisfactory and open to condemnation.'[76] However, any analysis of the supply problem must be tempered by an appreciation of both the magnitude and unexpected nature of the problem at Gallipoli. This also applies to the supply of the most precious of munitions — men.

THE HUMAN COST

Considering the heavy fighting in August, together with the very hot weather, shortage of varied rations and stress, an alarming increase in the already high incidence of sickness and disease was inevitable. In a confidential memorandum to the DA & QMG, General Carruthers, Howse wrote of an inspection he carried out of the 5th Battalion, and consequently recommended that 'the men require a good long rest and unless they get it soon many of them will suffer permanent ill effects and be unfit for further active service for at least one year...'[77]

At this time, troops were being sent across to Lemnos for short rest spells. They were a sorely needed respite and Diggers could hardly believe their luck, as related by Lieutenant T.W. Garling: '...We left the ship [at Mudros Harbour] at four pm and after a march of twenty-one/two miles found our rest camp on a hillside overlooking the Harbour. An advance party had been sent on and they had tents erected and a jolly good feed waiting for us. We were dog tired and turned in immediately after tea...Duties are very light the main object of the camp being to give the men a thorough rest.'[78]

By 10 September the 2nd Australian Division arrived as a relief force and small numbers of troops were taken to Lemnos for longer periods of one or two weeks for rest. Many were suffering from exhaustion, but were still keen to fight on. In an interesting comparison the *New Zealand Army Medical History* states that in the ANZAC Division alone the average losses through sickness amounted to 100 per 1000 per week, while the rate for troops in France at the **same time** (emphasis added) was five per 1000.[79]

There was a constant desperate demand for reinforcements by infantry commanders on the peninsula. Once the casualty rate began to climb, the repercussions for field commanders were brought home when expected replacements from men sent away to rest or recover failed to be realised. This important aspect of the work of the AAMC, namely to restore fighting troops to the front as soon as they were well again also highlights what at first seems a failure of the Australian medical services in 1915.

Such 'processing' of wounded was a vital and a poorly understood role (by the General Staff) of the medical services.

During April and May Howse complained that 50 per cent of the casualties leaving Anzac (suffering from slight wounds or illness) would, under normal circumstances 'have been returned to duty within three or four weeks' and at that time the weekly evacuation from Anzac was over 2 000 men. Despite this, few were actually returning to Gallipoli.

Howse considered it 'essential that urgent steps be immediately taken to return Officers and other ranks who are fit for duty…in fact it has become a byword at Anzac that, once evacuated, it is improbable that they will return for many months.'[80]

Problems of transport, the inefficient administration of paperwork and lack of reliable shipping timetables together with the relative ease with which some determined individuals could evade their duties did not help matters. This problem was encountered at Anzac as well. Major S.J. Richards of the 1st ACCS wrote to his wife that 'a few skunks broke [their dental plates] deliberately when they found I was sending them to Alexandria'.[81] This problem would become worse and the implications of the lack of medical statistics would take on critical importance to a military machine badly mauled by a high casualty/sick rate.

An early illustration is provided by this signal from Lt. Colonel A.J. Bennett, the CO of the 4th Battalion, dated 5 May: 'I desire to bring to serious notice the disadvantages and inconvenience caused by lack of info concerning the whereabouts, condition, and probable period of absence of officers and men who leave the battalion on account of wounds, sickness while on duty. It is only from hearsay and from returned officers and men, that information is gleaned and that cannot, of course, be relied on or acted on officially…'[82] Even in the largest Australian medical unit — No 1 Australian General Hospital in Cairo — convalescents were allowed to roam the city's streets at will for several months until the hospital's administrative procedures were tightened. On the other hand, conscientious Diggers complained that they were hampered by red tape when trying to make their way back to their units on the peninsula. Others didn't complain or could not cope, and sought to get away from Gallipoli.

'PSYCHOLOGICAL' PROBLEMS

There were also less tangible problems which had to be dealt with by the medical services at Gallipoli, which, although not as obvious as wounds and disease, nonetheless were part of the overall medical environment. The AAMC was unprepared for this type of battle casualty, even though the numbers actually involved were relatively small and certainly not on the same scale as that seen on the Western Front from 1916.

Shellshock was first recognised in the Great War, and those cases who appeared on Anzac were not diagnosed as such for some time.[83] Shellshock (a misnomer, which is perhaps better identified as shell concussion) is both mental and physical in origin, and is caused by being close to a bursting shell of high calibre. One authority at the time also wrote that 'in men already worn out or having previously suffered from the disorder, the final cause of the breakdown may be so slight, and its origin so gradual, that its origin hardly deserves the name of "shock"'.[84]

Before this, soldiers suffering from brain dysfunction were discharged simply as 'mental' cases. A contemporary authority added an important rider in 1917: 'Shell shock has been given prominence on account of its prevalence and the various hysterical symptoms that have followed the high explosions. Exactly the same symptoms have occurred however, after shrapnel wounds, falls, and without previous injury at all.'[85]

The soldier was practically always blown over by the blast from a shell and often buried by the debris and deafened by the explosion. A temporary vacuum is formed around him, which is rapidly filled by a great rush of air causing a transitory increase of atmospheric pressure. Any sudden severe change in the atmospheric pressure can cause a disturbance in the cerebro-spinal fluid and therefore may produce an injury to the underlying cerebral tissue.[86] The symptoms included dizziness, tremors, tachycardia (i.e. fast pulse), insomnia, nightmares, disordered personality, and amnesia. Not until the beginning of 1916 was 'the idea of a direct and causative connection between the "shock" from the "windage" (later called "blast") of a shell-burst, or ... the effect of being buried by the earth or debris of a shell explosion...officially recognised...'[87]

However, direct physical trauma was not always involved and even in those early days this fact was recognised, as an Australian medical editorial stated: 'It is already very obvious that the war will bring us many cases of little understood nervous and mental affections, not only where a definite wound has been received, but in many cases where nothing of the sort appears.'[88]

An instance was recorded by Sister May Tilton who remembered nursing a 20-year-old 'who regained his reason but lost his voice. This was attributed to shock. He told me in the faintest whisper that he saw his two elder brothers killed in one day on the Peninsula. He went mad and wanted to rush the Turks' trenches; remembered being prevented; then knew no more. He could not understand why he could not talk.'[89] A less sympathetic medical officer, A.J. Campbell wrote that 'Without being malingerers, these men generally exaggerated their disability, and as carriers of psychic contagion were a source of danger in a ward, therefore we always endeavoured as far as possible to isolate them.'[90]

The conditions of Gallipoli precluded the relief of tension afforded to troops on the Western Front, in terms of rest leave, recreational facilities, and military brothels. It was inevitable then that for some soldiers something had to give. In its milder form this usually took the form of poor morale and then, increasingly, minor infringements of military discipline. It affected both combatant and medical units, as both experienced the same dangers and shared the same environment. Throughout July a number of members of the 3rd Australian Field Ambulance and (in August) several men of the 5th Australian Field Ambulance, were punished for insubordination and refusing duty.

Not long into the campaign, the strain at Anzac became so great that men began to inflict wounds upon themselves in the hope of being evacuated. Typical examples are recorded in personal and war diaries. 'During the night nine self-inflicted wounded men were transferred to me from the 6th Fld Amb.'[91] Even troops new to Anzac felt the strain. Sergeant (later Lt.) H. Woods of the 4th Australian Field Ambulance noted in his diary 'A newly arrived man (16th Btn.) purposely blew off his foot, and was detained in custody.'[92]

The situation became so bad that as early as 26 May 'special instructions were issued with regard to the prevalence of self-inflicted wounds. They were repeated again in July and each succeeding month.'[93] In June one hospital patient was 'to be sent back to Anzac when better to be tried for shooting himself through the hand'.[94] Again, these incidents are in stark contrast to the popularly held view of the superman 'bronzed Anzac'. The official historians rarely use this material to highlight the fragile state of some men under the conditions of battle stress. Some medical officers would have viewed this type of behaviour very censoriously, and there are moral overtones in some of their letters and diary entries.

Under the MEF's *Standing Orders*, unless life-threatening situations were involved, all cases of self-inflicted wounds were to be retained and treated in medical units on Anzac. 'As many as half a dozen men were in the ambulance at one time with these injuries. They generally took the form of a bullet in the left hand or left foot.'[95] Even senior medical officers were aware of developments and Sir James Porter wrote to his wife that he had heard 'disturbing tales of self-mutilation — blowing off fingers so they cannot shoot'.[96] All such cases still had to be held and nursed by front-line medical units, units whose personnel were often subject to the same strains. Medical resources were now directed into what was then a highly specialised, if pioneer, field of medicine — and one totally beyond the training the AAMC had traditionally offered its members, doctors and medics alike.

Other Diggers took less drastic measures to get an early ticket off Anzac. Some troops not infrequently resorted to eating explosive (cordite). This had been done in the South Africa War, and produced cardiac symptoms in the individual concerned. Other men simply haunted 'sick parades' and thereby added to the work load of medical units in the field. A.G. Butler saw this at firsthand: 'Though scrimshanking was always a despised rarity, men worn out with fatigues and debilitated by disease, disillusioned as to quick success, and seeing no prospect of respite from the hopeless monotony of discomfort and danger, were more willing to go sick'.[97]

There were occasions when medical personnel too were less than enthusiastic in the front line. Captain A.Y. Fullerton, the medical officer of the 2nd Battalion (1st Aust. Division) wrote that prior to one battle he lined up his medics and the regimental stretcher bearers behind their old trenches and warned them they would follow 'close on the heels of the last company of our Battalion (the 2nd)' with as many dressings and iodine as they could carry. As soon as the last rifles of his Company had got up over the sandbags this doctor led his lads on only to find when he got to the enemy trenches he was accompanied only by his batman, and two medics! Later he 'rounded up the whole lot of the A.M.C. unit and the R[egimental stretcher bearers].S.B.s. The next day I told them I expected they would all be shot for cowardice...'[98]

Fullerton was perhaps unique in that prior to this particular engagement, the RMOs of the 1st Brigade had decided that they would not accompany their units but would wait until it was dark before rejoining them.

Rheumatism, which became very prevalent in November in the cold and wet weather, was also to be used by a few as a ploy to escape Anzac. 'On a sunny morning a Medical Officer would get his rheumatic cases out into a dry creek bed and make them walk slowly up and down while he sat on the bank closely scrutinizing them and trying to distinguish the malingerers from the genuine cases.'[99]

At grassroots level Private V.R. Laidlaw of the 2nd Australian Field Ambulance observed that there were 'always a few malingerers, every morning one can nearly always tell them, they usually ask the officer to put them on light duty, they usually get M & D which means Medicine & Duty and they walk away with a scowl on their face. Most of these chaps are reinforcements who haven't been [long] at Gallipoli or have seen very little service, the fellows who landed on the famous Sunday [25 April] very seldom parade sick.'[100] This is a telling point for among the originals staying at Anzac, whatever the cost, had become a point of honour. The bonding of mateship and therefore the mutually supportive social structure was much stronger amongst the veterans than for example the untried units of the Second Division. All that newly arrived Diggers saw at Anzac was a stalemate. They had not taken part in the initial assault or any of the big 'pushes'. For them Gallipoli was siege warfare with its inevitable and soul-destroying drudgery.

BACKGROUND OF RECRUITS AND MOTIVES FOR JOINING THE AMC

Members of the Australian medical services who served at, or near Gallipoli, were from a variety of backgrounds; many were recent migrants from Great Britain; all were white. In March 1915 the Nominal Roll for the 2nd Light Horse Field Ambulance for example showed that of 126 men only 14 were married, most having joined in October/November of 1914. There were many town dwellers among them including students and clerks but very few stockmen or bushmen.[101] The motives of volunteers joining a medical, or 'specialist' unit of the Army were probably those of Australian Diggers generally in 1914. The desire to be in the same unit as one's mates, to use their civilian skills (e.g. first aid), humanitarian ideals, or a number of other, less likely reasons.

One man joined a field ambulance because his local doctor had joined that unit.[102] Another noted in his diary that he enlisted in the AIF 'but owing to my father's prejudice against my joining a fighting unit had to go into the A.M.C.'[103] For many 'It was just being faced with the ordinary never changing things of life...I wanted the thrill of something new...'[104] For others it was a happier alternative to unemployment.[105]

Not everyone found enlisting an easy matter. 'After a great deal of hesitation I decided to volunteer for Active Service...I had gone to Victoria Barracks twice previously, but had turned away

for reasons of my own, before finally submitting myself for the
Medical Examination. Today I passed the Medical Test and
became attached to the Australian Army Medical Corps.'[106]
Others were keener: 'It was not long before I made up my mind
to be "Up and at 'em", for I am British born...'[107] A Perth artist,
Ellis Silas, wrote in his diary that he tried 'once more to get into
[the] A.M.C. but unfortunately, not being a Bushman or a coal
heaver or dropping enough H's, my application [was] not
considered'.[108] Eventually after evading submission for the
compulsory chest measurements required in the recruiting
medical, he was enlisted.

Still others found, nearer the Dardanelles, that they had
made the wrong choice. The Officer commanding the No 1
Australian Stationary Hospital at Mudros, wrote of one of his
privates who had 'been twice punished for drunkenness and once
for breaking bounds and drunkenness since February 1st 1915. He
is useless for hospital work and himself desires transference into
a combat unit.'[109]

On the home front social pressure, including the attitudes of
women, were not unimportant considerations. At the height of
the Gallipoli campaign a nurse stationed at Lemnos wrote home:
'My opinion of any man who stays unless *absolutely prevented* from
going isn't much — that is to say unmarried men — the others
can do their duty otherwise — and can keep things going in their
own Countries.'[110] Later, conformity was often preached by
some churches. A Melbourne newspaper reported a sermon from
the pulpit of the Collins Street Independent Church: 'The man
who is not fighting is already slackening and decadent.'[111]

The pressures to enlist extended to students at the
universities and the medical schools and a number left their
studies to join the ranks. The authorities, alarmed at the potential
loss of future doctors, tried to counter the drain. For instance at
a meeting of 7 July 1915 the Council of the University of
Melbourne amended its Medical Faculty Regulations to reduce
the length of its course from five years to one of four years and
one term.[112] Because of concerns being expressed as to future
supply of medical practitioners in Australia, the medical schools
made representations to the military so that towards the end of
1915 the army 'commenced returning all former medical students
who were sick, wounded or convalescent from the hospitals in
Egypt so that they might finish their course'.[113] At Gallipoli the
University of Melbourne medical faculty lost four of its
graduates, three first-year (medical) students, two second-year
students, and one from the fifth year.[114]

RECRUITMENT

Archie Aspinall, a doctor with the 1st Australian Field Ambulance, described the final months of 1914 in his unit. 'The O.C. and Captain Poate spent busy days at Victoria Barracks selecting the men, and, having so many to choose from, secured a magnificent lot, drawn from all classes of life — from professions to the manual labourer — all possessing some knowledge of first aid work.'[115]

Petty professional jealousies and squabbles continued despite the war. Colonel J.W. Springthorpe — the Senior Physician of No 2 Australian General Hospital — wrote while en route to Egypt in 1914: 'Two Victorian captains and myself as Senior Physician, had been switched on to No. 2 A.G.H. because of the failure of Sydney Hospital physicians to enlist. (Said also that our two Senior Surgeons were similarly not representative of Sydney Surgical Hospital staffs, and that their selection had been the cause of the more experienced not enlisting).'[116] It was also a man's world. As far as can be ascertained the only female doctor near the Dardanelles theatre was Dr Agnes Bennett of Wellington, New Zealand, who (attached to the RAMC) worked at the commandeered Austro-Hungarian hospital in Choubra, Cairo.[117]

Soon after the Great War broke out and as the Gallipoli campaign got underway, severe strains were placed on resources in Australia where thousands of volunteer troops encamped around Australia were hurriedly put through their basic military training. Naturally their health was the responsibility of the AAMC. However, to a large extent civilian medical practitioners carried out the initial medical examination of volunteers on behalf of the Army and Navy. The immediate benefits to the small medical staff of the AAMC which this system necessitated were outweighed by the haphazard procedures and ambiguous guidelines followed by many civilian doctors (not all of whom were competent) in certifying men fit who patently were not.

The subsequent strain these unfit men placed on both the Army generally and the medical corps both during the Gallipoli campaign and en route there, was considerable. As early as August 1914 before the AIF convoy left from Western Australia 'no less than thirty-seven men were put ashore as "medically unfit for active service." The cases comprised five phthisis, three middle-ear disease, two mental, two epilepsy.'[118]

Medics, nurses and stretcher bearers received only the basics of first aid. To the modern eye the various training schedules seem very simple indeed. In 1914–15 the teaching of the syllabus for a medical unit's training took place over a mere two weeks. The first half of each day's training was devoted to various drills: stretcher, squad, company, and signalling. In the afternoons practical instruction was given in first aid based on the *Training Manual of the Royal Army Medical Corps* (1911). This manual was standard throughout the Empire, and was regarded as adequate for the training needs of the Australian medical services.

Additional lectures were given by various specialists in different fields, for example anatomy and physiology, military law, the care of the horse, clerical functions etc. Captain Chapman, who became adjutant to the 5th Australian Field Ambulance, noted that the 'Colonel gave first lecture on bandaging using triangular bandages'.[119] This suggests a dearth of qualified medical instructors, at least in this unit, if such a senior officer delivered basic first aid lectures. In some circumstances those men who were recruited directly into a medical unit might then receive further training in a civilian hospital.

At the regimental level the suggested training was, as with medical units, based on the 1911 RAMC training manual. There were practical sessions on packing and unloading equipment, signalling (semaphore), collecting wounded, and various ways of transporting them. Other recruits went through a different process, as the War Diary of the No 1 Australian Stationary Hospital related that selection for its personnel began on 10 September 1914. The first men to be taken on were those applicants for positions in the 4th Field Ambulance who were not required for that unit. Additional men were then called for by advertisements in the daily papers. 'Preference was given those fitted for special work, and who had received instruction in ambulance work. Instruction was given in all branches of male nursing and some of the men were taught the methods of preparing patients for operations.'[120]

Many contemporary accounts illustrate the real lack of preparation for wartime duties amongst the various medical units. Typical of this situation was the 4th Australian Field Ambulance which was mobilised at Broadmeadows, near Melbourne late in 1914. 'The transport [section] laboured under the added difficulty of the necessity of breaking in all their horses which were drawn unbroken from Remount Depots, and difficulty was experienced in obtaining quickly the equipment for personnel of "A" Section who ultimately had to leave Australia possessing a somewhat rag time appearance, but this by no means affected their efficiency.'[121]

The men recruited as 'Other Ranks' into the various medical units often had a basic first aid knowledge. This had been provided by the St John Ambulance, as the Red Cross was not widely established outside New South Wales before August 1914. The St John Ambulance had trained men and women in most towns in addition to workers in State railway systems. 'On the outbreak of war this association furnished a valuable reservoir of skilled recruits for the medical services, and the training given by it proved invaluable in the field.'[122] Early in the war the Adelaide branch of St John advertised for a number of certificated men and women to volunteer to travel to the Mediterranean theatre as auxiliaries with the AAMC. This offer was however declined by the Army.

The method of selecting a man for a medical unit varied from unit to unit. Often it was simply a matter of an officer or NCO nominating a number of men. Others chose more carefully, as Major L.O. Betts, a Light Horseman wrote: 'Four from each Squadron, or twelve in all were chosen by troop leaders very often because they were not much use in the troop. Later we increased the number to eight per squadron and as at that time I had more experience, I insisted that men with more than average intelligence be detached for the work. They were trained by myself on the lines of RAMC theory by a series of Lectures, Demonstrations and Drills.'[123]

As late as October 1914, on the eve of the embarkation of Australia's second contingent, many medical units were still rather amateurish. Later that year the commanding officer of the 2nd Light Horse Field Ambulance (raised in Queensland), wrote to the District Commandant to inform him of various items of equipment which had been supplied to him not by the Army, but by the Red Cross! These included pyjamas for patients, bandages, honey, and a mincing machine 'to prepare food for invalids in hospital'.[124]

In 1914 and 1915 nurses were recruited from both the Army Nursing Service and from civil nursing groups. Military medical training was somewhat light in terms of both content and frequency. Prior to 1915 the Army Nursing Service had undertaken 'practically no peace training and had no pay, not even expenses'.[125] This was a marked and unfavourable contrast to the (British) Queen Alexandra's Imperial Military Nursing Service which had a permanent cadre staff and was thoroughly trained in military procedure and administration.

Female nurses played an extremely important part in the First World War. However, only a relatively small number of Australian nurses were employed near the front during the Gallipoli campaign (at Lemnos). Many more worked further to the rear in the Lines of Communication, and did invaluable work in hospitals at Alexandria and Cairo. The fact that so few worked closer to the front in 1915 may be partly explained by the Victorian attitudes of senior medical officers (both Australian and British), as well as their largely untried capacity in the period preceding the massive campaigns on the Western Front from 1916. This analysis precludes a detailed study of the role of nurses working close to the Gallipoli theatre.[126]

Officially the services of women doctors were refused; however there were too few women doctors in Australia at that time for this to become an issue as it did in Great Britain.[127]

SOME CONTEMPORARY VIEWS OF THE MEDICAL WAR

What at first sight might appear to be a peripheral subject to the thrust of this work does in fact have an important bearing on the history of the AAMC at Gallipoli. It concerns the various views held of Gallipoli and the part played therein by the Australian medical services. These views include those of war correspondents, editors, officers and other participants of the campaign itself. The medical services had sufficient problems with which to cope without criticism from home. This is not to suggest that the Australian press withheld fulsome praise, but the organisation of the medical services was often subject to criticism (unfair or otherwise), whereas on other occasions timely observations by the press may have materially assisted the AAMC and its morale.

Views, for or against, were invariably strongly expressed when the Gallipoli campaign was discussed — either in general or in the medical aspects. A New Zealand doctor (Major A.C. Purchas) when giving evidence before the Dardanelles Commission said 'I should say the medical arrangements for the Dardanelles business was about as puerile as anything ever was.'[128] This from an Army officer! However the Australian press were surprisingly moderate in their coverage of the medical problems *per se* and the actual mistakes of the Gallipoli campaign.

1. THE PRESS

For the most part the Australian press relied on syndicated correspondents such as C.E.W. Bean, Ashmead-Bartlett, P.F. Schuler and a handful of 'special correspondents' working from Alexandria and Cairo.

Reuters was used regularly. *The Times* (London) was also frequently quoted, particularly its editorials and coverage of the proceedings, statements and questions in both the Commons and Lords. There was to be significant controversy over two war

correspondents, the English Ashmead-Bartlett and the Australian Murdoch, both of whom seized upon some of the medical
arrangements together with the more blatant inadequacies of the
campaign and tried to have their views published uncensored.
Part of Murdoch's brief by the Australian Government [in a letter
dated 14 July 1915, Melbourne, Department of Defence], was to
furnish a report on 'Suggested despatch expert corps to
Hospitals'. After the publication of Hamilton's *Gallipoli Diary*,
there was quite a public war of correspondence between him and
Murdoch.[129]

Ashmead-Bartlett, in a letter to Winston Churchill, dated 11
April 1915, asked to represent the *Daily Telegraph*, ten other
British and European papers and 200 of the leading American
newspapers.[130] His articles were also re-published by most large
Australian newspapers. Charles Ross (NZ) and C.E.W. Bean
(Australia) were accepted by Admiral De Robeck at Mudros on
20 April 1915.

The Times was critical of the Dardanelles campaign
throughout 1915 and it described the experiences of the wounded
at the April landings as 'one of the most discreditable phases of
our participation in the war' and blamed the lack of cooperation
between the Admiralty and the War Office (in full):

> ...The Expedition was hopelessly mismanaged at the outset. The
> lack of co-operation between the Admiralty and the War Office
> extended to the hospital arrangements. The War Office seems to
> have assumed that the Admiralty was making such hospital
> arrangements as were necessary. The Admiralty seems to have
> depended on the War Office. Both departments [assumed]...that the
> British authorities in Egypt would do what was necessary. The
> ultimate result was chaos, and in consequence we are now receiving
> piteous tales of human misery such as should never have been
> possible...we trust that before more decorations are scattered
> broadcast some attempt will be made to fix the responsibility for the
> grievous muddle we have described (*The Times*, 2 July 1915,
> editorial).

'The prospect of great numbers of wounded apparently never
occurred to anybody.' While this newspaper did not propose to
'attempt to allocate the blame', it stated that the causes must be
sought. The rest of the article was scathing. However it was some
time before Australian papers picked up the gauntlet. The
editorial of the British *Lancet* under the heading 'A Medical View
of the Gallipoli Adventure', also attributed the failure of the
campaign to lack of attention to detail (*Lancet*, 15 January 1916,
p. 141).

The official response usually took the form of an assurance

by the British Government to the effect that 'the arrangements made for the reception of wounded at Alexandria had been adequate in all reports' (*The Times*, 9 July 1915). Then in late October *The Times* reported a lecture (which was extremely critical of Hamilton's campaign) given by Ashmead–Bartlett upon his return to London. Once the final evacuation had been completed an editorial left no doubts as to this paper's views. It stated that 'questions must be asked as to the way in which this campaign had been conducted'. It wrote of 'the infinitely graver and more fundamental problem of the allocation of responsibility for the faulty inception and blundering execution of one of the most monumental failures with which British arms have ever been associated' (*The Times*, 23 December 1915).

Interestingly, the Australian press rarely reported on the medical aspects of Gallipoli, except for the occasional feature like the 'Treatment of Wounded' such as the Melbourne *Age* ran. It is less understandable that those papers who maintained their own correspondents for various periods at the front could only reprint features from *The Times*, although the censor doubtless played a part, as argued in J. Robertson's *Anzac and Empire*.[131]

The Melbourne *Argus* newspaper occasionally published letters which had been written from medical personnel to their relatives. In matters medical it gave periodical coverage to the saga of Springthorpe versus Barrett in the arguments over the distribution of Red Cross stores and the AAMC administration of its Cairo hospitals. Between May 1915 and January 1916 only one editorial relevant to the AAMC was printed (on 2 September) and concerned Colonel (acting DMS Australia) Fetherston's voyage of inspection 'at very considerable cost' to Egypt.

The question of whether Australian wounded were being adequately looked after in England was also addressed periodically. 'The New South Wales Agent-General (Mr B. Wise) has informed the Commonwealth High Commissioner (Sir George Reid) that he has received well-founded complaints as to the neglect of wounded soldiers in England, which suggests that there is insufficient organisation to deal with the wounded' (the *Argus*, Melbourne, 23 October 1915). However, there were no articles on the evacuation of wounded troops from Gallipoli or anything to suggest that there were, or had been serious problems in the medical field. The only hint of trouble came in a few lines in the *Argus* of 6 November 1915, which related that complaints had been made public in New Zealand, concerning the poor quality of bully beef and its contribution to sickness on Gallipoli.

The censor must have exerted an influence. Under the War Precautions Regulations 1915 in their original form (they were later amended in 1917), the publication of matter could be made the subject of a prosecution if: '(a) it contains information useful to the enemy (Regulation 19); or (b) it contains a statement likely to cause disaffection or public alarm, to interfere with the success of the Forces, to prejudice relations with foreign powers, or to prejudice the recruiting, discipline, or administration of the Forces'.[132] Curiously, however, a number of private letters which indicated serious problems at the front were not only allowed back to Australia, but were published. At no time did the allegations or situations described therein lead to any special comment, further articles or enquiries by this paper.

By contrast the Melbourne *Age*, publishing material from its 'Special Correspondent' — P.F.E. Schuler (as well as C.E.W. Bean and E. Ashmead-Bartlett[133]) gives a different aspect of the AAMC and the problems it faced. Schuler devoted rather more time to the medical services. In contrast to the *Argus*, the *Age* published (beginning on 2 October 1915) a series of potentially damning articles concerning medical conditions, in which the problem of the shortage of boats on Gallipoli was identified.

Then it published a further piece from Schuler who thought that it was 'time to sound a note of protest against the medical organisation, or rather the lack of it, and the treatment of the wounded...The blame, if any, rests more on Imperial than Australian shoulders...' It went on to say 'Want of organization, foresight and supervision were the primary reasons for the breakdown in the medical arrangements. The work falls into two halves. The conveying of the wounded from the beaches to the bases, and the arrangements for the reception and treatment of the men at the bases. General Birrell was in command of the first branch, and General Ford, as director of medical services in Egypt, the second' (*Age*, 15 October 1915).

Under the headline 'Treatment of Wounded — Sheeting Home the Blame', the special correspondent of the Melbourne *Age* (18 October 1915) wrote about the inadequacies of the system by which Red Cross stores were being distributed both in Egypt and on board hospital and transport ships.[134] This was not so much an AAMC problem, but a Red Cross affair. There was also reference to a special 'board of enquiry' set up in July, and presided over by Lt. Colonel Springthorpe, 'to enquire into past errors and mistakes, and draw up suggestions for future guidance in regard to the care of the sick and wounded'.

Again, this was more properly in the realm of the Australian Red Cross, but the medical services were given undue prominence in an area which had been temporarily administered, albeit poorly by one or two Australian medical officers in Cairo.

The article also contained a number of questions directed to the Defence Department. The correspondent asked all the right questions, but in each case assumed that 'someone' was to blame, when in some cases only the unique circumstances of the campaign could explain mistakes.

A number of related articles continued to appear in the *Age* during the remainder of October. Schuler pleaded that he had not spoken out earlier and had 'suppressed any hint of the sufferings of the troops' because he wanted to spare additional suffering to a public regularly in receipt of casualty lists. Interestingly the *Argus* made no such report during the same time, in spite of Ashmead-Bartlett's increasingly critical reports to the British newspapers, which were being reprinted in the Australian press.

The *Sydney Morning Herald*, relying on the same sources for its news, reported those issues covered by the *Argus* and the *Age*. There was more emphasis on the Red Cross, and a number of soldiers' letters were published in which the transport of wounded from Gallipoli was vividly described. Again the theme was that all was well. The *Sydney Morning Herald* stated that 'although nothing official has been announced by the Defence Department with regard to the progress made by the Australian wounded, it is understood that the injured men are doing well...'[135] It later published a statement made by a British official denying that arrangements for the reception of wounded at Alexandria were inadequate.[136] The reproduction of some private correspondence from wounded Australians by this paper is curious, as some of these were related to the appalling situation aboard the *Seang Choon*. No letters from readers were published by this newspaper, nor were there any editorial comments or statements by politicians.

Throughout July it published a series of private letters, often written by AAMC personnel at Anzac or Egypt, which were extremely critical of medical arrangements and the conditions under which the Australian medical services had to work, but they were unaccompanied by any editorial comment.

The Sydney *Bulletin* was silent on the issue of Australian wounded at Gallipoli and their subsequent medical treatment. Its editorials appear to have been heavily influenced by *The Times* editorials and its publication of Sir Ian Hamilton's complete despatches in the preceding month (such as that of 12 January 1916.) The *Bulletin* regarded the latter 'as a piece of special pleading on his own behalf...The Generalship of the landing at Gallipoli failed to complete the work of the soldiery. In August it did the same thing, with more painful consequences' (Sydney *Bulletin*, 13 January 1916).

The Adelaide *Register* reflected other Australian newspapers in its coverage. Its tone was one of optimistic patriotism. 'London May 19. Reuters correspondent at Cairo reports that the difficulties which arose at the hospitals at Cairo and Alexandria owing to the unexpectedly high casualties, have been overcome. The cheerfulness of the wounded soldiers is remarkable' (Adelaide *Register,* 21 May 1915). It published 'extracts' from a private letter written by Howse (*Register,* 3 July 1915) concerning events in April and which contained no mention of any problems relating to the wounded or their evacuation; presumably the censor had edited any such references in this letter.

Along with other Australian papers it published a statement by Mr Tennant, the Under-Secretary of the War Office, that 'adequate arrangements had been made at Alexandria for the treatment of wounded men' and that there were sufficient hospital ships (he mentioned ten). Tennant had indicated that three of these were naval hospital ships. In fact there were only two naval ships operating between Gallipoli and Alexandria and England.

2. OFFICIAL AND NON-OFFICIAL VIEWS

The often frank commentaries and opinions in private diaries kept by Army officers were not translated into public statements. In the latter part of 1915, Fetherston (acting Director-General of Medical Services in Australia), left for Egypt and the Dardanelles on a fact-finding mission. His report to the Australian Secretary of Defence was for the most part accurate in its assessments, and certainly the more abysmal shortcomings were identified. The basic administrative shortcomings within the AAMC were recognised as well as the larger problems.

Colonel Fetherston noted: 'In addition to the naval medical Command, the Corps had to work in Egypt, England and Mediterranean Force [*sic*]. Each of these four were distinct Commands, independent of each other, and under their own G.O.C. There was no connecting link between our Corps or Units, and no one in Egypt with authority from one line to the other.'[137]

Fetherston also identified one of the underlying causes of medical mismanagement. He levelled severe criticism at senior British medical officers who 'were given positions for which they were not suited'. But more importantly he pointed out that the dissatisfaction, disorganisation, and wasteful expenditure which had occurred at Mudros could only be solved by sending out soldiers who were also businessmen and able administrators, 'for the professional sailor or soldier who from their training are not suited or fitted to work a large business concern' — Mudros with its many hospitals and other medical units had indeed become a business concern.[138] This was an evolution, reflecting as it did the complexity of modern warfare. The medical services were ill suited to conducting the type of integrated administrative and fiscal functions carried out nowadays by specialised hospital bureaucracies.

At the private level, both senior British medical men and Australian officials who were aware of the problems besetting both the RAMC and the AAMC often wrote of their concerns to superiors and colleagues. Surgeon-General Bedford — one of the more able senior British doctors during the Gallipoli campaign — wrote to Keogh in September 1915: 'I must say that I am very concerned with the wastage from sickness which is going on…Unfortunately the figures are gradually rising and the week ending 18/9/15 represents an annual wastage of 240.7 percent of the troops; this is from disease alone, and does not include any casualties from wounds…'[139]

He was also thoroughly pessimistic concerning the longer term at Gallipoli. 'Yesterday I spent on ANZAC…I am sorry to say that there is a good deal of sickness in this Army Corps…It was rather a surprise for me[?] to find this condition of affairs…I fear we shall be faced with great difficulties if we have any prolonged spell of bad weather.'[140]

The former Australian Prime Minister, Andrew Fisher (who succeeded Reid as Australian High Commissioner in London), wrote a memorandum concerning Gallipoli, admittedly with the benefit of hindsight — he was a member of the Dardanelles Commission. He believed that the 'initial provision of men, equipment, transport, medical services, and of intelligent proportion for contingencies inadequate [sic] — a fault that was never fully rectified'. As for the arrangements for wounded, there were 'unheard of hardships, unnecessary suffering by uncomplaining men…' Fisher was highly and unjustly critical of Porter, but rightly censorious concerning the luxuries enjoyed by staff officers aboard the Aragon.[141]

However Fisher, as a member of the Dardanelles Commission, was studiously diplomatic in his public utterances. As Pugsley points out in Gallipoli: The New Zealand Story, 'In Australia there were strong feelings that it was disloyal to rake over the ashes while the war was being fought and the Australian High Commissioner found pressing reasons for not attending the Commission's sessions and did not sign the final report concluded on 4th December 1917.'[142] Fisher's New Zealand colleague, Sir Thomas MacKenzie was more forthright: 'Until August 1915 the arrangements for dealing with the transport of wounded were in a very unsatisfactory state, and, indeed, the medical side of the campaign does not seem to have ever been thoroughly thought out.'[143]

At a semi-official level, editorial comment is also helpful in assessing the sometimes uneasy relationship between the AAMC in the field and even its closest supporters at home. Throughout 1915 editorials of the *Medical Journal of Australia* were concerned with patriotic calls for doctors to offer their services, as well as an occasional item on rations and Red Cross supplies. There was rarely any critical comment on the overall medical aspect of the Gallipoli campaign.

Hopes were expressed concerning the fruits of medical and scientific advances as a result of the conflict, and this journal was thoroughly supportive of the AAMC. At the end of 1915 it contended itself with the occasional patriotic editorial and reprinted articles by medical officers who had served at Gallipoli, Lemnos or Egypt.

One of the journal's articles included a private letter which was published to stress the image of self-sacrifice by the medical profession at home. 'While the profession is being depleted at an almost alarming extent at home, able and keen men in the A.A.M.C. are seeking something to do to pass the time.' Such was the observation of one medical officer at No 1 Australian General Hospital, writing to a medical colleague. He expressed his pleasure on learning that his friend was not coming out, at least immediately, and pointed out that many of the medical officers were 'tumbling over themselves, looking for work...It is somewhat disconcerting with this information to hand to receive official notifications calling on all men on the active lists and those in the reserve to declare whether they are prepared to proceed to the front...'[144]

Here is a singularly useful insight into the shortcomings of what had evolved (in Egypt particularly) as a huge and unwieldy machine partly out of control. Such disorganisation had been perceived early in 1915 by Howse and later observed by Fetherston during his inspections. However, by the time the appropriate recommendations were being set in place Gallipoli was already fading into the past.

Thus, in a sense, the AAMC fought its war on two fronts — one in the Dardanelles and the other against a jaundiced military hierarchy and a seemingly uninterested press. Such a position must not only have been frustrating for the fledgling service, but could only have been detrimental to the sometimes flagging morale among medical units, particularly those in the rear at Lemnos and Eygpt.

CHAPTER SEVEN

Politics and Rivalries

I think the outcry, both in Australia and amongst our own men —
not only in the medical Corps has led to a great deal of feeling
against the Imperial authorities. I have heard officers of some rank
...say they consider it was murder, and ... would lead them to report
to their Government that under no conceivable circumstances
would they advise the Commonwealth of Australia to enter again
upon any war where they were entirely placed under the authority
of the British Headquarters.[1]

T his comment was made by the pre-eminent
Australian medical personality at Gallipoli,
Colonel Neville Howse. It sums up the frustration of many
Australian medical personnel, although it disguises the lack of
communication between the services and the inefficiencies within
both the Army and the Royal Navy. There can be little doubt that
the problems of the Gallipoli campaign, a unique amphibious
undertaking, were exacerbated by personal animosities and
professional jealousies.

The British Army, the AIF, the Royal Navy, and the medical
services of each, were of course strictly hierarchical
organisations. Consequently inefficiencies or weaknesses at the

top were bound to have serious consequences for the smooth running of these organisations at all levels, with profound repercussions on the treatment and evacuation of sick and wounded from Gallipoli. An appreciation of the inherent weaknesses in the overall structure within which they worked is critical to understanding the activities of the Australian medical units at Gallipoli, Lemnos, and in Egypt. Again it is essential to bear in mind the magnitude of the problems associated with an amphibious assault which was on a scale and of a type unprecedented in British military history up to that time.

This chapter deals with the relevant issues within three broad categories. The first concerns the Mediterranean Expeditionary Force and the lack of communications between, and the tensions within, the various arms of the military. Second, it reviews the relations between the Army and the Royal Navy with respect to the evacuation of sick and wounded casualties from Gallipoli. This is best illustrated by the controversial appointment of Sir James Porter RN to coordinate medical evacuations. The third part provides an insight into the politics, rivalries, and professional jealousies between Australian and Imperial medical personnel and amongst the Australians themselves. To assist the reader Table 7.1 illustrates how the overall organisation of the medical services worked in 1915 as it affected the AIF.

The Dardanelles Commission was appointed in August 1916 by the British Government to investigate, among other issues, glaring inefficiencies and bungling in the treatment of wounded during the Gallipoli campaign. It published two reports, one in 1917 and a second in 1918, and the Commission's deliberations make interesting reading.

Surprisingly, perhaps, the Australian Government of the day did not appear concerned with what was a relatively thorough analysis of what had gone wrong at Gallipoli. Maurice Hankey (Cabinet Secretary and Secretary of the Committee of Imperial Defence) relates that he saw the British PM and 'showed him two newspaper telegrams from Australia to the effect that Australia did not approve' of any enquiry into the shortcomings of the campaign 'and thought we ought to get on with the war'.[2] The late John Robertson is one of the few Australian scholars to research this important source. He argues that the 'Australian reaction was polite and moderate...because the Australian psyche was so British-oriented. The Australians were in the war to see that the Empire won, and saw little point in launching furious criticism against the "home country"'.[3]

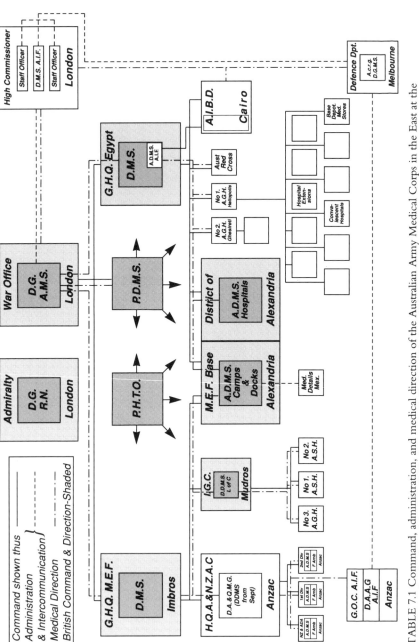

TABLE 7.1 Command, administration, and medical direction of the Australian Army Medical Corps in the East at the beginning of August 1915. *Source:* A.G. Butler, Vol. I, p. 381.

The High Commissioners of both Australia and New Zealand (Fisher and McKenzie respectively) were members of the Dardanelles Commission. Fisher was often unable to attend meetings and his signature is absent from the Commission's 1917 Report. The New Zealand High Commissioner however, would not be a party to the Commission's findings and distanced himself from the other Commissioners by signing a supplementary Report. He also endorsed statements made by Howse, similar to that quoted at the head of this chapter.[4]

The Commission's deliberations and findings highlight a number of cases of infighting and blatant attempts by British staff officers to pass the responsibility for mistakes onto others, or even to refuse to recognise the very existence of serious errors and shortcomings in their own departments.

PROBLEMS WITHIN THE MEDITERRANEAN EXPEDITIONARY FORCE

With hindsight the Gallipoli campaign was probably doomed even as it started. There was a conspicuous absence of planning and cooperation. Everything had been rushed. Hamilton had been despatched in great haste to Egypt and was expected to weld what material he had into a formidable Expeditionary Force. The responsible medical authorities — both Australian and British — trailed behind, for a while unenlightened as to their ultimate destination and forgotten completely when the critical initial medical arrangements and evacuation procedures were made for the Gallipoli landings.

Throughout the proceedings of the Dardanelles Commission different witnesses in the medical and other departments complained of two problems. The first was Hamilton's decision in March 1915 to leave behind his administrative staff in Alexandria, and the second was Hamilton's personal remoteness and inaccessibility.

The General Staff went off, first to Alexandria, then to Lemnos to organise the Gallipoli landings without any assistance from the usual logistic and auxiliary arms of the expeditionary force. Thus the Quartermaster-General, the Adjutant-General and the Director of Medical Services were not represented at a senior level until the eve of the April landing. When they arrived they found that the General Staff had already begun making administrative arrangements, which, as the AQMG Lt. Colonel Beardon said, 'caused considerable trouble out there because we had considerable difficulty picking up the ropes and...in many cases the Administrative Staff did not know what was going on, I think some of the plans they did make might have been made after consulting us first…the General Staff did not see the necessity of consulting the Administrative Staff so much.'[5]

This was to have appalling consequences for medical arrangements at Gallipoli, not only for the Australians but for the entire MEF. In reply to Howse's allegation of mismanagement at the landing, Birrell told the Dardanelles Commission that the 'confusion that has now come to light about the [medical] evacuation at Anzac at the landing could, I am certain, have been avoided if the DMS and staff had been allowed to carry out their duties, instead of these duties being taken over by the General Staff'.[6]

One of the first things to go wrong as described by Birrell was that as a result of General Carruthers' initiative on 26 April five transport ships had left Anzac for Alexandria (apparently short of their full complement of wounded) without orders from GHQ — Birrell, fearing that something was wrong, requested to go aboard the HQ ship *Queen Elizabeth* to superintend the evacuation, as it was not being carried out according to his scheme. His request was not passed on to Headquarters by the Deputy Adjutant General at Gallipoli, Brigadier-General E.M. Woodward, and in any case the General Staff saw itself as carrying out the evacuation exactly in accordance with Birrell's own plan.[7]

The second complaint concerns senior officers being denied access to Hamilton, mainly through the intervention of his Chief of Staff, Major-General W. Braithwaite. This supposition is supported by Woodward, who earlier had suggested to Hamilton that the landing at Gallipoli be postponed for two days so that medical arrangements could be placed on a proper footing. Braithwaite may have blocked (deliberately or otherwise) Woodward's request to Hamilton. Part of Woodward's evidence to the Commission concerning his own activities on the eve of the April landing states that he saw Braithwaite and pointed out to him that the arrangements were quite inadequate. Woodward suggested that the operations should be postponed until he could make more definite arrangements. One of his functions was to supervise medical arrangements. Woodward insisted on seeing Sir Ian Hamilton personally because he thought there would be trouble about the wounded, but Braithwaite refused to cooperate with him.[8]

Braithwaite later denied this but from the available evidence this officer may have been a key figure in the decision not to postpone the landing at Anzac until the medical arrangements were complete. At times, Braithwaite's obstruction could have been intended simply to shield Hamilton from the more minor worries of a large and complex campaign. In any case this approach had serious consequences for the Australian medical services, and especially those Australian doctors who tried, via Generals Birdwood or Godley, to have Hamilton put deficiencies right.

During the course of the Dardanelles Commission it was not unusual for staff officers prior to, or while attending sessions, to write to various members of their own staff asking them for assistance in clarifying some of the issues raised, particularly with respect to statistics and matters of a specialist nature. However, in one letter (to General Braithwaite) Hamilton actually coached Braithwaite through an entire report which the latter was to send to the Secretary of the Commission. In it, he completely denied the veracity of previous evidence damaging to Hamilton and rebutted Woodward's assertion: *'I have no knowledge* [emphasis added] of Woodward's having asked you to postpone this landing for two days — only a profound belief that *it is a lie.'*[9]

There were further problems in communications which were a major concern to those at Gallipoli. There was a chronic shortage of small boats and launches and often too the use of the wireless was forbidden because of the submarine menace. A typical comment was that by the DAG referring to Mudros Harbour just prior to 25th April 1915, when he explained that he could not communicate with other ships as he was on a ship crowded with troops and jammed with equipment and stores. There were 120 vessels lying in the harbour and they began to move off almost as soon as he got there. As he was not allowed to use the wireless, and a launch or boat was unprocurable, he could not transmit orders.[10]

A lack of personal communications is evident in Admiral De Robeck's letters: 'Soldiers do not help themselves and we have done so much for them and they lean on us always now! However here [on board his flagship which also served as GHQ] we have no friction and they cannot complain of our assistance.'[11] The honeymoon was soon over, for two months later he wrote that 'the soldiers are very trying at times & their methods or rather want of method make one nearly mad!'[12] But he seemed unaware that similar problems existed amongst his own staff. One observer, Vice-Admiral Wemyss, wrote to a naval colleague about the general confusion that 'the root of the evil has been the inability of De Robeck's staff to get their work done. They have been on board a battleship all the time.'[13]

Nor was the absence of adequate consultation confined to members of the General Staff. Surgeon-General Birrell was ill-served by the New Zealander Colonel Manders (ADMS to the ANZAC Division) whom Birrell had appointed DDMS of ANZAC. For on 22 April Manders suddenly informed Birrell that he was relinquishing this important post and gave Birrell a letter from Birdwood, the Corps commander, stating that as Manders was already ADMS ANZAC, he could not therefore fulfil the senior position of DDMS. In his defence, Manders had been reluctant to take on the post in the first instance (due to his age) and it was also refused by Howse when Birrell offered it to him.

However, Manders' timing could not have been worse, as he gave his 'notice' only three days before the Gallipoli landing. As discussed above, the lack of a DDMS would prove to be a serious shortcoming on 25 April and in the early days of evacuating wounded. Birrell and his staff have perhaps attracted an undue share of the blame for this particular episode.

In another instance Lt. Colonel Thom (RAMC) was quite happy to state that he had never left the *Aragon* for the three months after he arrived at Mudros.[14] He was not then in any position to see at first hand some of the medical problems being faced by the AAMC both at Anzac and at Lemnos — particularly concerning staffing, stores and evacuation transport. The results were predictable. Lt. Colonel Stoney Archer, with reference to Birrell said: 'I begged for the assistance of our Sanitary Section which was at Mudros along with many others; but though my ADMS supported me my request was refused'.[15] There were of course to be continual differences of opinion within the AAMC. Towards the end of May Lt. Colonel Corbin had laid out a number of suggestions for the improvement of the evacuation and then put them before his own CO who promptly vetoed them.[16]

Subsequently much was left to chance and on occasion things were cut rather fine. In a briefing of senior officers at General Birdwood's HQ prior to the August Offensive John Corbin, a doctor from the 1st ACCS told Birdwood he believed that as more casualties could be expected and as no preparation had been made, Corbin thought it was possible that they were going to have a bigger calamity than at April — if something was not done quickly. As Corbin understood it there had been absolutely no preparations made for the wounded on the left (or northern) flank of the proposed operations area. Colonel Keble, who was acting as Medical Control Officer at Anzac, piped up to say that there were two British Casualty Clearing Stations to deal with casualties there. Corbin queried him as to where they were. An embarrassed Keble had no idea.[17]

All this took place less than six hours before the commencement of the Offensive. Apparently the British No 13 and No 16 Casualty Clearing Stations landed under extremely adverse circumstances, very late, having been sent to Suvla Bay instead of Anzac by mistake and were subsequently unable to prepare themselves properly.

As Corbin had predicted there ensued utter chaos on the left flank; and subsequently at Colonel Keble's own request Corbin went there on 12 August with medical officers and tried to help the RAMC units. The conditions they met were appalling.[18] The war diary of the 1st ACCS for 15 and 23 August suggests why. The OC of the No 13 CCS (Colonel McNaught) was seriously ill and his unit had shelter only adequate for fair weather — bearing in mind the time of year. In the case of No 16 CCS, its evacuation pier was under rifle fire and it had been set up in the 'dry' bed of a stream![19] Fetherston also mentions this bungle and suggests that the (RAMC) casualty clearing station collapsed not from work but from nervousness and ignorance.

The confused official liaison between the various medical authorities, bad and chaotic as it was, had already reached a nadir some time before June, with the well-intentioned appointment of a senior naval medical officer whose task it was to streamline medical evacuations from Gallipoli.

RELATIONS BETWEEN THE ARMY AND THE ROYAL NAVY

Surgeon-General Babtie was the first officer to hold the appointment of Principal Director of Medical Services (PDMS) for the East and he arrived in Egypt in June. The creation of this post was the result of an attempt by the War Office to resolve the medical problems which had occurred in April. The Navy, for the same reason, appointed Sir James Porter to the post of Principal Hospital Transport Officer (PHTO). His arrival in Egypt on 24 July added to the confusion. Lt. General Altham, Inspector-General of Communications, wrote that 'at the present moment, I find, on my return this afternoon from General Headquarters, concentrated here Surgeon-General Babtie, Surgeon Birrell, Colonel Maher, D.D.M.S. and Surgeon-General Sir James Porter. I have in fact to face the most extraordinary embarrassment of a superfluity of expert advisers the relations of whom with each other are exceptionally ill-defined and unsatisfactory.'[20]

This statement was to characterise relations between the military and naval medical authorities throughout the Gallipoli campaign. The strained relations between the two services are perhaps best illustrated by the role of Sir James Porter, an ex-Medical Director-General of the Naval Medical Services.

On 15 June 1915, at the instance of the military, a conference was held at the War Office which was to have a number of implications for the Australian medical services at Gallipoli for the ensuing five months. It appointed Porter to be 'Principal Hospital Transport Officer to cooperate with Surgeon-General Babtie of the Dardanelles...'[21] with respect to the transport of the sick and wounded. However, Sir Alfred Keogh in hindsight disclosed that the Navy was unaware (prior to the conference) that Babtie had been in control of hospital ships in the Mediterranean — as he arrived on the scene three weeks earlier. Furthermore he states that 'if the capacity of this officer had been understood by the Admiralty, the suggestion [of Porter's appointment] would not have been made'.[22] This is one of several instances of poor liaison between the Army and the Navy.

The object of this June conference had been to organise a regular service of ships for severely wounded troops to work between the Dardanelles and Britain and to have a ferry service for the more lightly wounded cases to ply between the Dardanelles and Alexandria, and the Dardanelles and Malta. A subsequent submission which was sent to the First Sea Lord on 21 June, expanded Porter's role to ensure that there was a combined utilisation of the naval and military resources in respect of sea hospital transport in the Mediterranean, under the superintendence of a single authority to be known as the 'Hospital Transport Officer (Mediterranean)'.[23] The original Admiralty Nomination List for the 14th of that month states that Porter was to be lent for inspecting duties only.[24]

However, by the time Porter received his sailing instructions two weeks later, his 'duty statement' had been considerably expanded.

The Admiralty now wanted him to inspect and report on the naval hospital ships *Rewa, Soudan* and *Somali* and the provision made in them for embarking and disembarking, transport and treatment of wounded generally. In addition he was to direct the movements of all sick and wounded of both services by sea in the Mediterranean. The berthing and general movements of hospital ships would continue under Admiral De Robeck. Porter was also to satisfy himself that the medical and nursing staff and the outfit generally of all hospital ships were adequate for the work required.[25] As the military, not the Navy, was responsible for supplying medical officers, nurses and orderlies to most of the hospital ships, the potential for conflict can be appreciated.

Table 7.2   Local Responsibilities — MEF and Egypt

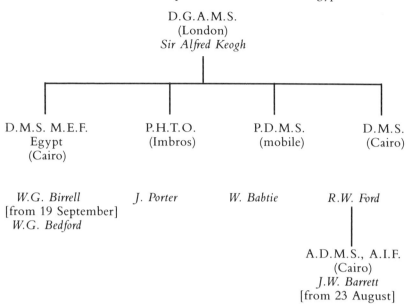

Hamilton was informed by cable on 28 June that Porter was on his way and he was told that 'the Naval and Military Medical officers will inform the Hospital Transport officer [Porter] of their wants, and arrangements will be made by him for sea conveyance on hospital ships, subject to the usual control of the Senior Naval Officer'.[26] Up to this time Surgeon-General Babtie had been in charge of hospital ship movements. Hamilton was quick to realise what such duplication of effort would mean and the next day cabled to London: 'I hope you realise that this creates one more link of possible friction which I will try to avert to the best of my powers. Babtie has just arrived and is a most capable man. He does not know anything yet of the new appointment. He has worked out a scheme of evacuation of sick and wounded by land and sea. Who is to be "boss"?'[27] His anxieties would later be played upon by Babtie's animosity towards Porter, while the War Office for its part was content throughout June to send Hamilton its assurances that the new arrangement would be for the good of all.

When Porter visited Babtie on 21 July in Egypt, both he and Surgeon-General Ford (DMS Egypt) disclaimed all knowledge of his official appointment and even General Maxwell, the GOC in Cairo, knew nothing at all of Porter being appointed PHTO.

However, in contrast with Babtie, Maxwell promised his cooperation.[28] At least Hamilton seems to have been giving some thought to future complications for on 3 July he had cabled to the War Office and asked that the respective responsibilities of both Porter and Surgeon-General Birrell be clearly defined.[29]

Then on the 28th Porter arrived at Mudros and reported to both De Robeck and Hamilton, and '…the administrative confusion became confounded indeed'.[30] Porter complicated matters further by setting up his own separate headquarters, not at Imbros in the flagship or with the DMS, MEF, at General Headquarters, or at Lemnos with the Inspector-General of Communications and Principal Naval Transport Officer, but in a small yacht, the *Liberty*.[31] Here, though personally 'mobile', he was without wireless communications and was therefore unable to respond to rapid changes in the situation as they arose.

Confusion persisted even after Porter had visited Hamilton, for the latter cabled the War Office in July with reference to Porter's powers asking 'if Sir James had now assumed direction'.[32] Even Woodward, the DAG who had studied Porter's instructions in detail confessed he was at a loss to explain how Porter 'is almost single-handed going to get through this great piece of work…nor apparently does Birrell'.[33]

On the next day in another cable to London, Hamilton quite rightly pointed out that under existing Army Regulations, any orders for medical evacuations were vested in his Quartermaster-General and that he would be unable to accept any responsibility in this matter on future occasions.[34] This, at a time when Hamilton was planning an offensive in which large numbers of casualties were expected.

To summarise to this stage, we have a naval surgeon being appointed over an army doctor to take charge of a medical evacuation scheme designed entirely along vague lines by the Army using the resources of the Royal Navy. Neither medical arm of the two services had worked with the other on such a scale before. Added to this was the failure by the War Office to notify all senior officers of Porter's appointment, an omission that heightened personal animosities among the participants.

Despite Porter's approach to the General Staff at this time, he could obtain little information concerning the proposed battle, apart from the intimation that there was going to be 'a push' made at Gallipoli on 6 August. Porter managed to obtain a plan of the operations to ascertain what arrangements had been made for the wounded, reviewed them, and decided they were grossly inadequate in terms of the necessary hospital ships.

After the War Maher (who was ADMS Mudros on board the *Aragon*) wrote to Porter that 'Babtie's scheme was inadequate as the Suvla landing was not foreseen at the time he made his proposal and as far as I could see, at the time, no hospital ships were forthcoming to carry it out. It was only [with] your appearance on the scene that we obtained sufficient hospital ships to carry on. What we should have done without the *Aquitania, Mauretania* and *Britannic* I do not know.'

According to Maher's letter Babtie's scheme added to that of Birrell by placing hospital ships as near the beaches as possible and sending them down the lines in what Babtie 'called a ferry service, i.e. a vessel or vessels leaving whether full or not and plied to a time table to Egypt and Malta'.[35] In consultation with the new DQMG, MEF, Major-General G.F. Ellison, Porter modified the original plan and arranged for eight hospital ships to lie off Gallipoli when the August Offensive began. This was the origin of the Porter-Ellison scheme.

The two main stumbling blocks throughout the five months that Porter was PHTO were first, duplication of control; and second, the demarcation of Army and Naval responsibilities 'at the high water mark' on the beaches. This opinion was echoed in a variety of sources. For example on 26 September 1915, a letter from Field Marshal Lord Methuen (Governor of Malta) to the DGAMS illustrated the difficulties inherent in the system of working hospital ship transport in the Mediterranean. He also condemned dual control of Porter and military authorities.[36]

These would continue to plague medical arrangements at Gallipoli until the end of the campaign. Even before Porter's appointment was terminated in November, certain medical officers, jealous of their own prerogatives and professional standing, failed to cooperate fully with Porter. This, together with Porter's own shortcomings, further hindered the efficient medical evacuation of Australian casualties off Gallipoli.

In a letter to Admiral Limpus, Porter wrote: 'Babtie for his own personal [reasons] real or imaginary has worked up Hamilton's attitude towards me for all he is worth — This is very bad.'[37] He noted that complaints had been made of the inadequate number of medical staff on transport ships, together with the state of these ships. However, these areas were wholly military, rather than Naval, responsibilities. Nevertheless he 'recommended that the appointment of Hospital Transport Officer should be abolished'.[38] This would again make Surgeon-General Babtie responsible for evacuation and distribution of casualties.

In response De Robeck sent a letter to the Second Sea Lord on 3 October 1915, arguing that prior to Porter's appointment the situation had been one of chaos where the RAMC was concerned as regards lending assistance. De Robeck believed that attempts to have Porter withdrawn emanated from Surgeon-General Babtie, 'a person whose sphere of interference could with advantage be curtailed' and whom he thought was anxious to have Porter's yacht the *Liberty*. He concluded by requesting the Sea-Lord to 'do anything to retain Porter'.[39]

The War Office, now vaguely aware of the frictions within the medical community at the Dardanelles, cabled Hamilton to ask if the system was working to his satisfaction, and did he want Babtie to resume control?[40]

In reply Hamilton, who seems to have switched personal alliances, stated that he fully concurred with De Robeck's opinion that Porter should stay. Other military medical officers also professed not to have had any difficulties in their dealings with Porter: 'He [Porter] and Colonel Maher and I got on splendidly, we never had any trouble, we were on the most cordial terms and then he was taken away, which was unfortunate.'[41]

Moves had already begun at the Admiralty to call an enquiry, because of suspicions that Porter had not received the loyal support of the Army's senior medical officers.[42] This inference is evident in a private letter the Director-General of the Admiralty's Medical Department, Sir Arthur May, wrote to his friend Admiral Limpus. 'You will I feel be pleased to hear that the Cabal of Babtie & Co. has failed and the War Office have withdrawn their request for Porter to be relieved and so the transport of wounded won't return to previous condition of chaos.'[43]

However, this assessment was premature for on 19 November 1915 the War Office informed the Admiralty 'that as a result of the experience gained during the past 3 [*sic*] months, they are desirous that…the normal system of control of hospital ships should be reverted to and that the responsibilities of Surgeon-General Sir James Porter, in the matter, should cease at as early a date as possible'.[44] In part this was a realisation that the dual system did not work, nor could it against the complexities of the overall Dardanelles campaign.

The Secretary of War frankly admitted this by recognising that the scheme represented a departure from the normal system by which responsibility for the movements of the sick and wounded was centred in the Quartermaster-General's Department, which dealt direct with the Naval Authorities when sea transport was involved.[45] Porter however did much good work, despite both the inflexibility of the British military authorities, and in some cases, their deliberate obstruction.

At a general level relations between the Army and the Navy reflected the situation which existed between Porter and his military contemporaries. (This is not to suggest a state of perpetual antipathy existed between all members, units of the two services.)

Even before Porter arrived at the Dardanelles, one of De Robeck's aides (Wemyss) wrote that the military medical arrangements were entirely inadequate and that Birrell was absolutely incompetent to deal with the situation. Wemyss admitted to almost coming to blows with Birrell because he refused Wemyss's offers of assistance in sending naval surgeons on board transport ships sorely in need of medical assistance. He also wrote of 'the fact of the General Staff refusing to go on shore and detaching themselves from everybody and everything... Naturally there have been great delays in communications, and none of the soldiers ashore dared to give any orders or to even say what they wanted without reference to the General staff who couldn't be got at!'[46] Porter was also somewhat disdainful of Headquarters life and this comment comes from one of his letters to a fellow Admiral: 'In Mudros itself all is as it ought to be — harmony between A[rmy] & N[avy]. As for G.H.Q. they are people apart living up at Imbros in solitary grandeur...'[47]

The Navy was the first to realise what the Army was only now coming to terms with, i.e. the conditions of Gallipoli — unprecedented as they were — demanded a different approach in handling medical matters, and medical evacuations in particular. The old methods were no longer valid, at least in this campaign. Under the new system the Admiralty would now make separate arrangements for the sick and wounded of the Fleet and those naval hospital ships and the naval medical staff which had been 'on loan' to the Army would be again placed under De Robeck's control [as senior Naval Officer], and they would be allocated for purely naval purposes. These problems of communication and cooperation in the medical services were not restricted to the High Command of the Army and the Royal Navy.

ANZAC AND BRITISH RELATIONS

There were periodic instances throughout the Gallipoli campaign where relations between the AAMC and the RAMC were less than cordial. Fortunately such occasions did not have lasting or important consequences for the medical services' proper functioning. The Australians themselves were often responsible; at other times the Imperial authorities were the source of friction.

At the beginning of 1915 the AAMC, AIF was to be absorbed wholly into the MEF — i.e. to become an 'Imperial' unit. Local Australian authority was to be responsible for the raising, outfitting and training of Australian medical units, but the plan was that once these personnel reached the base in Egypt, they would immediately come under the direct control of the British PDMS, Surgeon-General Babtie. However, for their part, the British senior medical officers had assumed that the internal administration throughout the AAMC under their 'control', would be the continued responsibility of Australian officers. (See Table 7.1 on page 164? for details of the (General medical) staff's area responsibilities.)

In Egypt especially, a number of Australian medical units were under the direct supervision of RAMC officers, a fact which caused a great deal of animosity and valid criticisms from the Australian medical services, such as this comment by an Australian doctor: 'It is hard being under R.A.M.C. men who though quite nice know not the officers nor the organisation and constitution and don't try very hard to find out.'[48] In a letter to Fetherston, Colonel Brudenell White wrote 'The cost to Australia of Medical arrangements in Egypt is enormous. All that cost is at present being incurred by R.A.M.C. Officers who are not responsible for their action to the Australian Government...From the Australian point of view this alone makes the provision of some effective administrative machinery, a necessity.[49]

The Australian military authorities had contributed to the confusion by not supporting their own DMS — General Williams — when he first went out to Egypt early in 1915. Fetherston also was convinced it would have been much better if the Defence Department in Melbourne had initially taken up the position that in Australian matters the AAMC would do things in its own way, and insisted on having its wishes carried out.[50] However, the Australian Government seemed content to throw in its resources unconditionally to the Imperial cause. Williams' British opposite (in Egypt), Surgeon-General Ford, had only just been appointed to act as chief medical officer for the British commander there, General Maxwell. The Australian commander, for his part, did nothing to support Williams.

The result was that Ford rapidly subsumed to his direct control all the Australian hospitals in Egypt. 'Brooking no apparent rival, he almost immediately questioned Williams' status...'[51] The problem was compounded by the absence of a DDMS ANZAC or a DDMS 1st Australian Division appointment early in the campaign. This was not the fault of senior

British medical officers, either at Gallipoli or in England, but in the first instance by both Manders and Howse refusing the position in April, and later to reluctance on the part of Hamilton, as per a diary entry by Birrell which states: 'D.D.M.S Corps [ANZAC] vetoed for [the] moment by C.in C.'[52]

Some of the general rivalry stemmed from misunderstandings brought about by men and women coming from very different backgrounds as recorded by an Australian doctor. 'One man arriving at the hospital ship was describing, with the usual picturesque invective, how the bullet had gone into his shoulder. One of the officers, who apparently was unacquainted with the Australian vocabulary, said: "What was that you said, my man?" The reply came, "A blightah ovah theah put a bullet in heah."'[53] From among the medical ranks opinions and prejudices ranged from the bemused to the bitter. A British medic, Private J. Hargrave, wrote 'Certainly the Australians we met were a cheerful, happy-go-lucky, devil-may-care crew. They were the most picturesque set of men in the peninsula.'[54]

The view of Sister F. McMillan, an Australian nurse working at Mudros, is also noteworthy. 'The English Tommy is very dull in intelligence. I have not met any of the better classes. They are good souls but when sick are much harder to nurse than our boys who never lose heart and are always ready to get up.'[55]

A similar opinion was expressed by H.E. Gissing. 'We have taken on [a hospital ship in June] practically all Englishmen, very boyish some of them & taking them on the average they are not as cheerful nor do they bear their wounds as well as the Australians.' (Diary entry for 4 June 1915.) There was also hostility, as J.G. Burgess, a Light Horseman in a British hospital on Mudros wrote: 'The more I see of the English Tommy the less I like him and I think it is evident that they have no great love for Australians either.'[56]

On the other hand there were instances of animosity towards the Australian medical officers, even at senior levels, indicated by this excerpt from a confidential memo by a Britisher, Captain F.P. Dunlop, concerning complaints relating to the access of obtaining medical stores for the *Galeka*. According to him this ship was crowded with medical officers and personnel of Australian units, among which he perceived 'considerable jealousy... and a want of discipline on the part of subordinates'. Dunlop admitted that there was a real difficulty in obtaining medical comforts at Mudros late in May. But according to him all could have been resolved through a display of appropriate manners. 'This difficulty could have been overcome if a young and ill-bred Australian Officer who called himself the Quarter-master [Captain (later Colonel) J.R. Muirhead, attached to the 1st Light Horse Field Ambulance] had approached the ships' captains and others in a less offensive manner, when they could have helped him as they invariably helped other officers in difficulty.'

Apparently Muirhead did not suffer fools and red tape gladly with the result that Dunlop reported Muirhead to his superiors. He also damned the rest of the Australians for good measure: 'of all the untrained officers with whom I have had to deal at Mudros, those of the Australian medical units were the most helpless in all matters of administration and discipline. This fact in my opinion, fully accounts for any trouble which occurred on the *Galeka*.'[57]

The comments of others were borne of prior acquaintance, thus Private H.P. Moloney of the 5th Battalion: 'Got Dr. Wilson to have a look at me, he was keen on admitting me to No.15 [a British Hospital], but my previous experience of English hospitals makes me shy of them.'[58] Perhaps this was becoming part of the Anzac folklore about the British medical establishment. Australian doctors were not always impartial either. 'The ship [from Anzac to Alexandria] was under the control of Australian medical officers who show much better attention compared with the English.'[59]

There were other reports of Australians in British field hospitals having insufficient to eat, not enough blankets and not having their wounds dressed.[60] No doubt some of these reports were based on hearsay. There were also those Australian troops who spoke highly of English hospitals and standards in both British and Australian run hospitals varied as to staff, supplies, and facilities as they do today.[61]

Chas. Ryan, a surgeon of much experience recounted one episode of working with the British. 'My experience on board the *Soudan* was the reverse of pleasant through the unwillingness of the Consulting Surgeon to co-operate with me.'[62] The most bitter comments were to come from Australian field officers such as Captain A.G. Carne, the RMO of the 6th Battalion: 'When we worked and fought side by side with the British troops at C. Helles the British stretcher bearers refused to assist our men, collecting only their own wounded, passing by Australians; while our men attended to British and Australian alike.'[63]

A curt entry in the war diary of the 3rd Light Horse Field Ambulance notes 'O/C bearers of 39th F.A. [a British field ambulance] had refused request for help by means of his unemployed and stretcher bearers.'[64] A similar charge was made by a young New Zealander (Charles Clarke) wounded in the battle for Chunuk Bair, early in August. In his case one of his own officers 'directed two English stretcher bearers to place me on a stretcher...these fellows just waited for him to go, and then turned me over and tipped me out, and off they went.'[65] Dr Cyril Checchi related in an interview with the author that the term RAMC was popularly believed to mean 'Rob All My Comrades', and its members were not held in high repute by some wounded — neither British nor Australians.

Even obtaining stores could be a problem, as related by Lt. Colonel V.O. Stacey of No 2 Australian Stationary Hospital based on Lemnos. 'We took our orders from the D.D.M.S. (Col. Hughes) who was stationed on the *Aragon* at Lemnos. On applying to this officer for stores (food & dressings etc.) I was first roundly abused for asking for them and was told to get them from the beach at Anzac.'[66] Lt. Colonel Muirhead of the 1st Light Horse Field Ambulance (as we have seen, the subject of Captain Dunlop's spleen) was faced with a similar situation but he was more resourceful.

Muirhead was on a transport ship packed with wounded and was ordered to find supplies for these men. In desperation he finally clambered aboard the HQ ship (*Aragon*), but was refused a hearing. He then told the British officer of the Army Supply Corps that if he did not do something promptly he would dump 15 corpses overboard and 'show him up'.[67] Consequently he was shown into the presence of Admiral De Robeck, who heard his story and issued him with a 'blank cheque' to draw supplies. Even then this officer could only obtain 17 tins of condensed milk and 10 pounds of arrowroot to help feed 500 wounded for 10 days.

Fetherston, writing an official report stated 'Proverbially R.A.M.C. Officers and also Q.A.I. [British] Nurses are not used to hard work and do not work as hard as Australians of similar standing.'[68] Sergeant O.P. Kenny, of the 3rd Australian Field Ambulance reveals both pride and contempt when he wrote about his men thus: 'The stamina of these bearers was wonderful. They worked in pairs carrying stretcher cases, a striking contrast to the R.A.M.C. method of four bearers to one stretcher.'[69]

Some were critical of the lack of professionalism of senior British medical officers. Surgeon-General Babtie eventually arrived at Gallipoli to see the situation for himself. His inspections, at least at Anzac, were somewhat perfunctory. According to Corbin of the 1st ACCS Babtie was at Anzac Cove for two and a half minutes, while Porter was not seen by him at all on Anzac.[70]

Howse was very critical of Birrell, but added that he 'considered he was ill, when I saw him, and I did not think he was physically fit to grapple with such a big situation as existed, which required a good deal of initiative'.[71] The reason is no doubt that Neville Howse was a very strong personality with strong views. It is not widely known that he had threatened to resign over the question of dual control (Australian and British) of the AAMC. He wrote to the Director General of Medical Services, stating that he would 'be glad to be relieved of my duties at the earliest possible moment unless the Minister of Defence is able to support my view'.[72] At the end of 1915 he got his wish.

While Babtie was not an organiser of any great calibre, his colleague Birrell was found out first, possibly because of Hamilton's dislike of him. Hamilton wrote in September 1915 to the Director of Medical Services: 'Dear Keogh, Birrell, as you know is leaving us...he does not, as I have already called home, in my opinion possess the exceptionally brilliant qualities desirable in the medical chief.'[73]

Surgeon-General Babtie had recognised this when he visited Hamilton as one of his first duties as newly appointed Principal Director of Medical Services, claiming that Hamilton had two complaints against Birrell. He 'had got up the backs of the Navy by lack of tact when in the days of stress they had offered help and second, that he had been slow in getting hospitals established at Mudros'.[74] The second complaint was unjust. There was an acute shortage of water on Lemnos at that time, making Mudros a poor base for hospitals. Birrell was replaced with someone almost as inept, Surgeon-General Bedford, Hamilton being cabled of this appointment on 30 August.[75]

Criticisms were not restricted to the grumbling of Australians and New Zealanders. An Englishman, Doctor H. Clough, on board the *Carmania* off Gallipoli wrote that they 'were blundering along in the most clumsy fashion. Splendid men and equipment and splendid officers, the young ones...Some old stale Admirals who...know more about social questions than naval warfare, and Generals who ought to be in Hospital for senility...and to see the lives of these splendid fighting men thrown away through sheer incompetence, makes one's blood ever boil.'[76]

Not a few resorted to using semi-official channels to air their grievances. Some of these were later deliberately or otherwise published.

In a letter addressed to Lady Helen Munro Ferguson (wife of the Governor-General), in her capacity as Chief of the Australian Division of the British Red Cross Society, Colonel Fiaschi, the officer commanding the 3rd Australian General Hospital, told her that when his hospital was ordered to Lemnos he applied for the two motor ambulances presented to the hospital by the branches of the British Medical Association in Australia. He was informed that Sir Ian Hamilton had issued orders that no ambulances were to be taken from England to Lemnos.[77]

There were rivalries elsewhere of course, as Fetherston noted: 'There is great jealousy between the Royal Army Medical Services and the Indian Medical Services...'[78] However, not all relations were antagonistic, indeed had they been the Gallipoli campaign would have been an impossibility. There were many instances of close cooperation between various medical units of the different armies. At least in England such rivalries and animosities did not have such an obvious profile. There, according to Fetherston, Sir Alfred Keogh, had 'a splendid Staff also keen and alert, and no doubt they did great work but could not control the details so far away and in so many places, and I am certain the reports and information they received were not reliable. They were very favourable to Australians.'[79]

Of Australia's other partner in Gallipoli, Lt. Colonel Bryant, the OC 1st Australian Stationary Hospital noted '[Mudros, French General] lent me three mule carts and drivers with two mules in each to assist us in shifting up equipment [eight tons]...we are greatly indebted to the French for their assistance and courtesy on all occasions as required it.'[80] It is noteworthy that there was little, if any criticism of the other principal actors in this drama, namely the Indians, the Gurkhas or the 500 strong Zion Mule Corps (which consisted of Russian Jewish volunteers who had fled Palestine at the outbreak of war and who subsequently arrived in Egypt). The Canadians, who operated hospital facilities on Lemnos, also appear not to have roused the antipathy of their Commonwealth colleagues.

The point made above by Fetherston with respect to Keogh not receiving accurate reports was reiterated by observations he later made in a confidential report to the Australian Secretary of Defence in 1916, when his suspicions were aroused. 'Every endeavour was made to forward my wishes and frequently great haste was made to carry out my suggestions...due to the fear of reports by me being sent to the Commonwealth Government and that the Government would complain to the War Office. All Senior Imperial Officers greatly fear any complaint by Australia. They do not as a body like Australians, but they certainly fear Australia.'[81]

This fear may have been justified, at least with respect to Fetherston himself. Concerning Fetherston's inspection General Sir John Maxwell wrote on 21 January 1916 to the Australian

Governor-General 'I wonder if Fetherston had stirred up any mud. [H]e left here apparently pleased but I hear he is not quite to be trusted.'[82]

Apparently the British wanted to continue having direct control over the AAMC. T.E.V. Hurley, as Fetherston's staff officer, attended some of the meetings held between the latter with General Sir John Maxwell, the GOC Egypt, and Surgeon-General Ford, the DMS Egypt. At these meetings it was made clear to the British that there was considerable dissatisfaction with Australian medical authorities not being allowed to administer their own affairs.[83] There was also some disquiet about Ford's methods: 'Our ambulances take Turkish Officer prisoners for drives by Gen. F. order.' Ford had commandeered Springthorpe's hospital car for his personal use and then billed the No 1 AGH for the petrol![84]

Fetherston therefore put a proposal to General Birdwood and Colonel White for the establishment of a DMS with full powers over the Australian Medical Services in Australian matters, and for an Australian ADMS in all areas where Australian (Army) patients were being treated. These proposals, approved by both Birdwood and White, were discussed with the newly appointed PDMS Surgeon-General Babtie.

Babtie, fresh from India, was nominally in charge of all the medical services in the Dardanelles campaign and therefore was to control Birrell (DMS, MEF, superseded by Bedford), Ford (DMS, Egypt), as well as the DMS Malta (Surgeon-General Whitehead). He agreed to support these proposals and recommended that they be approved by Keogh — the Director-General of the Medical Services. Fetherston proceeded to England believing this proposal had only to be rubber-stamped. However in the interim Babtie wrote to Keogh suggesting that the scheme was something of a sop to the Australians, and that any Australian medical chief would in fact be part of Babtie's staff and under his direct orders.[85]

Whilst in Gallipoli and Egypt Fetherston also had to face the impermeability of the 'old boy' network among the generals, the difficulty and at times the impossibility of obtaining anything in writing, and their predilection for resisting reforms and instructions. The root of the trouble, according to him, was the rule of seniority and he gives detailed complaints against Babtie, Ford, Birrell and Porter.[86]

The British for their part were also well aware of the defects in the Australian organisation. Writing of the April landing at Gallipoli, Hamilton said: 'True, owing to accidents, inexperience, shell fire and defective organisation of the higher medical authority in the Anzac Corps, there was a partial breakdown of the Australian section of the scheme during a few days.'[87] This observation was largely correct as the Australians were experiencing problems with their senior medical administration at the time of the April landing. This was due both to the organisational deficiencies mentioned above and to the refusal of either Colonel Howse or Colonel Manders to take on the responsibilities of DMS, ANZAC.

Hamilton's written observation that 'had the impetuous valour of Surgeon-General Howse not led him ashore, but remained afloat he would have been in a better position to witness what really happened, and subsequently direct operations' is both inaccurate and unfair. Hamilton's remarks were in fact a drastically watered-down version of an earlier draft of a letter which was quite controversial: '...talk such as that indulged in by Surgeon-General Howse must tend to create clouds of vague prejudice which I for one have to struggle the best I can to dispel'.[88]

Keble went further and accused Howse of losing 'an opportunity which comes very seldom to anybody, but I do not blame him because he was not a soldier nor was he a trained Staff Officer'.[89] Howse, a South Africa VC, was known for his bravery and it may be that he felt he could not sit still on a ship while all the action took place on the beaches. There may be comparisons in this revealing entry in the war diary of No 1 Australian Stationary Hospital, by its commander — a statement which may also explain why these posts were not filled: 'D.D.M.S. offered A.D.M.S. [4 June] A.& N.Z.D. to any of my majors. Declined as no practical [i.e. surgical] work in it.'[90] This explanation for Howse's action is speculative of course, but it is difficult to understand why Howse refused the position of DMS, thus leaving the AAMC largely rudderless over several weeks after 25 April.

The preparations for the landing were also deficient. Before the actual fighting began everything had been underestimated, and very little provision made for hospital ships, as it was thought that the wounded could be kept ashore (as per Birrell's orders — see Appendix III), and he blamed the Australian medical officers for being alarmed unnecessarily.[91]

Surgeon-General Birrell, when questioned on the problems at the landing, tried to redirect the blame. He considered that his own plan, which had been vetted by Hamilton's General Headquarters, was fully equal to any requirements. Its manifest failure at Anzac was, in Birrell's opinion, due solely to both Howse and Manders who did not work in conjunction with the

Quartermaster-General. Birrell thus flatly denied any responsibility 'for the local confusion that may have arisen at Anzac'.[92]

Even so, Birrell could see the obvious defects in the Australian arrangements at Gallipoli, and there is little doubt that the senior officers of the AAMC were to blame for some of these inadequacies. Two years later he wrote to Hamilton that there had been no trouble with the evacuations further south at Cape Helles which were carried out under the same conditions but there the ADMS of Divisions remained with the HQ. Birrell went on to write that 'if the two ADMS at Anzac had done the same and not landed to do the work of junior officers on the beaches the confusion Surgeon General Howse states occurred at the landing would have been avoided'.[93]

However, criticisms of the British have to be tempered by an analysis of the frictions within the different Australian medical units and among medical personnel serving throughout the Gallipoli campaign. The latter were chiefly medical officers, as most of the trouble emanated from professional jealousies brought intact from Australia.

INTRA-AUSTRALIAN RELATIONS

As early as May frustrations building up within the AAMC were becoming known far afield. The Governor-General, in a letter to King George V, wrote that: 'The medical service both here and in Egypt has been disappointing. In Egypt, [this is] largely because of the friction between medical men, all of whom being great swells in the profession find military discipline irksome...'[94] Thus relations between individuals and units within the AAMC were not immune to those organisational and personal weaknesses which have been discussed above. The War Office cabled to Australia that the state of No 1 Australian General Hospital was unsatisfactory and offered to hold an enquiry, and then shortly after it recommended that certain officers be relieved from duty.

This request was carried out by Australia, and Lt. Colonel Barrett was relieved of duty as ADMS, also Lt. Colonel Ramsay Smith of Command of No 1 AGH, and Miss Bell as Principal Matron No 1 AGH. The following letter from Babtie to Keogh, dated 11 September 1915, Alexandria is of interest because it focuses as much on professional jealousies as on any real incompetence or wrongdoing. Barrett was an extraordinarily talented (if over-committed) doctor:

> I have heard about the Australians. I was well aware that Ramsay-Smith and Barrett were hated by every other Australian,

and they were just as efficient, or inefficient as their colleagues, and
Barrett is certainly a man of great administrative ability...but it was
a mistake as I told Ford to make him A.D.M.S. Australians [*sic*], if
only because of his unpopularity — Everything is politics out here.
I thought the [Australian] Heliopolis Hospital poor from the
beginning but the domestic standard of order out there is obviously
low and is reflected in their hospitals...[95]

This view is not so jaundiced as it might at first appear, as
reflected in another letter (dated 30 July 1915), this time from
Rupert Downes, the CO of the 3rd Australian Light Horse Field
Ambulance. In it he wrote that he knew little about the No 1 AGH
except that it had a vast medical staff apparently doing nothing.
Despite this the hospital managed to grab all the reinforcements
originally earmarked for medical units on Gallipoli. He also
wrote that the mention of the hospital's registrar (Barrett) 'throws
most of the M.O.s here into an instant fit of fury and the feeling
about his A.D.M.S. job and promotion is very great...the temper
of the senior men is such that I am nervous for the name of the
A.A.M.C. through what they may do.'[96]

Fetherston later noted that he 'quickly found that there was
considerable confusion in the Corps, and discontent amongst all
ranks in the A.A.M.C.'[97] One of Colonel Fetherston's staff
officers believed that most of this trouble in Egypt (which
reflected the larger situation) was due to the fact that there was
no Australian authority responsible for the administration of its
own medical units and for the treatment of Australian casualties
from Anzac.[98]

Complaints included quarters, seniority, and promotions.
Unfortunately such strife was not confined to those directly
involved. In September 1915 the Australian Governor-General
wrote to General Sir John Maxwell that the 'Medical Department
seems to give by far the most trouble...These doctors...are
singularly destitute of any sense of discipline.'[99] This strife
sometimes spilled over into the public arena: 'There has been
considerable controversy in the Public Press over the English
administration of the Red X supplies...extraordinary acerbity
developed amongst Australian Doctors at the Front. There are
eminent Surgeons among them, but personal rivalries and mutual
antipathies   destroyed   their   sense   of   decency   and
discipline...Probably it will take a series of libel actions to calm
some of them down!!'[100]

Others too had seen the writing on the wall. Colonel (later
General Sir) Brudenell White, of the 1st Australian Division,
wrote to Fetherston in September that he particularly wished to

speak with Fetherston about the medical arrangements for the
Diggers, as the 'present position is by no means satisfactory'. He
did not blame individuals, but 'the lack of organisation'.[101]

In a letter to the Australian Minister for Defence (Senator
G.F. Pearce), Ferguson complained that 'our medicos seem to
continue to set the worst example in discipline...'[102] Some of the
grievances, for instance those concerning promotion, were not
unreasonable. One senior officer expressed a common complaint
of those serving at the front concerning the promotion of
Australian officers and Other Ranks of the AAMC taking place
in Australia, Egypt, and England. Subsequently they were
superseding men serving at Gallipoli and on the Lines of
Communication.[103] As Colonel Downes pointed out: 'There is
much dissatisfaction among some of the men at their juniors
coming out after them promoted over their heads through no
fault of their own. It is the same in the combatant ranks...partly
because there is no supreme A.A.M.C. head to recommend
[promotions]'.[104]

A typical gripe was this one penned by Dr T.E.V. Hurley
from his Gallipoli dug-out: 'I was fortunate in receiving my
A.M.J. [*Medical Journal of Australia*] for the last few mails and saw
articles contributed by the two members of staff of the No.2 Gen'l
Hospital, am not surprised they caused some commotion. As
usual the people who are doing the work are saying and writing
the least about it...'[105]

In England Sir Alfred Keogh was also told that the Australian
medical services were permeated with politics and state
jealousies.[106] This view (which was actually that of Surgeon-
General Babtie) had been held for some time both by Australians
and the British. It had been a problem since 1914 in the early days
of enlistment, when medical units were initially rent by parochial
State jealousies. The 4th Australian Field Ambulance for example
was composed of three sections, each of which was manned by
Victorians, South Australians and West Australians. Most of this
evaporated with the landing at Gallipoli. However, as late as
October 1915, Babtie was suggesting that State units be broken
up by the importation of men from other States.[107]

At this stage of the analysis it is relevant to discuss briefly a
fundamental problem which gave rise to animosities both
between the British and Australians and among AAMC officers
themselves. There was a lack of local (i.e. Australian) control at
the hospitals, and for this both they and the Australian
Government must take the blame.

Surgeon-General Ford, the DMS Egypt, was not familiar
with the AAMC, Australian regulations or with the sometimes

vaguely-stated wishes of the Australian Government. According to Fetherston 'the D.M.S. subsequently found great difficulty in directing the A.A.M.C. (added to this he had no authority outside Egypt), and was therefore anxious that a senior officer A.A.M.C., should be appointed and placed upon his Staff to act as his adviser in Australian matters and to control the internal or purely Australian side of the Corps'.[108] Subsequently Lt. Colonel Barrett, already overburdened with other duties, was made ADMS, AIF Egypt — he was later relieved of his duties.

Various letters written from the front to Fetherston are not the most salutary. Again Lt. Colonel Downes of the 3rd Australian Light Horse Field Ambulance wrote:

> Taken as a whole the officers of the AAMC are seething with discontent and growling. A lot arises from it being natural to them but a great deal is due to the fact that there is no supreme AAMC authority, but except those under Howse, we are under R.A.M.C. men who get all the plum positions and unfortunately are nearly all hopelessly incompetent and largely so from age...the AAMC men seem to be so much more able to look after the wounded and to extemporize in difficulties than the RAMC...[109]

In a memorandum of 23 September 1915 Howse wrote to his superior officer, referring the latter to Howse's earlier correspondence in which Howse had urged the appointment of an Australian officer who would be responsible to Australia. As a result of Australia's medical services being placed entirely under RAMC control, Howse believed that officers had been selected for appointments they were palpably unfitted to fill and a great deal of friction resulted. If these problems were allowed to continue they 'must ultimately mitigate against success, which can only be obtained by co-ordination'.[110]

The 'cream' of the RAMC officers had been committed to France or were filling specialist positions in London. The remainder, often brought out of retirement, were sent to the Dardanelles, whereas Australia at this time could concentrate all her resources at Gallipoli, and so she sent the best of her medical (and other) men. Hence the often stark contrast in the calibre particularly in the officers of the AAMC and the RAMC.

This is not to suggest that every doctor and member of the AAMC was absolutely competent; and in these difficult times even the most resourceful of medical officers would be pushed to their limit. For example, Howse told Fetherston that Colonel A. Sutton, who 'stood in' for Howse as a/DDMS whilst the latter was in Egypt in November 1915, 'made an absolute failure of it'.[111]

Fetherston himself was criticised for his objectivity and professionalism in compiling such reports. General Sir John Maxwell advised the Australian Governor-General not to '... put too much faith in Colonel Fetherston's reports: like some others, he is too inclined to jump at [*sic*] conclusions without full knowledge of the country or its conditions...'[112] The Governor-General (Munro-Ferguson) for his part seems to have had an antipathy to the Australian Medical Service, and particularly to Williams. When the latter's name was put forward for a knighthood in 1916, Munro-Ferguson 'noted with some bewilderment the appearance of Surgeon-General Williams in the *Gazette* as K.C.M.G. Always a "difficult" person of somewhat tarnished reputation...'[113]

The previous year Munro-Ferguson had expressed an ill-balanced interpretation of the AAMC's activities in Egypt to the King:

> [Doctors] are said to have demurred to being detailed to do work which they considered themselves too good for. [A gross generalisation, as in many cases specialists were under-utilised by the British authorities either through lack of knowledge of their skills or poor administration.] Reports of dissensions are, however quite unofficial, and arrive here through private sources only. It is therefore difficult for the Defence Dept. to take action. Some Imperial Officer will probably establish better discipline amongst Surgeons and Matrons.[114]

A subsequent internal memorandum of the Colonial Office stated that despite a search through its files on Williams, it could 'find nothing in them as to what Sir. R. Munro-Ferguson says about him in his letter to Mr. Bonar Law [cited above]. He was highly spoken of by the military...'[115]

From the British perspective, mainly (it appears) from the more senior medical officers, personal observations were equally circumspect. While Colonel Keble, the ADMS, MEF, professed admiration for many of his Australian counterparts, Howse included, he felt no hesitation in criticising those who had questioned his own abilities at Gallipoli. He spoke of one Australian doctor thus: '...if you will judge the evidence of Major Corbin in the light of his mental condition and ill-health you will see that he is taking up rather an exaggerated position, not only of his own importance but otherwise'.[116] Dr Cyril Checchi, then a young Australian medical graduate working in a RAMC unit (17th Stationary Hospital) at Cape Helles also remembers the veiled hostility shown to him and being 'treated more or less as not quite one of them' by British surgeons there.[117]

Such were the machinations, politics and personal rivalries

which bedevilled the medico-military operations at Gallipoli and in the rear. These factors together asserted undue influence on what ultimately was done for the sick and wounded on Anzac. Subsequently the relative success of the treatment and evacuation of Australians is almost remarkable, given such obstacles. One of the triumphs of the AAMC was its ability to overcome such problems, some of which sprang from its members' perceptions of their own role in the war.

CHAPTER EIGHT

Conclusions — Post Mortem

All this was somebody's fault, but God knows it was not ours, who already had a superhuman task before us. Someday, perhaps, it may be fixed to somebody holding a much higher position than any of ours. Surely a want of preparation & foresight on somebody's part?[1]

T his cry of anguish was surely an attempt to seek an explanation for what occurred at Gallipoli. Such interpretations are sometimes sought in an unreasonable quest for fixing 'blame'. The medical scenario at Gallipoli was played out with heroism, devotion and doggedness.

This work has necessarily used the military intricacies of Gallipoli as a common thread in order better to isolate the problems faced by the AAMC and to show how those problems were fashioned by tactics, inexperience, incompetence, and the sheer magnitude of the endeavour. The size of the task and the nature of the preparations undertaken were of prime importance to the role of the AAMC. 'However easy it may be to draw attention to blunders made or problems left unconsidered — and insufficient preparations to attend to casualties is an obvious example — it should be recognized that the scale of the task was unprecedented.[2] This chapter brings together a number of conclusions about the medical aspects of the Gallipoli campaign.

PROBLEMS AT THE APRIL LANDING

Well before the landing itself, the medical establishment within which the AAMC was obliged to work, was poorly prepared and ill-suited to provide the flexibility which both the nature of the campaign and the temperament and outlook of Australian medical officers demanded. The laissez faire attitude of the Australian Government to its medical services, and the Commonwealth's artless belief in the capacity of the British war machine to administer adequately the needs of Australian wounded had profound implications for the AAMC and that Corps' ability to carry out its function.

The magnitude of this amphibious exercise and its novelty caused massive difficulties, particularly for a medical service so manifestly subservient to other arms of the MEF. The uniqueness of the amphibious campaign (which despite its complexity was woefully ill-prepared) was arguably too great a challenge at times for the largely untried Australian medical services. Added to the deficiencies in numbers, experience and equipment, there was the necessary subordination of the AAMC to an Imperial machine which knew little of Australian ways. Individual events, taken together, also made a significant contribution to the later medical debacle during the first days after 25 April. Important among these was the late arrival at Lemnos of the *Hindoo*, the absence of any overall medical controlling officer at Anzac Cove, and the radio communications blackout during the landing itself.

On a smaller scale there were other contributing factors. Inadequate physical screening of AIF volunteers for poor eyesight, dental problems, rheumatism, and other deficiencies provided a peripheral, but contributory load for the AAMC.

Unfortunately Australia understood that the provision of treatment, transport and accommodation of wounded and sick troops would be undertaken by the War Office. This state of affairs was compounded by lack of arrangements as to what extent either Australia or Great Britain should be responsible for them or their administration. This applied particularly to hospital ships. Serious administrative deficiencies also derived from this lack of clearly delineated areas of responsibility and coordination between Australia and Britain.

General Bridges did not help matters by ignoring the advice of Surgeon-General Williams prior to 25 April. General

Birdwood in a desperate and well meant attempt to clear the backlog of casualties in April ordered his QMG General Carruthers into action. We have seen that Carruthers' solution was to send to Alexandria all five transport ships which were then off Anzac, thus totally upsetting even the last shreds of Birrell's overall medical evacuation plan.

Hamilton, by his decision to leave behind those directly responsible for the medical arrangements for the MEF, is guilty of poor management. It was this decision, together with secrecy and wild optimism surrounding the success of the landing, that was responsible for many of the subsequent problems encountered by the Australian medical services at Gallipoli in April.

Unit training within the AAMC had been interrupted in Egypt by the spate of illnesses there, including venereal disease, with which the medical services had to cope. Fortunately, perhaps because of the unusual circumstances of the landing, some of this unit training may have been wasted anyway. It is arguable therefore that such medical units were not seriously disadvantaged in this respect on 25 April. It can equally be said however that these units lacked, or had not practised techniques for keeping in touch in rugged terrain and in scattered formations. In addition, the usual British medical organisation for field service upon which the AAMC operated was based on land warfare, not an amphibious operation. As there was simply no space in which to deploy many of its units (e.g. tent subdivisions) it ran into trouble at the landing.

LESSONS LEARNED?

In some aspects the costly lessons of April had been learned by August; in others it was obvious that little had been gleaned from the first landings. The reason for this dichotomy may be found in the larger picture of the campaign.

Throughout the entire Dardanelles action Australia had no real control over the larger medical policies which so often affected her troops. Australian wounded and sick were at once both the beneficiary and the victim of British policies. Britain supplied and controlled the means of evacuation, directed the location and staffing of the base hospitals, provided supplies of drugs and medical equipment for a large part of 1915, and above all it established the infrastructure in which the AAMC performed as a small and very subordinate player.

Australia's Colonel Fetherston had correctly diagnosed a major weakness within the AAMC early in the campaign:

Australia should have insisted that in Australian matters it would do things in its own way, with AAMC officers in charge. Had the Australians followed the Canadian example and demanded autonomy for their medical units, the situation may well have been altogether different. The problems this caused at the April landings were still not entirely resolved by August, and a solution would not be found until 1916.

In August the Australian medical services were better prepared than many British units, despite inadequacies in areas beyond the control of the Australian medical services. Whereas in April the stretcher bearer subdivisions of the field ambulances had been restrained on board ship until the confusion of the landing had been sorted out, this was not a problem in August. At a higher level Babtie's preparations were substantially incomplete by the time of the August Offensive, with some medical reinforcements not arriving at Mudros until 7 August, and even then with equipment missing or lost. Porter's contributions have been mentioned and these must have helped avoid a repeat of the disastrous April landing. Despite his other shortcomings, Babtie had organised an expansion of hospital accommodation on Lemnos. Many of the same administrative and tactical errors were repeated and these too adversely affected the medical scenario.

Disease and sickness, absent in April, also made a contribution in that some front-line medical units were understrength in August. Conversely, finding medical personnel to care for invalid casualties on transports had been a major problem in April. This was less so in August due to more comprehensive planning and additional medical personnel at the rear. The dental issue was beginning to be addressed, and the fitness of reinforcements arriving both at Gallipoli and in Egypt from Australia, was more rigorously assessed. This eased the pressure on the AAMC at the front and the medical services on Lemnos and in Egypt. On the peninsula itself, matters were still less than satisfactory however due to the late arrival of British medical reinforcements.

Unlike the April disaster there were adequate medical stores on depot ships offshore prior to the August Offensive. The difficulty was getting the appropriate requisition orders to the ships. Stretchers were in as short supply in August as they had been in April. In August too there were traffic 'jams' caused by large numbers of reinforcements and munitions being forced up narrow defiles shared by stretcher bearers. Scenes of an overcrowded Casualty Clearing Station on the beach were reminiscent of the original landing. This unit was also faced with the same difficulties as in April — particularly in a shortage of sea transport.

Nonetheless some progress was made offshore. For instance, after the arrival of Lt. General Altham in Mudros in mid-July, the situation improved there. In addition, several Australian motor ambulances later arrived from Egypt which made life easier for the services working on Lemnos.

A number of problems which occurred early in 1915 were largely the result of the unreasonable expectations and optimism of the General Staff. There were also factors beyond the control of any of the medical authorities, such as the unexpected tenacity of the Turkish defence, the absence of a properly prepared forward base, bad weather, poor communications, and a lack of suitable medical transport.

One of the major reasons for the mismanagement of the medical services on 25 April was the failure by Birrell, Manders and Howse to appoint a senior Army medical officer to oversee the sorting and disposal of wounded on the beaches where the Australians and New Zealanders were to land. Fortunately this was one lesson well learned, and it was not repeated during the August Offensive.

To summarise then, despite better planning, the August Offensive had something in common with things which went wrong in April. There were insufficient hospital ships and small boats, a lack of effective communications and a shortage of stretchers. However, in August there were more personnel in some areas (particularly as all sub-sections of the field ambulances were utilised), there had been better and more comprehensive planning, accurate maps had been made available and there were more stores. The nomination of sufficient officers both to sort casualties and to direct them to shore or ship had at last been recognised and this was a definite improvement. There was also at least an awareness of the implications of large numbers of casualties for medical units such as stationary and general hospitals along the Lines of Communication.

'FLIES IN THE OINTMENT'

The problems faced by the medical services during the Gallipoli campaign were exacerbated by personal animosities and professional jealousies. Relations between individuals and units within the AAMC were not immune to professional and personal weaknesses and complaints about quarters, seniority, and promotions.

These strains impaired the efficacy of medical units from Gallipoli through to Cairo. Not even Howse was immune from charges of professional animosities. One of the players at Anzac, Colonel (later General Sir Brudenell) White believed that Howse was not such a great organiser, and that it was 'possible that he may have suppressed some others who might have been better administrators than he'.[3]

Undoubtedly the AAMC was subject to the same mistakes in judgement and the same professional and personal jealousies as every other wartime organisation. Too often in the past an uncritical eye has scanned the activities of the various medical services of the AIF and cast them as the unwitting (but always innocent) prey of a heartless and rigidly bureaucratic juggernaut. *Gallipoli: The Medical War* has sought to show that serious mistakes were made by the Australian Government and its own Defence Department. Most of these errors were founded on an almost naive faith in the ability of Great Britain to provide resources in abundance — Australia assumed that it was the only country or Dominion which mattered (this applied particularly to the supply of hospital ships).

For their part the British military authorities must answer for the lack of adequate arrangements in coordinating Lines of Communications units which caused the loss of many surgical cases. The AIF must shoulder responsibility for a number of 'casualties', particularly dental cases. Poor screening of men at Australian recruit depots, 'cheating' by over-eager volunteers, and laxity on the part of civilian doctors employed for medical inspections were at the source of later medical trouble at Gallipoli.

Certainly in 1914 there is a case for stating that the Australian medical services were beset with State jealousies. This argument weakens after April when an *esprit de corps* began to consolidate itself. Whilst it cannot be denied that there were bouts of infighting within the AAMC, the effect on its capacity to function was not seriously impaired, as most of the acrimony was confined to Egypt. However this tried the Corps' morale as a whole. One of the triumphs of the AAMC was its ability to overcome such problems, some of which sprang from its members' perceptions of their own role in the war.

The selflessness and highly visible bravery and dedication displayed by the AAMC on the peninsula and in the Lines of Communication, was to hold an important place in the later folklore of the Anzacs. Both at the initial landing and throughout the subsequent campaign there is no doubt that individual

medical personnel acquitted themselves admirably. The following awards and decorations which were made to officers and men
of the AAMC at Gallipoli testify to that.[4]

These included two KCMGs, the Distinguished Service
Order (one of which was won by Butler himself for gallant
service), two Military Crosses, nine Distinguished Conduct
Medals, and 46 Mentioned-in-Despatches. No member of the
AAMC or the RAMC won a VC (although Howse had received
this decoration during the Boer War) at Gallipoli. Several British
medical officers were so honoured on the Western Front. As only
one DSO and one MC were awarded to RAMC personnel at
Gallipoli, Butler had no reason to fear that the AAMC had been
'hard done by'.

Private Kirkpatrick at Gallipoli and Private Latimer at Cape
Helles were the most obvious candidates for the Victoria Cross,
although there were undoubtedly many others. It is interesting
to note that ('Simpson') Private J. Kirkpatrick's CO was killed by
a bomb shortly after asking for details to recommend him for the
Victoria Cross.

COPING DURING THE CALM

The period after the August Offensive and the hot summer on
Gallipoli together constituted a 'lull' in heavy and large-scale
fighting. In the absence of large numbers of battle casualties the
medical services were kept more than busy. Many of the original
medical units, in common with their fighting colleagues, were
exhausted. As discussed above, professional rivalries continued,
but these mainly affected the medical units at the rear.

With the hot weather came disease and sickness — mainly
dysentery, diarrhoea and enteric fever. The policy of retaining
men at the front worked against standard practice in epidemi-
ology, which was isolation. Thus re-infection was almost
guaranteed. In several field ambulances 'holding' facilities were
set up where sick (as opposed to wounded) men could have a few
days' break on 'soft' rations. The onset of disease exacerbated the
shortages of medical manpower at the front and caused a backlog
of sick men in the field ambulances and other smaller medical
units at Anzac.

The largely unsuccessful battle against the fly continued
during this time. This period also coincided with an acute
shortage of water, and inadequacies in the supply and variety of
rations.

The daily routine continued with delousing, sick parades, and the preparation for winter. This meant the laying in of stores, the consolidation of old dug-outs, and other medical housekeeping chores, and sanitation. A highlight was the arrival of the 2nd Division in August. Subsequently the 1st and 2nd Ambulances were relieved by the 6th, while the 4th Australian Field Ambulance went to Lemnos after being relieved by the 7th Ambulance.

Overall then this was a time for consolidation and battling against disease, both tasks which fully occupied the medical services — particularly those AAMC units at the front.

SUMMING UP

With regard to Sir Ian Hamilton's generalship, some commentators maintain that 'a picture of unrelieved incompetence by Hamilton and his staff at every level cannot be maintained'.[5] This author may be placed in the school of those like Colonel (later General) C.C. Brudenell White who noted 'that Gen. Hamilton's concern in his L. of C. [Lines of Communication] appears to have been of the slightest. He took everything for granted, and took but the slightest concern in the arrangements for preventing the emasculation of his Force by unnecessary losses through sickness and wounds.'[6]

Such an attitude was reflected in an unsympathetic General Staff. This is not to suggest total indifference, but up to that time it was not popularly recognised by General Staff officers how valuable a part the auxiliary branches must play in an operation of such complexity in 'modern' warfare. The multiplicity of command within the medical services and the total dependence of the AAMC on British (medical) Lines of Communication units plus the dependence of medical units generally on the Royal Navy for transport, did little to keep before Hamilton the importance of the role of the medical services of either Britain or Australia.

Surgeon-General Birrell was, if not incompetent, then out of his depth in his appointment. This was known for some time before action was taken to remove him. The Dardanelles Commission and its conclusions suggest that Birrell at least was treated as something of a scapegoat, as a number of other senior officers were equally culpable, for example Ford, Keble and Braithwaite among others. Conversely, there were examples of a more competent type of British medical officer, perhaps best personified at the very senior level by Sir James Porter and Sir Alfred Keogh.

The bronzed Anzac is still a strong popular myth in Australia. Few texts point out that the men suffered the same psychological and disciplinary problems as other troops serving in the MEF. J. Murray was one of a number of British authors who published their own experiences of these phenomena (Murray belonged to the Royal Naval Volunteer Reserve).[7] One of his colleagues put his thumb over the muzzle of his rifle and pulled the trigger, and Murray had to cut the remnants of the finger off with a marlinspike. Episodes of disobedience, shirking of responsibility, cowardice, self-mutilation, fear, jealousies and dishonesty did occur — all traits which extended to members of the medical services.

One caveat perhaps is the particular disadvantage of the AAMC in respect to competent management, at least until Howse assumed proper control in 1916. In a letter to Fetherston from General Brudenell White, dated 18 September 1915, Cairo, the latter had identified this problem: 'I particularly wished to talk over with you the medical arrangements for the Australian Troops [sic]. The present position is by no means satisfactory. It is useless to blame individuals for what has occurred...It is the lack of organisation and not so much the defection of individuals which causes the present unsatisfactory position.'[8]

There were also cases of medical officers beating a hasty retreat to the safety of Cairo's hospitals. While Butler either explicitly mentions, or alludes to, such things, the reader is left with the impression that the *Official History* supports rather than distracts from the Anzac Legend.

At a grass-roots level the vast majority of men who found themselves sick or wounded on the peninsula, and who were committed to the care of their medical services, were treated in the best way possible given the conditions of time and place. The preceding chapters have demonstrated that this aim could only be achieved by the medical service making do with (and sometimes in spite of) circumstances completely beyond its control.

The medical war at Gallipoli was a strange amalgam of lost opportunities, wasted lives and hidden glory. There is no doubt that some of the major problems which beset the medical arrangements at Gallipoli could have been avoided. Some responsibility rests with the Imperial authorities. However, Williams, Howse and Manders must bear responsibility for a number of the problems which occurred in Egypt in the months preceding April, and particularly in complicating last minute changes to plans being made in the week preceding the infamous landing on the morning of Sunday, 25 April 1915.

As a volunteer force, the medical units of the AIF reflected a variety of different backgrounds — from blacksmiths to barmen. Their training had been relatively short and the lack of time meant that few had been trained in specialist areas prior to April. Despite this they adapted quickly and carried out a variety of tasks to the satisfaction of their officers. 'They dressed hideous wounds efficiently, helped us intelligently to adjust splints to hateful compound fractures, gave chloroform hundreds of times and assisted at operations. All this was done in a quiet matter-of-fact way, no fainting, no vomiting, just a steady attention to duty.'[9] Added to such pressures were the additional occupational hazards of bullet or shrapnel which such personnel shared with all who found themselves on Gallipoli.

The Australian Army Medical Corps received its 'baptism of fire' at Gallipoli, which moulded it into the efficient organisation it became after 1915. The stage at Gallipoli was set by Great Britain which supplied the major performers, while a relatively small part was accorded to Australia. The AAMC therefore evolved under the shadow of its larger ally. In the few areas in which it had autonomy the Australian medical services too reflected some of the contradictions of efficiency and pettiness which characterised several senior officers in the British MEF. However under the resolute leadership of capable officers, together with a growing appreciation of the independence of their Corps, these problems were grappled with and largely solved by the time the Gallipoli campaign drew to a close.

It was out of the brutal tragedy of Anzac that a tradition of medical care and organisation was born, a tradition which began to utilise many uniquely Australian qualities. The Australian medical services came out of the Gallipoli campaign sobered by its experiences, having served its sick and wounded admirably.

Appendices

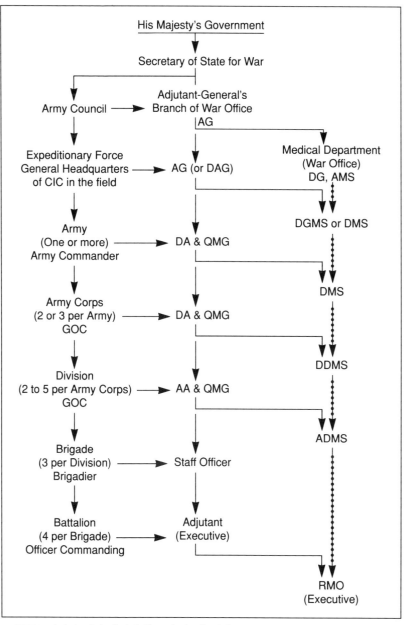

indicates chain of technical (or professional) control.

APPENDIX 1   The chain of control in respect of the medical department of the
adjutant-general's branch of the British army during the Great War.
Source: A.G. Butler, Vol. I, p. 812

Appendix II(a)

A Chronological Outline of the Events Leading Up To, and During the Gallipoli Campaign

1914

November 2 – The first shelling of the Dardanelles forts by British and French squadrons.

5 – Britain and France officially declare war on Turkey.

December 3 – Australian and New Zealand troops disembark at Alexandria in Egypt.

1915

February 19 – Naval attack on the Turkish forts at the entrance of the Dardanelles.

April   12 – First transports arrive at Mudros Harbour on the island of Lemnos.

24 – Troops leave for the Dardanelles.

25 – French troops land at Kum Kale, British at Cape Helles, the 1st Australian Division half a mile offcourse at Anzac Cove.

May   5 – 2nd Australian Brigade and NZ Infantry Brigade leave for Cape Helles.

12 – 2nd and 3rd Light Horse Field Ambulances land at Anzac.

24 – Armistice to bury dead of both sides.

August   6 – The August Offensive begins with a series of feints in the Anzac sector.

6/7 – Australian attack at Lone Pine, Quinn's Post and Russell's Top, as part of an Allied Offensive.

October   11 – Lord Kitchener, Secretary of State for War, asks Sir Ian Hamilton the estimated cost of evacuating all troops from the Dardanelles.

12 – Hamilton replies that evacuation was inconceivable.

16 – Kitchener recalls Hamilton.

17 – Hamilton leaves the Gallipoli theatre.

20 – General Monro named as replacement.

23 – Monro's first visit to Gallipoli.

November   – Winter weather deteriorates further.

27 – Commencement of 'The Great Blizzard'.

13 – Kitchener visits Anzac.

December 8 – Monro orders General Birdwood, GOC ANZAC, to evacuate troops from Anzac and Suvla Bay.

10/11 – Sick/wounded, surplus troops, stores removed.

15 – Detailed orders issued for evacuation.

19 – The last night of evacuation.

20 – Evacuation of Anzac and Suvla completed by daylight. Troops disembarked at Lemnos.

1916

January   9 – Evacuation from Cape Helles completed.

1918

October   31 – Turkey surrenders.

Appendix II(b) Medical and Military 'Who's Who'

(Non-Australians are designated thus:★)

★ Altham Lt. Gen. Sir E.A., Appointed Inspector General of Communications, MEF on 15 July 1915. An able administrator, he was highly critical of the disparate nature of the medical evacuation 'system'. He was responsible for the shipping and casualty accommodation immediately prior to the December withdrawal from Gallipoli.

★ Aldridge, Lt. Col. A.R., ADMS Sanitary MEF. Formerly the Professor of Hygiene at the RAMC College in London. He arrived at Imbros on 30 July to superintend disease prevention which was becoming a significant cause of non-battle casualties and was of major concern to medical officers in the field.

Aspinall, Maj. A. (Archie) J. Attached to the 1st AFA. He wrote of the appalling conditions on board the *Itonus* and contributed a number of articles to the Medical Journal of Australia both during Gallipoli and for the remainder of the War.

★ Babtie, Lt. Gen. Sir W., PDSA Levant. A 56 year old South Africa VC, was the Director of Medical Services in India before his Dardanelles appointment.

Barrett, Lt. Col. G.I. Melbourne ophthalmologist. Made 'ex officio' ADMS to the Australian Forces in Egypt by Ford. This did nothing to diminish his unpopularity amongst his colleagues. An able man but overburdened with numerous responsibilities including the administration of the Australian Red Cross in Egypt (until his forced resignation in September 1915). He was also the Registrar and oculist to No 1 AGH. After two enquiries in 1915 cleared him of any wrongdoing he went to England and finished the war in the RAMC. After the Great War he continued a vigorous public life until his death in 1945 (see also chapter eight).

Bean, Lt. Col. H.K., CO, 2nd LHFA.

Bean, Maj. J.W.B., RMO 3 Btn. Brother of the famous war historian; he was wounded at Gallipoli on 25 April and wrote of his experiences of medical evacuation. He returned and was wounded for a second time in August. Adopted the issue of rum in his Battalion from early August, mainly in order to get the men to eat their tedious rations.

★ Bedford, Maj. Gen. W.G.A., DMS MEF. This officer replaced Surgeon-General Birrell on 19 September 1915.

Beeston, Col. J.L. K.O., 4th AFA. He kept one of the more interesting diaries at Gallipoli. He was also a frequent contributor to the Medical Journal of Australia. He succeeded Col. Begg (NZMC) on 16 August as ADMS ANZAC Division.

Begg, Col. C.M. (NZMC), acting ADMS ANZAC Division. He was wounded on 16 August.

Bell, Principal Matron J., No 1 AGH. An innovative Scottish migrant who, upon the outbreak of war, fought hard to have the nursing service in the military sphere properly organised and recognised. She recruited Victorian nurses to No 1 AGH. Largely thwarted in establishing greater autonomy and clear responsibilities for the AANS, she was summarily dismissed in absentia from the No 1 AGH and was recalled to Australia in August 1915. As with Barrett, she was cleared by a formal enquiry, but elected to continue her career at the Melbourne Hospital as lady superintendent.

★Birdwood, General Sir W.R., GOC ANZAC Corps. He took unofficial command of the AIF after Bridges' death on 18 May. While he initially opposed the withdrawal from Gallipoli, once he was made responsible for it, its success was due mainly to his leadership rather than tactical skills. He was instrumental in appointing Colonel Brudenell White as his chief-of-staff.

★Birrell, Maj. Gen. W.G., DMS MEF. At 56 years of age he did not enjoy good health, and the responsibilities of his position were completely beyond him; in addition he did not have the confidence of the General Staff. Used as a scapegoat by the Dardanelles Commission in 1917.

★Braithwaite, Maj. Gen. W.F., Chief of the General Staff. Possibly one of the most disliked men at Gallipoli, certainly on Hamilton's staff. Evidence points to this staff officer refusing to delay the 25 April landing so as to ensure the medical arrangements were properly finalised. Braithwaite was instrumental in separating the 'non-fighting' arms from the General Staff in the crucial preparatory stages of the campaign. His evidence to the Dardanelles Commission was sometimes contradictory. Often regarded as having no concern for the welfare of the troops in his command; was instrumental in shielding Hamilton from 'troublesome' medical and supply officers.

Bridges, Maj. Gen. Sir W.T., GOC AIF. This officer (who created the name AIF) was not a popular man and in 1914 was acting-Chief of the General Staff in Australia. He had (unusually) a good working relationship with Howse. He was shot by a sniper on 15 May and died from gangrene three days later.

Bryant, Lt. Col. H.W., CO No 1 ASH.

Butler, Col. A.G., RMO 9th Btn. Australia's only medical DSO at Gallipoli; author of the three volume *Official History of the Australian Army Medical Services*.

Butler, Lt. Col. H.N., CO 3rd AFA.

Carbery, Lt. Col. A.D. (NZMC) Sanitary Officer to the ANZAC Division. He later wrote *The New Zealand Medical Service in the Great War*.

*Carruthers, Brig. Gen. R.A., DA & QMG ANZAC Corps. He was the chief administrator of Birdwood's staff. When matters deteriorated on 26 April he was instrumental in advising Hamilton that a successful withdrawal at that stage was impossible. He was also responsible for the overall medical arrangements at the April landing. In the absence of any clear scheme of orders he ordered the retirement of several improvised hospital ships from Gallipoli thus incurring the wrath of Birrell (see chapters three and five).

Corbin, Lt. Col. J., 1st ACCS. A frequent witness before the Dardanelles Commission as his post was in the thick of the casualty work in both the April and August operations at Gallipoli.

Dawson, Lt. Col. A.L., DADMS AIF in Egypt, later ADMS.

Downes, Col. R.M. A Melbourne surgeon who was to command 3 LHFA during 1915 and acted as ADMS during Begg's absence for several days in November. He wrote about disaffection in the AAMC ranks over junior doctors fresh from Australia being promoted over the heads of officers who had been at Gallipoli for some time. An innovative officer whose military career blossomed in 1916 when he became ADMS of the ANZAC Mounted Division. In 1934 he was appointed DGMS and went on to train many of the medical officers who saw action in the Second World War.

Fenwick, Col. P.C. (NZMC) One of the first staff officers to land at Anzac; frequently experienced British anti-colonialism at its worst and documented several cases. He was evacuated sick from Gallipoli on 15 June. Together with a very small staff this officer was later responsible for the health of thousands of Australian and New Zealand troops who were stationed in the great Training Camp at Zeitoun (about 15 kilometres north of Cairo).

Fetherston, Maj. Gen. R.H.J., Acting DGMS Australia. Took over from General Williams in 1915 as Australia's de facto chief military doctor. Critical of Imperial administration both on Gallipoli and in Egypt. Sought to place an Australian in sole command of AAMC units in these areas (see also chapter eight). A staunch supporter of Howse, he was promoted major general in 1916.

Fiaschi, Col. T.H., CO No 3 AGH. A colourful Sydney surgeon with a Boer War DSO and Italian decorations for his service in the Abyssinian War (1886). He set up the No 3 AGH on Lemnos in July 1915. He was later invalided to England in November 1915. After serving as an independent agent for the Italian government, he re-joined the AAMC in 1917.

★Ford, Maj. Gen. Sir R.W., DMS Forces in Egypt. Superintended all AAMC units, hospitals in Egypt. Opposed and hindered any moves to autonomy by the Australians. Complicated matters by appointing the inexperienced Barrett as ADMS AIF.

Fraser, Lt. Col. Succeeded H.K. Bean as CO 2nd LHFA.

Giblin, Col. W.W., OC. No. 1 ACCS, Medical Control Officer at Anzac.

Gibson, Lockhart Major J. An eye specialist who did wonderful work on Lemnos. He brought most of his own equipment with him which enabled him to undertake operations which none of the Allied medical units could carry out.

★Godley, Gen. Sir A.J., GOC ANZAC Division (and from November 1915, the ANZAC Corps). A professional but very austere soldier who welded New Zealand's forces into an efficient fighting machine.

★Hamilton, Gen. Sir I., C-in-C, MEF. A South Africa veteran who at very short notice was sent by Kitchener to the Mediterranean to weld an invasion force. Hampered throughout by the lack of reinforcements and equipment, he was eventually recalled on 17 October. He suffered from periods of lack of confidence during which he repeatedly deferred to the wishes of his junior staff officers — Braithwaite in particular. He had no real conception of matters medical and took few steps to find out for himself what the real situation was, particularly in terms of evacuation procedures and the often inadequate treatment accorded to the wounded on board ship. He disliked and distrusted Howse.

Howse, Col. N.R., A South Africa VC PMO AN & MEF, later DDMS, ANZAC Corps. A high profile personality in this conflict and one of the prime movers in establishing the AAMC as an entity separate from RAMC administration. He has been eulogised in official chronicles but suffered from a number of shortcomings, most noticeably inability to delegate and a tendency to be in the thick of things rather than supervise. This is demonstrated most dramatically by his actions on 25 April.

*Joly de Lotbiniere, Maj-Gen. A. Director of Works MEF. A competent engineer who turned Lemnos into a proper military base with docks, water supply, roads and other facilities.

*Keble, Col. A.E.C., ADMS, MEF. An ambitious officer who rose to become DMS (superseding Surgeon General Bedford). He was at various times Medical Control Officer at Anzac, ADMS, MEF. He was the first doctor to see the General Staff's original plan for the evacuation of wounded from Gallipoli and denounced it as wholly insufficient. He drew up a revised plan under Surgeon-General Birrell's signature. He was critical of the actions of Howse and Manders on 25 April, but was himself partly to blame. He was an inconsistent witness before the Dardanelles Commission.

*Keogh, Lt. Gen. Sir A., DGAMS Britain's chief military doctor. Generally supported efficiency moves by Williams and Howse and the eventual appointment of an Australian to look after the interests of the AAMC in the Dardanelles/Egyptian theatre.

*Koe, Maj. Gen. F.W.B., Director of Supply & Transport MEF.

*Maher, Lt. Col., DDMS L of C MEF, acted as a Medical Control Officer at Anzac, later ADMS, MEF. One of the betes noirs of the AAMC, an ambitious and overtly anti-colonial officer. He was responsible for controlling medical evacuation from Anzac and the working of all temporary hospital ships and for the return to the front of recovered convalescents, for administering Lemnos as an advanced medical base and particularly for sending medical supplies and medical reinforcements to Gallipoli. He was conveniently absent during the hearings of the Dardanelles Commission.

*Manders, Col. N., (NZMC) Manders had been DDMS for the British Army in Egypt. Technically senior to Howse he acted for a short time as DDMS for the Australian and New Zealand Corps up to the April landing, when he relinquished this position to resume his duties as ADMS for the NZ & A Division. He was not replaced, a situation which had serious consequences for the evacuation of wounded from Anzac Cove in the days following

25 April. A thorough and able commander he was killed by a sniper's bullet to the head on 9 August.

Martin, Col. T.M., CO No 2 AGH. As SMO, AIF he was the formal liaison officer in dealings with General Ford (until Lt. Col. Barrett was appointed ADMS, AIF); he was also responsible for all medical supplies.

*Maxwell, General Sir J., GOC, Egypt. Presumably on the advice of General Ford he vetoed General Williams' appointment as DMS, AIF and was instrumental in sidestepping Williams by recommending that he stay in London. In September he also blocked a recommendation from Birdwood to Hamilton that Howse be despatched to Egypt to sort out the situation there. The subsequent problems experienced by the AAMC in Egypt were derived for the most part from these actions. He repeatedly worked against Hamilton, particularly in failing to supply the latter with reinforcements.

*May, Surg. Vice-Admiral Sir A., Director General Medical Department, Royal Navy. He was Sir James Porter's superior.

*Mayo-Robson, Col. Sir A. W. Consulting Surgeon to the MEF. Robson established a number of surgical principles to be carried out in the Gallipoli campaign as some of the surgical procedures then in use in France were not or could not be used to the same advantage at Gallipoli — notably the standard practice on the Western Front of opening up all wounds to allow drainage (see chapter four).

*Methuen, Field Marshal Lord, Governor of Malta. Critical of the lack of medical transport preparation prior to the April landing and suggested ships steam direct to Malta rather than proceeding to Egypt then on to Malta.

Monash, Col. J. CO 4th Infantry Brigade. Wrote home about the poor state of his troops and the necessity for them to be properly rested. This was later carried out when 'Rest Camps' were set up for Diggers who had been on Gallipoli since April.

*Monro, General Sir C.C. Took control of the MEF from Hamilton after commanding the 3rd Army in France. He suggested a withdrawal from the peninsula.

Newmarch, Lt. Col. B.J. CO 1st AFA.

*Phillimore, Commodore R.F. PNTO Dardanelles. One of his functions was to assist in directing casualty traffic back along the Lines of Communication, and in forwarding and distributing medical stores to the front.

Porter, Vice-Admiral Sir J., PHTO Levant. Appointed to sort out inefficiencies with the medical evacuation of casualties from Gallipoli to hospitals in the rear. Did good work but was frustrated by dual control and recalled at the instigation of the military.

*Purves-Stewart, Col. Sir J. Consulting Physician to the MEF. He was the first senior doctor to pick up the over-representation of Diggers in non-battle casualty statistics and to identify reasons for this.

Reid, Sir G. Australian High Commissioner, London.

Reilly, Col. C.C., DDMS Dardanelles in medical control of the peninsula.

Ryan, Col. C.S. Consulting Surgeon to the AIF. A sixty year old veteran of the Russo-Turkish War of 1878 and decorated by the Sultan, Ryan was appointed as Medical Officer to the staff of General Birdwood, after serving for a short time as the ADMS to the 1st Australian Division (then taken on by Howse). He was evacuated to England in June 1915 with typhoid fever and from July 1916 he served as Consulting Surgeon to the AIF.

Sturdee, Col. A.H. OC 2nd AFA. Appointed ADMS to the 1st Australian Division in February 1916.

Sutton, Col. A., CO 3rd AFA, later acting DDMS ANZAC Corps (a post for which Howse thought he was thoroughly unsuited). Despite this Sutton was appointed ADMS 2nd Australian Division in 1916.

*Thom, Col. G. St. T., ADMS. L of C MEF. Controlled medical evacuation from Cape Helles.

*Vyvyan, Capt. V. RN Naval Beach Master at Anzac. Was of the view that the arrangements made for the evacuation of the wounded at Anzac at the outset were totally inadequate.

White, Lt. Col. (later General Sir) C.B.B., GSO 1st Aust. Division. White was one of the first senior officers to realise — on the evening of 25 April — that the campaign had failed, at least in obtaining its objectives. He was responsible for the detailed scheme for the final withdrawal from Gallipoli.

Williams, Sir W.D.C. A South African veteran, he was Surgeon General, DMS AIF from 1914–1915. One of the 'forgotten' characters of the medical war and of the AAMC generally despite the fact that he was almost a founding father of that Corps. He did good work in England as DDMS, AIF from November 1915 working directly under the War Office. The Australian Governor-General later carried out a smear campaign against him.

Winter, Brig. Gen. S.H., Deputy Quartermaster-General.

*Woodward, Brig. General E.M., Deputy Adjutant-General. Opposed the General Staff's initial casualty evacuation plan for April as 'altogether inadequate'. He managed to see Hamilton despite Braithwaite's objections and was successful in having the casualty estimates upgraded to a more realistic figure.

Appendix III(a)
MEDICAL ARRANGEMENTS FOR THE LANDING OF THE M E F

(Issued by the Director of Medical Services, MEF)

1. With each covering force the bearer sub-divisions of a Field Ambulance and one tent sub-division will be landed with as much medical and surgical material as can be man-handled by the personnel, giving a total of 150 medical personnel with each covering force.

2. At 2 P.M. on day of landing the personnel of the Casualty Clearing Stations (one for the 29th Division and one for the Australian and New Zealand Army Corps) will be landed with as much surgical and medical material as can be man-handled.

3. When the remainder of the division lands the rest of the Field Ambulances and the equipment of the Casualty Clearing Stations will be put on shore as soon as it can be disembarked.

4. 2 hospital ships will be available
With the 29th Division *Sicilia*
    Accommodation serious cases   400
With the A.N.Z. Army Corps *Gascon*
    Accommodation serious cases   500

5. I understand from the Senior Naval Transport Officer that the Navy will commence the transport of wounded from the shore to the ships about 2 P.M.

The means of evacuation are as follows:
3 launches each capable of holding 12 cots are available for the 29th Division andthe same number for the A.N.Z. Army Corps. These launches are to be towed to the hospital ships in which the men are to be accommodated.

The following transports are allotted to the 29th Division for accommodation of casualties:

(a) B2 *Caledonia*	400 serious cases	1200–1500 slight cases	
B7 *Aragon*	400 ” ”	1200–1500 ” ”	
B9 *Dongola*	400 ” ”	1200–1500 ” ”	
(b) Allotted to the A.N.Z. Army Corps:			
A25 *Lutzow*	200 serious cases	1000 slight cases	
A1 *Ionian*	100 ” ”	1000 ” ”	
A15 *Clan McGillivray*	100 ” ”	600 ” ”	
A31 *Seang Chun*	100 ” ”	600 ” ”	

Medical personnel and medical and surgical equipment for the *Caledonian*, *Aragon* and *Dongola* have been provided by No. 15 Stationary Hospital and for the *Clan McGillivray* and *Seang Chun* by the A. & N.Z. Corps field ambulances at present, and later by No. 2 Australian Hospital. The *Lutzow* and *Ionian* to be supplied later with medical and surgical equipment from No. 2 Australian Hospital. The personnel and equipment of No. 16 Stationary Hospital is kept in reserve.

6. No. 4 Advanced Depot Medical Stores in *Anglo-Egyptian* is placed at the disposal of A. & N.Z.A. Corps, and No. 5 Advance Depot Medical Stores at disposal of 29th Division.

7. It is proposed to evacuate ships with casualties direct to Alexandria and Malta.

8. No.1 Australian Hospital at Mudros to be used for sick from shipping to Lemnos.

W.G. Birrell,
Surgeon-General.

General Headquarters,
S.S.*Arcadian*,
24/4/15

ORDERS FOR THE FRENCH DIVISION
Corps Expeditionnaire D/Orient — Alexandria,
15.4.1915, sqnd. D'Amade:

Ordre general no–12.

Medical Service

During the covering phase and at the beginning of the development stage, the regimental medical service will be set up. An individual field dressing must be used for each of the wounded; the Corps doctors will endeavour to group the wounded at appropriate points close to a beach.

As many as possible of those men who have received initial treatment should be evacuated to first aid posts, established on board boats where the personnel and medical material will be used. A post of this nature will be set up on every boat where there is a naval doctor, where there are the means of easy transportation between the boat and the shore.

The most seriously wounded will be directed to the hospital ship "Duguay-Trouin", kept sufficiently far from the action so that there is no risk of enemy fire and it will set up the appropriate means of transport between it and the coast. This will apply to all other hospital ships of which the CEO can make use.

No. 1 Ambulance arrives with the first group of ships. It will unload as soon as circumstances permit; it will operate on the ground to hospitalise and to dress wounds.

No. 2 Ambulance arrives with the second group of ships. When it has disembarked, it will make itself available to follow progressive troop movements.

As regards the field hospital it will arrive with the third group of ships. It will set up as soon as circumstances permit. 10

Marabout tents will be given to it as its first issue. It will set up at the site of No. 2 Ambulance which will be relieved. From this time two ambulances will be available to follow up progressive troop movements.

Finally, as soon as one can come from Mudros, an evacuation hospital will be set up and operate.

APPENDIX III(b)
MEDICAL ARRANGEMENTS FOR THE EVACUATION OF THE M E F

SOURCE: AWM 27 370.2[16]

EXTRACT FROM DARDANELLES ARMY ORDER NO. 2

"During the Intermediate stage and the first night of the Final Stages the arrangements for the evacuation of the sick and wounded will be normal. During the final stage lightly wounded cases must embark with the fighting troops.

Two Hospital lighters will be provided for conveyance of badly wounded cases to the hospital ships. Other Hospital ships will be held in readiness at Mudros or Imbros to come up at short notice.

Hospital accommodation for 2 000 patients, together with the medical personnel required for their care will be organised to receive such cases as cannot be evacuated during the final stage.

Arrangements will be made to store in selected areas 14 days' rations and water, with a due proportion of medical comforts for the above number of patients . . .

Lt. Col. C.F. Aspinall"

APPENDIX IV   AUSTRALIAN CASUALTIES

The following figures are synoptic, but they illustrate the most relevant aspects of medical and military operations discussed in this thesis. All figures are derived from A.G. Butler, Vols I and III.

Table 1: Total Battle Casualties:
Killed:	5833
D.O.W.:	1983
W.I.A.:	19 441
P.O.W.:	70

Table 2: Total Non-Battle Casualties

Died of Disease:	569
Died of other causes (accidents etc):	31
Sickness:	63 969

Table 3: Deaths per thousand of 'Exposed to Risk' among AIF overseas during 1915:

	AIF	South African Campaign
Enteric Fevers	2.32	18.06
Dysentery	1.19	3.02
Diarrhoea	0.12	0.05
Other 'intestinal'	0.17	0.05
Other 'infections'	5.00	0.20
Other diseases	2.28	0.20
All diseases	11.68	24.58
D.O.W.	38.69	3.92
K.I.A.	113.65	9.95
Total Deaths	164.65	38.09

Table 4: Types of Wounds Incurred by Australian Troops in 1915: ★
[★This analysis is typical for the Dardanelles theatre]

Region of body	Total wounds & accidents	Total died from wounds in medical units	Mortality rate %
Head (including scalp)	2120	381	17.9
Face	1346	76	5.6
Neck	398	28	7.0
Chest	1104	159	14.4
Abdomen	736	287	38.9
Perineum (bladder, rectum)	90	9	10.0
Back	1367	107	7.8
Upper extremities	6323	122	1.9
Lower extremities	7663	302	3.9
Unclassified		433	6.8
	21 580	1471	

Table 5: The Increase in the Rate of Sickness At Anzac:

MONTHLY EVACUATIONS: NATURE

	Sick	Wounded	Total
August	12 968	30 585	43 553
September	22 209	3639	25 848
October	21 991	2620	24 611
Total:	57 168	36 844	94 012

Table 6: Deaths from Wounds at Sea between Gallipoli and the Bases — 1915

	APR	MAY	JUN	JUL	AUG	SEP	OCT	NOV	DEC
1	–	5	6	–	4	2	1	–	2
2	–	12	2	2	3	–	–	–	–
3	–	13	3	1	1	6	1	–	2
4	–	24	3	–	–	3	1	1	2
5	–	7	4	2	2	2	–	1	–
6	–	10	3	1	12	1	1	2	–
7	–	11	2	2	23	3	1	–	–
8	–	7	2	2	38	3	–	1	–
9	–	4	2	1	26	2	–	3	–
10	–	9	2	3	32	3	2	–	–
11	–	5	–	1	28	1	1	3	–
12	–	10	1	4	9	–	–	–	–
13	–	4	3	2	7	–	2	1	1
14	–	9	–	7	7	2	–	–	–
15	–	6	2	3	8	2	–	–	1
16	–	7	–	–	1	2	2	1	2
17	–	4	5	1	1	2	3	–	1
18	–	1	–	6	2	6	1	–	–
19	–	7	3	1	2	–	2	1	1
20	–	12	5	4	4	4	1	2	–
21	–	7	1	2	1	1	1	2	–
22	–	5	1	2	3	4	1	–	–
24	–	4	2	5	5	2	1	–	–
25	13	9	4	3	1	2	–	–	–
26	20	3	3	2	–	2	–	–	–
27	22	4	1	3	1	–	–	1	–
28	14	5	6	1	7	–	–	1	–
29	32	6	11	4	5	–	–	–	–
30	18	8	3	4	19	2	1	–	–
31	–	–	1	–	1	3	–	1	–
	119	232	81	73	259	5	29	20	12

Total = 876

(Source: AWM 27   376.04[6].)

*Table 7: Statistics of Troops treated by the Australian Army Dental
Services in 3rd AGH Lemnos, August–December 1915*

Australians	4040
New Zealanders	552
British Troops	1691
	6283

APPENDIX V
VESSELS USED FOR THE RECEPTION, TREATMENT AND MOVEMENT OF CASUALTIES DURING THE GALLIPOLI CAMPAIGN[1]

Hospital ships and carriers	Transports, troopships and other vessels
Aquitania	*Alauria*
Braemar Castle	*Aragon*
Britannic	*Arcadian*
Delta	*Ascarius*
Devanah	*Caledonian*
Dongola	*Clan*
McGillivray Dunluce Castle	
Derflinger	
Galeka	*Franconia*
Gascon	*Georgia*
Gloucester Castle	*Hindoo*
Grantala (Aust. Navy)	*Itonus*
Guildford Castle	*Kyarra*
Karanowna (Aust) (Yacht)	*Liberty*
Karoola (Aust.)	*Lutzow*
Letitia	*Mashobra*
Maheno (NZ)	*Osmanieh*
Mauretania	*Seang Bee*
Neuralia	*Seang Choon*
Sicilia	*Southland*
Somali (Royal Navy)	
Soudan (Royal Navy)	

Appendix VI
Colonel Howse's Proposed (Medical) Scheme for the Final Evacuation,[2] dated 13 December 1915

'Submitted following proposals to G.O.C. Army Corps.

1. On last 2 days of evacuation only 2 Med units will remain at Anzac. (a) 1st A.C.C.S. (b) 13th C.C.S. These stations are fully equipped for treatment of over 1200 patients in all.

2. Tents of F. Ambs and their Dressing Stations have been left standing in many places at Anzac. There is a sufficient supply of dressings and with a few personnel these places would serve for the immediate treatment of wounded.

3. A small no. of A.A.M.C. of No. 1 A.C.C.S. and N.Z.M.C. and Indian bearers will be left with battalions and shd. [sic] if possible embark with them.

4. Major Campbell A.A.M.C. O/C No. 1 A.C.C.S. will be the S.M.O. of units named in plan.

5. O/C No. 1 A.C.C.S. and 13th C.C.S. have received instructions from me to be ready at very short notice for embarking on last day of evacuation, but under no conditions to embark without written instructions from G.O.C. Anzac.

6. I presume both these units will remain in the event of a no. of casualties occurring, but if only 1 unit required I wd. suggest No. 1 A.C.C.S. as being better equipped and more sheltered from shell fire and weather.

7. In the event of a large number of casualties remaining after we have completed evacuation I have advised the S.M.O. to apply for bearers from the G.O.C. enemy so that our wounded may be collected and treated in C.C.S.

8. A M.O. who speaks French perfectly has been detailed to each unit.

9. In my opinion the officer selected for command at final evacuation should grant Major Campbell S.M.O. and myself an interview at an early date so that we both may clearly understand the final arrangements for the protection and treatment of our wounded.'

APPENDIX VII(a)[3]
DESCRIPTION OF A FIRST FIELD DRESSING

'The field dressing, pattern 1911, consists of an outer packet of sewn khaki cotton cloth, containing two small dressings, each complete in itself. Each single dressing consists of: (1) A loose-woven bleached cotton bandage, 2½ yards long by 2½ inches wide; (2) a piece of bleached cotton gauze, 36 inches by 23 inches, not less than 260 grains [0.2 kilo.], folded into a pad 4 inches by 3¼ inches and stitched to the bandage 18 inches from one end; (3) one safety pin. The bandage and gauze pad are enclosed in waterproof jaconet [thick cotton cloth], the edges cemented with rubber solution so as to render the packet airtight, having a portion of one of the corners turned back and not cemented. The pin is wrapped in waxed paper and attached outside the jaconet.

The gauze contains 1 per cent by weight of sal alembroth and is tinted with aniline blue. The gauze pad is folded once, so that the bandage lies outside the gauze. The short end of the bandage is folded in plaits for 18 inches from the pad and then loosely rolled for the remainder of its length. The rolled portion of the bandage is secured by a stitch to prevent unrolling. The contents are compressed so that the outer packet does not exceed 4¼ inches in length, 3⅛ inches in width, and ⅞ of an inch in thickness. Printed directions for use are upon [both the inside and outside covers].'

Appendix VII(b)
CONTENTS OF A PAIR OF
FIELD MEDICAL PANNIERS[4]

[1898 Pattern. Weight: approx 41.3 kgs.]

MEDICINES

Acid, Boric — ounces 2
    "   Carbolic (crystals), in 2 bottles — ounces 8
    "   Gallic, 5 gr. tablets — doz 9
Ammon: Carb:, 3 gr. tablets — doz. 16
Antipyrin, 5 gr. tablets — doz 10
Argent: Nit: — ounces 1
Brandy, in 2 oz. bottles — ounces .16
Chloral Hydras:, 5 gr. tablets — doz 16
Chloroform: in 2 oz. bottles — ounces 16
Ext: Opii Liq: — ounces 4
Hydrarg: Perchlor:, soloids — doz. 12
Ipecac: Pulv: sine Emetine, 5 gr. tablets in 2 oz
    bottles — doz 34
Iodoform: in vulcanite dredger with screw cap — ounces. . . .3
Mistura pro Diarrhoea — ounces. .4
Oleum Menth: Pip: — ounces 1
    "   Olivae — ounces 8
    "   Ricini, in 2 bottles 16
    "   Terebinth: — ounces. 4
Pil: Blaud:, gr. 4 — doz 4
Pill and tablet tin [containing a variety of
    tablets]. 1
Potass: Bicarb:, 10 gr. tablets — doz 8½
    "   Bromid:, 5 gr. tablets — doz 8
    "   Permanganas:, 2 gr. tablets — doz 16
Pulv.: Ipecac: Co:, 5 gr. tablets — doz. 21
Quininae Acid: Sulph:, 2 gr. tablets in 4 bottles — doz 92
    "   "   "   5 gr.   "   "   " 33
Sodii Bicarb:, 10 gr. tablets — doz 9
    "   Salicylas, 5 gr. tablets — doz 19
Spirit Ammon: Arom: — ounces. .8
Tinct: Aconiti, 5 minim tablets — doz 17
    "   Chlorof: et Morphinae — ounces 3
    "   Opii — ounces. 4
Zinci Sulph:, 5 gr. tablets — doz 8
Scissors — pair 1
Spare Bottle 1

INSTRUMENTS, ETC.

[Various articles of stationery]
Specification Tallies and pencil-book 1
Spoons, tea — No 2
Stethoscope, aluminium, — No. 1
Tongue Depressor — No 1
[Hypodermic syringes, needles and tablets for same]
[Ophthalmic tablets — various]
[Measures, test tubes, rubber tubing, spirit lamp]
[Bandages, catgut, scissors, thread, needles]
Instruments, tooth, small pouch of — pouch 1
Tape, pieces of — No. 12
Tourniquet, screw — No 6
Wool, boric, in 2 oz. packets — oz .6
Bandages, triangular — No 12
Bovril, invalid (in 4 oz. tins) — lb. .1
Knife, for opening tins — No 1
Meat, extract of (in 4 oz. tins) — lb 1
Warmers, food (spirit lamp) — No .1
Wool, double cyanide (in 4 oz. packets) — lb 1
[Adhesive plaster, gauze, basins]

CONTENTS OF A PAIR OF
FIELD SURGICAL PANNIERS[5]

[1898 Pattern. Weight: approx 41.0 kgs.]

Air cushions, 2 round, 2 square — No 4
Lantern, candle — No 1
Sheets, old linen — No 2
Bovril, invalid (in 4 oz. tins) — lb . . . . ½
Candles — No 5
Catgut, in carbolized oil — tubes 2
Corkscrew, folding — No 1
Drainage tubing in aseptic solution 3
Eye shades, celluloid, tapes to tie. 12
Gauze, double cyanide — yards .18
Horse hair, in carbolized glycerine — tubes. 2
Hypodermic cases — No 2
containing:
Syringe; platina needles (2) in glass tube; cocaine tablets,
¼ gr. (2) tubes; morphia tablets, ⅙ gr. (2 tubes)
and glass mortar.
Ice-bags, black rubber, head — No 2
Ice-bags, black rubber, spine — No. 1
Meat, extract of (in 4 oz. tins) — lb. . . . . ½
Pencils, indelible — No 6
Plaster, adhesive, each 1 inch tape, 6 yards — tins 6
Plaster, isinglass, transparent, each 1 inch tape,
12 yards — tins. 2
Razor — No. 1
Scissors, counter, long and short — No 2
Silk, twisted, fine and medium, in aseptic
solution — tubes 2
Silkworm gut, in carbolized glycerine — tubes. 2
[thermometer, matches, spirit lamp]
Bandages, loose woven, fast edge — No 72
Chamois skins — No. 2
[scissors, thread, tape surgeon's needles]
[aspirator, various catheters, basins, strop, tourniquets]
[eye baths, gauze, waterproof cloth, sterilizer]
Acid, Carbolic — oz 8
Chloroform, in 2 oz. bottles — lb. 3
Iodoform, in two vulcanite dredges — oz 6
Hydrarg. Perchlor. solids — doz 12
Potas. Permanganas, 2 gr. tablets — doz 16
Brandy — oz 8

Appendix VIII
GLOSSARY OF MEDICAL TERMS

Adrenalin — For the purposes of this thesis, a therapeutic Drug, employed to arrest bleeding, and to prolong the action of local anaesthetics.

Amputation (Circular/Flap) — The removal of a limb or portion of a limb, or of any other appendage. A circular a. is one in which a single tubular flap is made by a circular cut through skin and muscles directly across the limb, the bone being divided at a high level. A flap a., in which the flaps, made of the soft tissues, cover the stump.

Anaemia — A condition of the blood in which there are quantitative and qualitative changes in the red blood cells and haemoglobin in the circulating blood and bone marrow, due, inter alia, from severe bleeding.

Anaerobic Organism — A micro-organism able to exist and multiply although deprived of either free oxygen or air.

Anaesthetic — Any drug or chemical used to produce anaesthesia (i.e. loss of feeling or sensation).

Antiseptic — Able to prevent the multiplication of the micro-organisms that produce disease or putrefaction.

Atropine — For our purposes, used in ophthalmology to dilate the pupils. Also used to reduce secretions from the mouth prior to general anaesthesia.

Barcoo Rot — A type of septic sore found on soldiers at Gallipoli.

Catgut — Sterilised surgical catgut, produced from sheep's intestines, as an absorbable material for ligatures or sutures.

Cellulitis — An inflammation of connective tissue, especially of tissue lying just beneath the skin.

Cerebro-spinal Fluid — A clear fluid which bathes the brain and spinal cord.

Cholera — A severe infectious epidemic disease, with symptoms of vomiting, diarrhoea and collapse; eventually leading to the collapse of the kidneys.

Comminuted Fracture — Crushed or broken into many small pieces (of bone).

Compound Fracture — a Fracture (i.e. broken bone) associated with a skin wound.

Conjunctivitis — Inflammation of the mucous membrane lining the eyelids.

Cresol — Consisting mainly of carbolic acid; used as a potent bactericide.

Diphtheria — An infectious disease concentrated in the upper respiratory tract. Can result in disturbances to both the heart and the nervous system.

Disinfectant — Any substance which kills bacteria, not applied directly or undiluted to wounds or tissue because of its toxicity.

Dressing — A covering which is applied to a wound for protection and to promote healing.

Dysentery — Inflammation of the colon. Symptoms are pain and severe diarrhoea. May be either amoebic or bacillic type. Usually spread by flies.

Dyspepsia — Indigestion.

Emetine — Medicine used to treat amoebic dysentery.

Enteric — Term used for typhoid and paratyphoid fevers.

Enucleation — The removal of an organ from its capsule (esp. eyeball).

Eserine — Used to reduce intra-ocular pressure.

Eucaine — One of the earliest synthetic substitutes for cocaine, used as a local anaesthetic.

Eusol — An antiseptic solution made by dissolving equal parts of chlorinated lime and boric acid in water.

Fascia — A layer or sheet of connective tissue separating or enclosing groups of muscles or other organs.

Femur — The thigh bone.

Foments — The therapeutic application of warmth and moisture to any part of the body in order to overcome inflammation or pain.

Fracture — A broken bone.

Frostbite — A local morbid condition of varying severity, including complete gangrene, caused by freezing of a part due to exposure to extreme cold.

Gangrene — Death and putrefaction of tissue due to the cutting off of the blood supply (e.g. severe wounds, frostbite).

Gas Gangrene — Spreading swelling, necrosis (i.e. death of a portion of tissue), and gas formation due to infection of wounds by anaerobic bacilli.

Gauze — A loose-meshed muslin used for surgical dressing, either dry or saturated in an antiseptic solution.

Haemorrhage — Bleeding.

Haemothorax — Bleeding into the pleural cavity (i.e. between the lungs and the chest wall).

Hypochondria — A person pre-occupied with his state of health to the extent that this in itself becomes a disability.

Infection — The invasion of the body by pathogenic (causing or producing disease) or potentially pathogenic organisms, and their subsequent multiplication in the body.

Jaundice — A syndrome characterised by an excess of bile pigment in the blood, and consequently deposited in the skin, giving it a characteristic yellow colour.

Keratitis — Inflammation of the cornea of the eye.

Laceration — A rent or tear, usually of the skin, or other tissues.

Ligature — Any material tied around a structure with the intention either of occluding its vessels, or of obstructing its duct or artery.

Louse (Lice) — An insect capable of carrying, inter-alia, Typhus (via Rickettsia) and Trench Fever.

Lumbar Puncture — Withdrawal of cerebro-spinal fluid for diagnostic or therapeutic purposes through a special needle inserted into the spine.

Lymph — The fluid flowing in the lymphatic channels.

Meatus — A passage or opening (often refers to the ear).

Meninges — The membranes which form the covering of the brain and spinal cord.

Morphia — A drug used mainly to alleviate pain.

Para-typhoid — A disease resembling typhoid fever, usually with milder symptoms however.

Perineum — Groin area.

Phlyctenular Conjunctivitis — An allergic form of conjunctivitis.

Phthisis — Consumption, T.B of the lungs.

Primary Union — Healing which occurs promptly and without complicating infection, healing by first intention.

Prolapse — The sinking down or protrusion of a part.

Pyrexia — A fever or condition characterised by fever.

Respirations — Gaseous interchange of oxygen and carbon dioxide between the tissues of the body and the atmosphere, via the lungs.

Rigours — A shivering fit.

Saline Solution — A (normally sterile) mixture of water and salt (sodium chloride).

Scopolamine-Hyosine — It relaxes the smooth muscles of the respiratory and gastro-intestinal tracts, and of the urinary tract and the bladder. Used as a pre-anaesthetic medication.

Sepsis — Infection.

Septic — Caused by, or in a state of sepsis.

Serum — Used to denote various forms of injectible substances.

Shock — A reduction in the effective volume of blood circulating around the body.

Splint — A rigid appliance used to immobilise a broken limb.

Steriliser — An apparatus used to sterilise instruments and other objects, such as dressings, linen, etc.

Suture — A surgical stitch, or group or row of such stitches.

Swab — An absorbent pad, sometimes on the end of a stick, by means of which materials may be applied to or removed from parts of the body.

Tachycardia — Abnormally rapid heart beat.

Tetanus — An infective disease due to the toxins of the *Clostridium tetani*, the organisms entering through an abrasion or wound of the skin; causes muscle spasms, facial paralysis.

Trench Foot — A condition of frostbite affecting the feet.

Tourniquet — An instrument for the circular compression of a limb with interruption of its blood supply, to prevent bleeding from a wound. Often improvised.

Trephining — The cutting of a circular disk of bone from the skull, to allow for drainage, release of pressure within the skull etc.

Typhoid Fever — An acute infectious disease which flourishes in situations of poor hygiene. Caused by ingestion of contaminated (by Salmonella typhi) food or water.

Typhus Fever — Epidemic, or louse-borne disease, often fatal if not treated. Caused by species of the parasitic micro-organism *Rickettsia*.

Venous — Of the veins.

Viscera — Internal organs of the body.

APPENDIX IX
COSTS OF THE CAMPAIGN

The sufferings of those men and their relatives and friends cannot of course be measured. Non-fatal casualties, as a proportion of the strength of the AIF — Gallipoli Campaign (May to December 1915) were:

DATE	EFFECTIVES	TOTAL SICK & WOUNDED	
1.5.15	21 066	4021	19.08%
1.6.15	24 334	5126	21.06%
1.7.15	25 498	4606	18.06%
1.8.15	29 067	6255	21.52%
1.9.15	21 814	7134	32.70%
1.10.15	27 843 +	7960	28.59%
1.11.15	30 451	7317	24.03%
1.12.15	27 035	7285	26.95%
1.1.16	33 540	8213	24.48%

+ First reinforcements begin to arrive at this time.

Source: Australian National Archives, Series AA 1977/110. Item No. 1464/15/2. Percentage figures were not included.

Deaths from enemy action at Gallipoli were as follows:

	KILLED IN ACTION	DIED OF WOUNDS	WOUNDED	TOTAL
A.I.F.	5833	1985	19 441	27 259
A.A.M.C.	33	35	225	293
N.Z.A.C.[6]	1904	495	4852	7251

Butler, op. cit., p 449. There is a discrepancy between this figure and those given by Butler in Volume III of the *Official History*, Appendix: Seven, which gives fatalities. 'The Turks and Allies suffered savagely, approximately 252 000 casualties each ... French casualties numbered 47 000 including 10 000 dead, out of 79 000 soldiers engaged.'[7] Of these fatalities, 94 were members of the AAMC (less than 2.0 per cent of the total casualties of the AIF). See also Appendix IV above.

Financially, the total cost to Australia [Memorandum dated 23 March 1916 to the Secretary, War Office. Australian National Archives, Canberra. Series AA 1977/110. Item No. 1464/15/2.] (which was to be reimbursed by Britain) of the Gallipoli campaign was assessed at £2 416 428 5s. 10d.

An idea of the scale of munitions supplied may be gauged from these statistics. In the Dardanelles theatre itself seven General Hospitals (1040 beds each), five Stationary Hospitals (400 beds each), eight Casualty Clearing Stations and 15 Field Amb-ulances had to be fully equipped with medical and surgical stores and equipment, all of which comprised 3228 cases, weighing 108 tonnes. These stores included 4.25 million bandages, 5972 kilometres of gauze, 340 tonnes of lint and wool, and 186 000 shell dressings.

Bibliography

UNPUBLISHED SOURCES:

AUSTRALIAN WAR MEMORIAL
AG Butler Papers [AWM 41]
RHJ Fetherston Papers [AWM 2] 2DRL 1200 and AWM 41 2/7.4.
Tait Papers [AWM 32]
AWM 25, AWM 27, AWM 44, AWM 51 (No. 103)
AWM 27 Miscellaneous Military Records Subject Classified files
Dardanelles Commission Proceedings and Reports AWM 51 No
103

[Diaries, Letters and Personal Recollections]
Aitken M Nursing Sister 41 Box No 5
Allardyee GG File No 12/11/206
Barton ASD 25 L/12/11/3251 and 27 Item 1/4.6
Beeston JL 2DRL 206 and File L/12/11/3719
Bell GS 6th AFA 2/172 and 2/242
Bennett F 3DRL 7507
Betts LO 41 Item 1/4.9
Bowman RM 41 Item 1/4.12
Buchanan AL 41 Item 1/4.18

Butler AG 2DRL 1188
Carne AG 6th Btn AIF
Chambers RW 41 Item 1/5.7
Chapman CL 41 Item 1/5.8
Clark E 41 Item 1/5.9
Conrick V 3DRL 3329
Davenport P 41 Item 2/6.4
Davies E 3DRL 3398
Douglas G 3DRL 3275
Duncan HR File No. 419/82/48. PR 84/60
Fry Lt Col 41 Item 2/7.15
Gardiner R 1DRL 304
Gutteridge EW 41 Item 2/8.8
Hampson WK 1DRL 331
Helsham WM 41 Item 2/8.16
Hensen BE 3DRL 4063
Hurley Dr 41 2/8.27
Howitt E 41 'Nurses' Narratives' Box 5
Jeffries LW 41 Item 3/9.4
Kenny OP 41 3/9.10
Kitson EH 41 Item 3/9.14
Lawson JR 3DRL 7681
Lockhart-Gibson J 41 Item 2/8.2
Loughran HG 41 Item 3/9.22
Lovell IG 41 Box 6, Folder 6/89
Lowell IE 41 Butler Papers [Box 6] Folder 6/89
MacMillan CC 41 3/10.9
MacMillan FE 41 Box 5
McWhae DM 41 Item 3/10.10
Magill EL 7th A.L.H. 2/212
Muirhead JR 41 Item 3/10.24
Nelson HF 41 Item 3/11.2
Newmarch BJ 41 Item 3/11.5
Purves-Stewart J 41 Box No 4 File No 4/62
Ryan CS 27 370.5 [1]
Selwyn-Smith NF 41 Box No. 5
Stephen C 41 Item 4/12.18
Stacey VO 41 Item 4/12.5
Young LE 41 Box 5
Vyvyan V 41 Box 5, File No. 5/13
War diaries for all medical units at Gallipoli (AWM 4)
Whitelaw 41 Box No.5
Wilson GM 3DRL 7819
Woods HHV 3 DRL 35.8

The La Trobe Collection, State Library of Victoria

[Diaries and Letters]
Allison Pte HR MS 10168
Blundell MP MS 10485 MSB 221
Brotchie J MS 11628 Box 1834/2
Collins RM MS 8133 940/1 (a)
Crome C MS 10026
Dunk RJ MS 11105 Box 356/8
Gourley AJE MS 10530 TMS134
Irving H MS 10431 MSB 210
Jenkins AM MS 10130 MSB 502
Kitchen AE MS 9627 MSB 478
Laidlaw VR MS 11827 Box 2163/3–5
Liddell TW MS 11568 Box 1674/10–13
Mathers RH MS 10904 MSB 331
McMillan AM MS 10473 MSB 219
McPhee JE MS 9876 Bay 18
Mills DG MS 10500 TMS 129–130
Moberly GF MS 57960 485
Moloney HP MS 10984 MSB 359
Randall W MS 11287 MSB 401
Scrapbook of Press Cuttings (Gallipoli) MS 11218 MSB 389
Taylor A MS 12286 Box 1829/6
Telfer GS MS 9604 MSB 422
Whittle AL TMS 550

Mitchell Library, Sydney

[Diaries and Letters]
Bennet J MLDOC 1293
Burgess JG MSS 1596
Cicognani H MSS 1238
Clune F MSS A 2660
Garling TW MSS A 2660
Gissing HE MSS 1845
Gordon AD MSS 1629
Gower G MSS 1651
Hall P MSS 2768
Holt OLS MSS 1986
Hurley PJ ML MSS 1997
Laseron CF MSS 1133
Mackinson FT MSS 2878
Maddox JO MSS 2877
McKenzie J MSS 1985
McMillan FE MSS 2068

Mitchell KJ MSS 1790
Morris APK MSS 2886
Partridge DJ ML MSS 2939
Rainsford BW MLMSS 1006
Richards SJ MSS 2908
Schaeffer LE MSS 3037
Silas E ML MSS 1840
Smith FH MSS 2742
Springthorpe JW MSS 1709
Walsh G A.2660

THE NATIONAL LIBRARY OF AUSTRALIA

Bonar-Law Papers Ms 1123
Fisher Papers Ms 2911
Novar Papers Ms 696

AUSTRALIAN ARCHIVES — CANBERRA, ACT

Memorandum dated 23.3.1916 to the Secretary, War Office
Australian National Archives Canberra Series AA 1977/110
Item No 1464/15/2
Series No A.2939 Item SC 352 'Hospital Ships'

AUSTRALIAN ARCHIVES — BRIGHTON, VICTORIA

Paper on Nurses' Salaries A.2023/0 Item A 20/5/70 War
Regulations MP 367 Item 430/2/702
Howse/Williams Correspondence B543 Item 239/8/78 Box 11

UNIVERSITY OF MELBOURNE ARCHIVES (NOT NUMBERED)

HB Allen Papers
JW Barrett Papers
University Council Minutes — 1915

MONASH UNIVERSITY — HISTORY DEPARTMENT LIBRARY

Egan B 'Nobler Than Missionaries — Australian Medical Culture
c.1800 to c.1930' Diss Monash University

AUCKLAND INSTITUTE AND MUSEUM, NEW ZEALAND

Papers of J Duder First Officer NZ Hospital Ship *Maheno*

IMPERIAL WAR MUSEUM, LONDON

Letters of Surgeon H Clough IWM P15
Diary of Lt N King-Wilson IWM P232

Public Record Office, Kew, London
Admiralty Papers — various

National Maritime Museum, Greenwich, London
Papers of Admiral Sir James Porter PTR/8/
Papers of Admiral Sir Arthur Limpus Ms75/139

Liddell Hart Centre for Military Archives, London
Papers of Sir Ian Hamilton (various):
17/3/1/86, 17/3/1/87, 17/3/1/89, 17/3/1/137, 17/3/2/56, 17/3/2/
57, 17/4/1/51, 17/4/2/34, 17/7/28/1, 17/4/3/36, 17/7/29/4,
17/7/29/1, 39/12/394

Recorded Interviews; private diaries and letters lent
to, or in the possession of the author
Dr C Checchi Willaura Victoria Personal Interview, January 1988
Les and Louis Lambert Strathmore Victoria Letters to author
Copies of letters written by Lt Colonel GA Syme lent by Mr M
Syme Malvern Victoria
Letter of Lt Colonel J Gordon (1st ACCS) dated 10 November
1915 Anzac Cove Original in the possession of Mrs JA Pillar
Curlwaa NSW
Diary of Nurse C MacNaughton No 2 AGH in the possession of
Mrs P Barnes Werribee Victoria
Personal interview with Mr T Meagher late of the 6th AFA April
1990
Personal interview with Mr E Thompson, late of the 6th AFA
April 1990

Newspapers
Adelaide *Register*
The Times, London
Melbourne *Age*
Melbourne *Argus*
Melbourne *Herald*
Sydney *Bulletin*
Sydney Morning Herald

Published References

1. THE WAR YEARS
Allan RM *Letters from a Young Queenslander* Watson Ferguson &
Co Brisbane 1915
'Anzac' *On the Anzac Trail* William Heinemann London 1916

Barrett JW *The War Work of the Y.M.C.A. in Egypt* HK Lewis & Co Ltd London 1919

Barrett JW *The Australian Army Medical Corps in Egypt*. HK Lewis & Co London 1918

Beeston JL *Five Months at Anzac* Angus & Robertson Sydney 1916

Bowden SH (ed.) *The History of the Australian Comforts Fund* Scotow & Preswell Sydney n.d.

Carrel A and G Dehelly *The Treatment of Wounds* Bailliere Tindall & Co London 1917

De Loghe S *The Straits Impregnable* Murray London 1917

Delorme E *War Surgery* HK Lewis London 1915

Eder MD *War Shock* William Heinemann London 1917

Hargrave J *At Suvla Bay* Constable & Son London 1916

Hastings S *First Aid in the Trenches* Murray London 1916

Jones D *The Diary of a Padre at Suvla Bay* The Faith Press n.p. n.d.

Jones RJ *Notes on Military Orthopaedics* Cassell & Co London 1917

Masefield J *Gallipoli* Heinemann London 1917

Memorandum — Treatment of Injuries in War HMSO London 1915

Nevinson HW *The Dardanelles Campaign* Nisbet & Co London 1918

Commonwealth of Australia — Parliamentary Debates Volumes 76–78 (6th Parliament) Melbourne 1915

Royal Army Medical Corps Training 1911 rpt. HMSO London 1915

Schuler PFE *Australia in Arms* T Fisher Unwin Ltd London 1916

Springthorpe J W *The Great Withdrawal* Brown Prior & Co Melbourne 1916

Vassal J *Uncensored Letters from the Dardanelles Written to his English Wife by a French Medical Officer of Le Corps Expeditionaire d'Orient* W Heinemann London 1916

War Office *Royal Army Medical Corps Training* HMSO London, 1911

2. THE INTER-WAR YEARS

Ashmead-Bartlett EH *The Uncensored Dardanelles* Hutchinson London 1928

Aspinall-Oglander CF *Military Operations: Gallipoli* 2 Vols. Heinemann London 1929

Bean CEW *The Official History of Australia in the War of 1914–1918* Vol II Sydney 1924

Bean CEW *The Story of Anzac* Vols 1 and 2 1924 rpt. University of Queensland Press Brisbane 1981

Bell CJP trans *The Campaign in Gallipoli* By H Kannengeisser Hutchinson & Co Ltd London 1928

Butler AG *Official History of the Australian Army Medical Services* Vols I and III Australian War Memorial Melbourne 1930 and 1943

Carberry AD *The New Zealand Medical Service in the Great War 1914–1918* Whitcombe & Tombs Auckland 1924

Chatterton EK *Dardanelles Dilemma (The Story of the Naval Operations)* Chatterton Rich & Cowen London 1935

Cutlack FM (ed.) *War Letters of General Monash* Angus & Robertson Sydney 1935

Fayle CE (ed.) *History of the Great War — Seaborne Trade* Vol II John Murray London 1923

Hamilton Sir I *Gallipoli Diary* 2 Vols Edward Arnold London 1920

Jeans Surgeon Rear-Admiral TT *Reminiscences of a Naval Surgeon* Sampson London 1927

Kirkcaldie RA *In Gray and Scarlet* Alexander MacCubbin Melbourne 1922

MacPhail A *Official History of the Canadian Forces in the Great War 1914–1919 — The Medical Services* Acland Ottawa 1925

MacPherson WG & TJ Mitchell *Medical Services General History* 12 Vols HMSO London 1924

Midwinter C *Memoirs of the 32nd Field Ambulance (1st Irish Division)* G E Foulgar London 1933

Ministere de La Guerre *Les Armees Francaises dans La Grande Guerre* Tome VIII Vol I Paris n.p. 1923

Mitchell TJ & GM Smith *The Official History of the Great War — Casualties and Medical Statistics* HMSO London 1932

Nicholls TB *The Army Medical Services in War* n.p. 1937

North J *Gallipoli: The Fading Vision* Faber & Faber London 1936

Report of the Joint War Committeee of the British Red Cross Society and the Order of St John of Jerusalem 1914–1919 London 1919

Report by the Joint War Committee and Joint War Finance Committee of the British Red Cross Society and the Order of St John in England HMSO London 1921

Scott E *Australia During the War* Angus & Robertson Sydney 1936

Smith TJ & GM (eds) *History of the Great War — Medical Services* HMSO London 1931

Tilton M *The Grey Battalion* 2nd Ed. Angus & Robertson Sydney 1934

Tubby AH *A Consulting Surgeon in the Near East* Christopher London 1920

University of Melbourne Record of Active Service 1914–1918 Government Printer Melbourne 1926

Waite F *The New Zealanders At Gallipoli* Whitcombe & Tombs Auckland 1921

Wemyss Lord W *The Navy and the Dardanelles Campaign* Hodder & Stoughton London n.d.

White CCB *Some Reflections Upon the Great War* Homer Sydney 1921

3. 1939–1945

Birdwood Lord *Khaki and Gown* Ward Lock & Co London 1941

Hankey MPA *Government Control in War* Vol II CUP Cambridge 1945

Hurst A *Medical Diseases of War* 3rd Ed. Edward Arnold & Co London 1943

Myers CS *Shell Shock In France 1914–18* CUP Cambridge 1940

4. POST WORLD WAR TWO

Adam-Smith P *The Anzacs* Thomas Nelson Melbourne 1978

Ashworth T *Trench Warfare 1914–1918: The Live and Let Live System* Macmillan London 1980

Bassett J *Guns and Brooches* Oxford University Press Melbourne 1992

Benson CI *The Man with the Donkey — John Simpson Kirkpatrick* Hodder & Stoughton London 1965

Bowerbank F *A Doctor's Story* Wingfield Press Wellington 1958

Cassar GH *The French and the Dardanelles* Allen & Unwin London 1971

Denham HM *Dardanelles — A Midshipman's Diary* Murray London 1981

Dixon NF *On the Psychology of Military Incompetence* Futura London 1985

East R (ed.) *The Gallipoli Diaries of Sergeant Lawrence* MUP Melbourne 1981

Fielding J & R O'Neil *A Select Bibliography of Australian Military History* ANU Canberra 1978

Gammage B *The Broken Years* Penguin Melbourne 1975

Gandevia B et al (ed.) *Bibliography of the History of Medicine and Health in Australia* Royal Australian College of Physicians Sydney 1984

Gurner J *The Origins of the Royal Australian Army Medical Corps* Hawthorn Press Melbourne 1970

Halpern PG (ed.) *The Keyes Papers, Vol.1, 1914–1918* London Navy Records Society 1972

Hankey MPA *The Supreme Command* Vol I Allen & Unwin London 1961

Hargrave J *The Suvla Bay Landing* MacDonald London 1964

James RR *Gallipoli* Angus & Robertson Sydney 1965

Jenkins JJ *Pte JJ Jenkins — RAMC — 318915* Privately Printed Newcastle 1982

Laffin J *Damn the Dardanelles* Sun Papermac Melbourne 1985

Laffin J *Surgeons in the Field* JM Dent London 1970

Liddle P *Men of Gallipoli* Allen Lane London 1976

McCarthy D *Gallipoli to the Somme* Ferguson Sydney 1983

Mitchell AM *Medical Women and the Medical Services of the First World War* Privately Printed Sydney 1978

Moore W *The Thin Yellow Line* Cooper Ltd London 1974

Moorehead A *Gallipoli* Macmillan Melbourne 1978

Murray J *Gallipoli as I Saw It* William Kimber London 1965

Nairn B and G Serle (eds) *Australian Dictionary of Biography* Vols 7–11 MUP Melbourne 1979

Plumridge JH *Hospital Ships and Ambulance Trains* Seeley London 1975

Pugsley C *Gallipoli — The New Zealand Story* Hodder & Stoughton Auckland 1984

Regan G *Someone Had Blundered* B T Batsford London 1987

Robertson J *Anzac and Empire* Melbourne Hamlyn 1990

Russell KF *The Melbourne Medical School 1862–1962* MUP Melbourne 1977

Serle G *John Monash: a Biography* MUP Melbourne 1982

Taylor AJP *The First World War* Hamish Hamilton London 1963

Watson AO (ed.) *A History of Dentistry in New South Wales 1788–1945* Australian Dental Association Sydney 1977

Periodicals and Articles

Aspinall A 'The Transport of Sick and Wounded on Ordinary Troop Ships' *Medical Journal of Australia* Jan 1916

Aspinall A 'First Field Ambulance, A.A.M.C., A.I.F.' *Sydney University Medical Journal* Jan 1917

Australian Journal of Dentistry Editorials Issues for 31 May 1915 and 31 Jan 1916

Barton ASD 'Work at a Casualty Clearing Station' *Medical Journal of Australia* 23 Aug 1919

Beeston, JL 'A Field Ambulance [4th] With the Fourth Infantry Brigade in Gallipoli' *Medical Journal of Australia* 24 June 1916 Vol I No 26

Begg C Mackie (NZAMC) quoted from the *British Medical Journal* for December 4 1915 and reproduced as part of a letter to the Editor *Australian Journal of Dentistry*, Vol XX 31 Jan 1916

British Medical Society 'British Medicine in the War' *British Medical Journal* 1917

Bryant HW 'Some Notes Taken Whilst On Active Service with the No. 1 Australian Stationary Hospital' *Medical Journal of Australia* Vol 1 No 13 25 Mar 1916

Campbell AW 'Remarks on Some Neuroses and Psychoses in War' *Medical Journal of Australia* Vol I 3rd Year 15 April 1916

Chapman CL 'Case of a Bullet Wound of the Skull, 5th Field Ambulance, Gallipoli' *Medical Journal of Australia* 26 Feb 1916

Chitty H 'A Hospital Ship in the Mediterranean' *British Medical Journal* 9.10.1915

Corbin J (1st ACCS) 'Experiences with the A.A.M.C. at Gallipoli' *Medical Journal of Australia* 5 Feb 1916 Vol I No 6

Craig MB 'A Short Account of the Hospital Ship *Karoola*' *Medical Journal of Australia* Vol II No 22 1916

Deakin EJF 'Some Experiences with the No. 2 Australian Stationary Hospital' *Medical Journal of Australia* 27.1.1917

Gordon KF 'Days at An Advanced Dressing Station' in Supplement to the *Australian Medical Journal* 3 Dec 1927 p 466

Howe HV 'The Anzac Landing — A Belated Query' in *Stand-To* Vol 7 No 5 September 1962

Jones WE 'A Case of Shell Shock' *Medical Journal of Australia* 4 Mar 1916

Journal of the Association of Military Surgeons of the U.S. Vol XXXVI Chicago 1915

Lancet Editorial 'A Medical View of the Gallipoli Adventure' 15 Jan 1916

MacMunn G 'The Lines of Communication in the Dardanelles' *The Army Quarterly* Vol XX 1930

Morley J 'Surgery on the Gallipoli Peninsula' *British Medical Journal* September 1915

Stacy HS 'Notes from the No.2 Casualty Clearing Station' *Medical Journal of Australia* Vol II 2 Sep 1916

Stewart HJ 'Personal Experiences and Clinical Observations with the Third Australian General Hospital, Lemnos and Egypt' *Medical Journal of Australia* Vol 1 No 19 1917

Summons W 'Notes on the Medical Work of the First Australian General Hospital' *Medical Journal of Australia* 20 Nov 1915 p 482

Syme GA 'Surgical Experiences At the War' *Medical Journal of Australia* Vol 1 No 14 1 April 1916

Journal Of The Royal Victoria Trained Nurse Association Vol II (1904) Nos 4, 6 and 11 and Vol III (1905) No 4

Medical Press London 14 Oct 1925

Watson-Cheyne W 'A Trip to the Dardanelles with the View of Testing the Value of Hypochlorite of Soda in the Treatment of Wounds in War' *Journal of The Royal Naval Medical Service* Vol II April No 2 1916

White B 'Combat Stress Reaction' in *Defence Force Journal* No 55 Nov/Dec 1985

Zwar BT 'Remarks On War Experiences' *Medical Journal of Australia* 29 April 1916

Notes

PREFACE

1   Laffin J *Damn the Dardanelles* Sun Papermac Melbourne 1985 and Regan J *Someone Had Blundered* BT Batsford London 1987

CHAPTER 1

1   W G MacPherson & G M Smith (eds) *History of the Great War — Medical Services* Twelve volumes HMSO London 1931 p 198

2   Diary entry Captain CL Chapman 28 March 1915 AWM 41 1/5.8

3   Diary of Major LO Betts, AWM No 41 Item 1/4.9

4   Personal narrative AWM 41 2/8.27

5   Extract from an unidentified letter to Butler dated 10 February 1916 from HQ 54th (British) Division, Mena Camp AWM 2 DRL Howse Collection Bundle IV File 184/11

6   Telegram (11 October 1915) from the Secretary-of-State to GHQ MEF 'Medical Aspects of Gallipoli Operations — Extracts from War Office Documents Feb–Dec 1915' AWM 25 Written records of the 1914–1918 War Item 367/40

7   See Commonwealth Parliamentary Debates, Vols 76–78 6th Parliament 1915 esp. pp 2641–53, 3380–82, 5495, 6147, 6664, and 6943

8   W G MacPherson & T J Mitchell, Vol IV p 18 quoting the conclusions of the Special Commission (Dardanelles and Mesopotamia) Act 1916

9   Letter dated 25 September 1915 Mudros F M Cutlack (ed.) *The War Letters of General Monash* Angus & Robertson Sydney 1935 p 70

10   ibid letter dated 3 October 1915 Mudros p 75

11   ibid letter dated 6 December 1915 from Anzac p 92

12   Entry for 8 June 1915 Diary of Colonel J W Springthorpe (No 2 AGH), MSS 1709 ML

13   Entry for 21 April 1915 War diary DMS MEF (Birrell) op cit

14   Entry for 21 April 1915 War diary No 1 ASH AWM 4 26/70

15   ibid

16   Diary entry for 24 April 1915 on board the *Seang Choon* by HE Gissing MSS 1845 ML

17   Dardanelles Commission (hereafter cited as 'DC') AWM 51 No 103 *Final Report* p 84 para 196

CHAPTER 2

1   Letter written by Peter Hall (No. 2 ASH) to his mother on 2 May 1915 op cit

2   C Pugsley in *Gallipoli: The New Zealand Story*, Hodder & Stoughton Auckland 1984, p 15 says that 'The errors in landing were never made an issue of by the Army.' The only statement made in the *Official British Medical History* is that the landings on all beaches were carried out on 25 April 1915 according to plan. WG MacPherson & TJ Mitchell op cit vol IV p 9. Pugsley (p 139), states further that the Royal Navy blamed a non-existent current and the midshipmen in charge of the pinnaces. Butler refers only to a deflection of a mile to the north caused by the tide, but goes on to mention the intricacy of the terrain, and the imperfection of the maps, which 'combined to confuse and dislocate the tactical scheme'. AG Butler *Official History of the Australian Army Medical Services* Australian War Memorial Melbourne 1930 vol 1 p 131

3   25 April 1915 War diary 1st AFA AWM 4 26/44

4   4 May 1915 Personal diary of Col J Beeston CO 4th AFA AWM 2DRL 206 File L12/11/3719

5   27 April 1915 Diary of A Gower AAMC stretcher bearer with the 15th Btn ML MSS 1651

6   War diary 3rd AFA op cit Entry for 28 April 1915 Howse's diary states: 'Owing to the number of cases and smallness of space available for CCS a rapid evacuation was essential. With the limited staff available it proved to be impossible to record the number killed and wounded from [25–29 April].' War diary of ADMS 1st Australian Division AWM 4 26/18

7   Notes of Captain (later Colonel) DM McWhae 3rd AFA op cit

8   Entry for 25 April 1915 Diary of AHE Gissing 1st AFA op cit

9   AWM 25 Written records of the 1914–1918 War. Item 367/40 'Medical Aspects of Gallipoli Operations — Extracts from War Office

Documents. Feb–Dec 1915.' This was despite numbers of officers being appointed to act as 'traffic controllers' and liaison officers on the beaches. 'At the three southern beaches, these personnel totalled 160 officers and 1,000 o.r.s, although the Anzac beaches were '"equipped on a similar scale"'. CF Aspinall-Oglander *Military Operations: Gallipoli* Heinemann London 1929 Vol I pp 146–7

10 Entry for 26 April 1915. Over the next two days it treated a further 1500 casualties.

11 25 April 1915 War diary of ADMS 1st Australian Division op cit

12 J Corbin (1st ACCS) 'Experiences with the A.A.M.C. at Gallipoli' *Med. J.Aust* 5 February 1916 vol I No 6 p 114

13 Extract from a letter to his father, n.d. but probably May 1915 AWM File Nos 2/172 and 2/242

14 30 April 1915 War diary 1st AFA op cit

15 Letter written by Peter Hall (No. 2 ASH) to his mother on 2 May 1915 MSS 2768 ML

16 Col C Ryan (principal medical adviser to General Birdwood) AWM 27 370.5[1]

17 27 April 1915 Diary of Pte AD Gordon 1st AFA, MSS 1629 ML

18 Diary of AHE Gissing 1st AFA op cit

19 A Aspinall 'A First Field Ambulance, AAMC, AIF' in *Sydney Univ Med J* January 1917 p 187

20 DC Question No 27671 to Howse

21 Personal Narrative of Sir V Vyvyan, a 'Beach Master' at Anzac AWM 41 Butler Papers (Box 5) File No 5/13

22 One can speculate whether Howse pre-empted orders at this time, for according to an entry for 25 April 1915 in the war diary of the 1st ACCS its OC 'was especially instructed by [Howse]...to evacuate as rapidly as possible'. By 3.00 am the next morning this unit 'had completely evacuated'. See also DC Question No 27667 (Howse)

23 Letter from Fleet Surgeon CC McMillan SMO Naval — Anzac dated 25 March 1924 AWM 41 3/10.9

24 *OHAAMS*, Vol I p 143

25 *Scheme for Evacuating Wounded at Gallipoli*, p 2 prepared by Birrell for Hamilton on 19 July 1917, presumably for the DC LHC Hamilton Papers 17/7/3

26 DC Question Nos 29895 and 29899

27 War diary DMS, MEF. Carbery also states that it was doubtful if Birrell had the message until two days later. AD Carbery *The New Zealand Medical Service in the Great War 1914–1918* Whitcombe & Tombs Auckland 1924 p 46

28 Letter from Fleet Surgeon CC McMillan SMO Naval — Anzac, to Butler, dated 25.3.1924 AWM 41 3/10.9

29 Carbery op cit p 40

30 Sir Ian Hamilton *Gallipoli Diary*, Edward Arnold London 1920 Vol I p 152

31 Carbery op cit p 44

32 ibid pp 51–52

33   *Scheme for Evacuating Wounded at Gallipoli* p 3 prepared by Birrell for Hamilton on 19 July 1917 presumably for the Dardanelles Commission LHC Hamilton Papers 17/7/3

34   War diary 3rd AFA op cit

35   J Corbin (1st ACCS) op cit

36   Personal diary of H Cicognani, a stretcher bearer of the 1st A.F.A. ML MSS 1238. Later, during the attack on Krithia on 8 May there 'were an exceptional number suffering from abdominal injuries, for in the final advance the troops had waded through a stream of bullets waist high'. *OHAAMS* vol I p 155

37   Diary entry 1 July 1915 AD Gordon 1st AFA op cit

38   War diary 3rd AFA op cit Entry for 30 April 1915

39   *OHAAMS* Vol I p 146

40   25 April 1915 Diary of Pte AD Gordon 1st AFA op cit

41   26 April 1915 Personal Diary of H Cicognani, a stretcher bearer of the 1st AFA op cit

42   Diary entry 26 April 1915 Sgt CF Laseron 13 Btn ML MSS 1133; Pugsley p 148n includes an account of Turks bayoneting wounded

43   J Duder, first officer of the *Maheno* Diary entry for 1 September 1915 Auckland Institute and Museum New Zealand

44   Entry for 27 April 1915 War diary 3rd AFA op cit

45   27 April 1915 War diary 1st AFA op cit

46   Entry for May Sgt DJ Partridge AAMC attached to the 2nd Btn 1st Inf Brigade ML MSS 2939

47   Carbery op cit p 51

48   Letter of 2 May 1915 by P Hall No 2 ASH on board the *Seang Choon*

49   Copy of a letter in the possession of Mrs AJ Pillar Curlwaa NSW

50   *OHAAMS* Vol I p 149

51   9 May 1915 Personal diary of H Cicognani op cit

52   21 May 1915 Diary of James McPhee 4th AFA MSS 12286 Box 1829/6 SL

53   F Waite *The New Zealanders at Gallipoli* Whitcombe & Tombs Auckland 1921 p 98

54   AWM 25 367/26

55   Personal interview with Dr Cyril Checchi of Wilaura Victoria 23 February 1988

56   Diary of FT Makinson ML Mss 1985

57   War diary 5th AFA AWM 41 26/48

58   Narrative of Sir V Vyvyan RN Beach Master at Anzac op. cit

59   Sister A Kitchen. This may have been accidental MS 9627 MSB478 SL

60   AWM 2DRL 1351 Folder 185/8

61   War diary 3rd AFA Entry for 1 May 1915 op cit. The standard work on 'Simpson' is that by CI Benson *The Man with the Donkey — John 'Simpson' Kirkpatrick*. Benson also shamelessly edited his subject matter to suit his own purposes. See also statement by Lt Col V Conrick AAMC AWM 3DRL 3329

62 C Pugsley op cit p 145

63 Page four of a *Scheme for Evacuating Wounded at Gallipoli*, prepared by Babtie for Hamilton on 19 July 1917 presumably for the DC LHC Hamilton Papers 17/7/3. The story was factual. The veterinary was Major (later Colonel) Young, a New Zealander and the ship involved was the *Lutzow*

64 Diary entry for 20 May 1915 by JR Lawson 4th AFA AWM 3DRL 7681

65 *OHAAMS* Vol I p 153 This figure includes action at Anzac

66 Captain P Davenport AWM 41 2/6.4

67 Entry for 27 August 1915 War diary 1st AFA op cit

68 5 September 1915 War diary ADMS 1st Australian Division op cit An entry in the war diary for 24 August 1915 the 1st ACCS reported that it was 'short' of 32 men

69 AWM 41 Butler Papers (Box 9) File No 9/12

70 War diary 2nd LHFA OC Lt Col HK Bean AWM 4/26/40

71 AWM 41 Item 1/4.8

72 *OHAAMS* Vol I p 184

73 1 May 1915 Diary of Col JW Springthorpe, Senior Physician at No 1 AGH op cit

74 *OHAAMS*, Vol I p 193

75 Diary of Sister Alice Kitchen op cit

76 Surgeon Rear-Admiral TT Jeans *Reminiscences of a Naval Surgeon* Sampson London 1927 p 263

77 J Corbin op cit p 114

78 Letters from Babtie to Keogh letter dated 17 August 1915 AWM 27 370.2[14]

79 Letter from Pte F Clune 16th Btn 20 August 1915 ML MSS A2660

80 29 August 1915 Personal Diary of Col JL Beeston (O.C. 4th AFA) op cit

81 F Waite op cit pp 241–3

82 Entry for 12 August 1915 Diary of Sister Alice Kitchen op cit

83 C Pugsley op cit p 308

84 Para 166 p 74 *Final Report* of the Dardanelles Commission — Part II However, it did criticise the plan of attack at Anzac in August. p 87 Para 6

85 *OHAAMS* Vol I p 323

86 TT Jeans op cit p 268

87 Memoirs of Lt N King-Wilson MO on board the *Caledonia*, relates to 28 August 1915 IWM P 232

88 Diary of JR Lawson 4th AFA op cit According to another witness the same hospital had been shelled on November 10 'when a number were killed and many wounded'. Entry for 5 December 1915 Diary of Pte JM McKenzie op cit

89 GG Allardyee 4th AFA AWM File No. 12/11/206

90 Interview in January 1988 with Dr C Checchi who worked as a surgeon with the RAMC at Helles

91   Pasha H Kannengeisser in *The Campaign in Gallipoli* trans CJP Bell (London 1928) p 245. CEW Bean gives a full account in Volume II (particularly relevant is 884n) of *The Story of Anzac*

92   GH Cassar *The French and the Dardanelles* Allen & Unwin London 1971 pp 167–8

93   Diary entry for 19 November 1915 by Lt Col RW Chambers, 2nd AFA AWM 41 Item 1/5.7

94   Entry of 26 November 1915 War diary of Lt Col A Sutton (ADMS 2nd Aust Div.) acting as DDMS during Howse's absence. AWM 4 26/14

95   Diary of Sgt (later Lt) HHV Woods 4th AFA AWM 3 DRL 358

96   Diary entry for 21 December 1915 Pte PJ Hurley attached to the No 1 AGH Mitchell Library ML.MS 1997. See also Bean *The Story of Anzac*, Vol II op cit p 884n

97   Entry for 12 December 1915 Diary of WK Hampson 5th AFA AWM 1 DRL

98   Diary of JR Lawson 4th AFA op cit

99   War diary Col N Howse DDMS op cit

100   Personal Recollections of Sister E Howitt AWM 41 Nurses' Narratives

101   War diary Col N Howse op cit

102   Entry for 17 December 1915 War diary Col N Howse, DDMS op cit

103   ibid

104   See also C Pugsley op cit p 342

105   Diary of Captain ASD Barton AWM 25 L/12/11/3251

106   Diary of JR Lawson 4th AFA op cit

107   Entry for December 1915 op cit

108   J.W. Springthorpe *The Great Withdrawal* Brown Prior & Co Melbourne 1916 p 14

109   Letter dated 25 December 1915 to his mother by Cpl R. Gardiner Clerk to the ADMS 1st Australian Division AWM 1 DRL 304

CHAPTER 3

1   Diary of Lt Col JL Beeston 4th AFA Entry for 17 May 1915 op cit

2   War diary of the 3rd LHFA Entry for 9 August 1915 AWM 4 26/41

3   War diary 4th AFA Entry for 28 June 1915 AWM 41 26/47

4   Letter from Pte F Clune 16 Btn 20 August 1915 op cit

5   Letter dated 14 January 1916 by Pte Fred Bennett 6th AFA AWM 3 DRL 7507

6   Butler's diary as RMO 9th Btn Memorandum to ADMS 14 October 1915 AWM 2DRL 1188. See also chapter six below

7   *Memorandum — Treatment of Injuries in War*, HMSO London 1915 p 4

8   Diary entry for 1 June 1915 Col JL Beeston op cit

9   Major Battye's [Indian Medical Service 108th Indian Field Ambulance] *'Treatment of Wounds Prior to Evacuation from the Point of View of Field Ambulances'* 'Anzac Medical Society' address p 7 AWM 27 3DRL 1181 370 [3]

10 'Some Notes Taken Whilst On Active Service with the No.1 Australian Stationary Hospital' Lt Col HW Bryant in *Med J Aust* vol 1 No 13 25 March 1916 p 261

11 Taken from AWM 2DRL 1188 *Correspondence & Reports — RMO 9th Btn. 9.11.15–8.12.1915*

12 HJ Stewart 'Personal Experiences and Clinical Observations with the Third Australian General Hospital, Lemnos and Egypt' *Med J Aust* Vol 1 No 19 1917 p 393

13 Personal Narrative of Major J Lockhart-Gibson AWM 41 2/8.2

14 Diary entry for 15 August 1915 Sister IG Lovell AWM 41 Butler Papers [Box 6] Folder 6/89

15 Entry for 22 July 1915 War diary of the 1st ACCS AWM 4 26/62

16 Recollections of Captain P Davenport 5th AFA op cit

17 *Memorandum — Treatment of Injuries in War* op cit p 6

18 Diary of J McPhee 4th AFA op cit

19 War diary 2nd LHFA AWM op cit

20 Diary entry for 29 July 1915 L/Cpl JG Burgess 6th LHR MSS 1596 ML

21 Letter of 2 May 1915 by P Hall No 2 ASH op cit

22 Letter to the author by Mr L Lambert [Gallipoli veteran and late of the 6th Field Ambulance]. See also *Med J Aust* 23 August 1919 p 153

23 War diary 1st ACCS 7 July 1915 op cit

24 JL Beeston op cit p 498

25 1 December 1915 Diary of J McPhee 4th AFA op cit

26 War diary Lt Col A Sutton (ADMS 2nd Aust Div) op cit

27 Entry in the war diary of the 2nd LHFA for 29 November 1915 op cit

28 War diary 5th AFA 9 October 1915 AWM 41 26/48

29 Diary of J McKenzie op cit

30 Notes for November War Diary 2nd LHFA op cit

31 JL Beeston op cit p 497

32 War diary 2nd LHFA op cit

33 ibid

34 *Memorandum — Treatment of Injuries in War* op cit p 4

35 Entry for 24 June 1915 Sister A Kitchen on H S *Gascon* off Gaba Tepe op cit

36 *Memorandum — Treatment of Injuries in War* op cit pp 24–25

37 JEF Deakin op cit p 77

38 J Morley 'Surgery on the Gallipoli Peninsula' *Br Med J* September 1915 p 462

39 'Case of a Bullet Wound of the Skull' by CL Chapman 5th AFA Gallipoli *Med J Aust* 26 February 1916 p 185

40 JL Beeston *Five Months at Anzac* Angus & Robertson Sydney 1916 p 64

41 Recollections of Lt Col JR Muirhead AWM 41 3/10.24

42 AWM 41 Item 4/12.18

43 *Memorandum — Treatment of Injuries in War* op cit p 103

44 J Laffin *Surgeons in the Field* JM Dent & Son London, 1970 pp 215–6

45 Diary entry for 3 May 1915 Col JL Beeston op cit

46 'Surgical Experiences At the War' Lt Col GA Syme AMC *Med J Aust* Vol 1 No 14 1 April 1916

47 EJF Deakin *Med J Aust* op cit 27 January 1917 p 77

48 *J Ass Milit Surg US* vol XXXVI Chicago 1915 p 572

49 The Anzac Medical Society, Minutes of 5 December at No 1 ASH AWM 27 370[6] (AWRS 891/1/13)

50 Personal Narrative of an (anonymous) Australian nurse aboard the *Guildford Castle* dated 26 April 1918 AWM 41 Butler Collection [Box 5] Folder 5/50

51 Entry for 8 July 1915 War diary PDMS MEF AWM 4 26/2

52 ibid Entry for 10 July 1915

53 'Surgical Experiences At the War' Lt Col GA Syme op cit. This extract refers to the *Gascon*.

54 DC Question No 29326 Surgeon-General Ford fully agreed with the accuracy of the text. DC Question No 29327

55 EJF Deakin op cit p 77

56 AH Tubby *A Consulting Surgeon in the Near East* Christopher London 1920 p 41

57 Entry for 28 September 1915 Diary of VR Laidlaw 2nd AFA MS 11827 Box 2163/3–5 SL

58 Letter May 1915 by P Hall No 2 ASH on board the *Seang Choon* op cit

CHAPTER 4

1 Diary of Col JL Beeston [commanding the 4th AFA], entry for 30 April 1915 op cit

2 Statement by Lt General EA Altham Inspector-General of Communications DC p 1

3 Adapted from *OHAAMS* Vol I p 116

4 Diary entry for 28 April 1915 Sgt CF Laseron 13th Btn op cit

5 Letter from Charles Crome to his parents written on 21 May 1915 SL MS 10026

6 War diary 1st AFA 25 June 1915 op cit

7 War diary 5th AFA 2 December 1915 op cit

8 Diary entry for 30 April 1915 James McPhee 4th AFA op cit

9 Memoirs of Cpl HR Duncan 8th Sanitary Section AAMC AWM File No 419/82/48. PR 84/60

10 Letter to his family from Pte J Brotchie 14th Btn MS 11628 Box No. 1834/2 SL

11 27 May 1915 War diary of the 1st AFA op cit

12 9 May 1915 War diary 4th AFA op cit

13 Note for 28 July 1915 War diary of the 1st AFA op cit

14 Col CM Begg (NZAMC) 'Statement with regard to provision for sick and wounded during the Gallipoli Campaign' 1915 DC p 2

15 Letter dated 9 April 1915 AWM 41 Butler Papers (Box 9) File No 9/18

16 Letter from Colonel RM Downes (CO 3rd LHFA) dated 30 July 1915 AWM 3DRL/518

17 29 April 1915 War diary DDMS 1st Aust Div (Howse) op cit

18 AWM 32 Tait Files (Box 4) File 1 'Medical Arrangements at Gallipoli'

19 DC Final Report p 70

20 DC Question No 28637

21 DC Birrell Replies to the Evidence of Lt Col J. Corbin 25 August 1917 p 7

22 Recollections of Captain JWB Bean concerning the April landing. AWM 41 Butler Papers [Box 5] File 5/53

23 Extract from a letter from the Governor of Malta to Vice-Admiral Limpus dated 6 May 1915 Limpus Papers MS 75/139 A NNM

24 Diary entry for 24.9.1915. MSS 3037 ML

25 DC Question Nos 28745 and 28746 to Lt Col C Ryan

26 Lt Col J Corbin DC Question No 28537

27 Letter from Fleet Surgeon CC McMillan SMO Naval — Anzac to Butler dated 31 March 1923 AWM 41 3/10.9

28 Aspinall-Oglander op cit p 146

29 AWM 41 (Box 5) Personal Narrative of Captain Whitelaw

30 Personal Recollections of Colonel BJ Newmarch OC 1st AFA AWM 41 3/11.5

31 Misc Porter papers p 14 AWM 51 Item No 103

32 AWM 27 370.2[14]

33 Fayle CE (ed.) *History of the Great War — Seaborne Trade* Vol II John Murray London 1923 p 174

34 Hamilton Papers 17/3/2/38. LHC

35 Cairo 1 May 1915 Diary of Pte McKenzie No 2 AGH MSS 1985 ML

36 JEF Deakin op cit p 77

37 Letter of 2 May 1915 by P Hall No 2 ASH on board the *Seang Choon* op cit

38 BT Zwar 'Remarks On War Experiences' *Med J Aust* 29 April 1916 pp 361–2

39 Notes written by Lt Col G.A. Syme, Surgical Consultant on board the *Gascon*, for 25 April 1915 [from MSS lent by Mr Martin Syme] Ambulance Carriers were better prepared

40 Diary of AHE Gissing 1st AFA op cit

41 Entry for 28 July 1915 Diary of L/Cpl JG Burgess of the 6th LFHA op cit

42 Lt Col C Ryan DC Question No 28696

43 Letter dated 15 July 1915 from Lt Col J Humphrey (RAMC) OC No 11 (British) CCS to the DDMS Lines of Communication, Mudros.

This was part of a larger report requesting more small boats. The latter supported by a cable of 25 July 1915 from RF Phillimore PTO AWM 27 371.5

44   Howse Collection Bundle IV File No. 184/14

45   AWM 27 370.2[17]

46   Letter from Birrell to Keogh dated 22 August 1915 aboard the *Aragon* AWM 25 Written Records of the 1914–1918 War Item 367/40 'Medical Aspects of Gallipoli Operations — Extracts from War Office Documents Feb–Dec 1915'

47   *OHAAMS* Vol I pp 288–9

48   CF Aspinall-Oglander (ed.) op cit Vol II p 309

49   Letter to Butler 29 December 1915 from Lt Col LW Jeffries re the pier at the North Beach in the August fighting at Anzac AWM 41 3/9.4

50   Sir G MacMunn 'The Lines of Communication in the Dardanelles' in *The Army Quarterly* Vol XX 1930 p 57

51   DC Question No 28553

52   AWM 51 Item No 103 DC p 2

53   ibid

54   Mayo-Robson DC Question No 18109

55   Letter to her sister by Sister GM Wilson dated 6 August 1915 at Mudros Bay. AWM 3DRL 7819

56   August 1915 Diary of Sister IG Lovell 3 AGH op cit

57   Based on JH Plumridge *Hospital Ships and Ambulance Trains* Seeley Service & Co London 1975 pp 34–5

58   Letter written to Limpus by Field Marshal Lord Methuen Governor of Malta dated 25 June 1915 Limpus Papers MS 75/139 A. NMM

59   Lord Wester-Wemyss *The Navy and the Dardanelles Campaign* Hodder & Stoughton London n.d. pp 149–50

60   Letter from Birrell to the DAG AWM 27 371.5

61   AWM 27 371.5

62   DC Question No 30603

63   HW Nevinson *The Dardanelles Campaign* Nisbet & Co London 1918 p 164

64   AWM 27 370.2[17]

65   Recollections of Sister Woniarski for 6.7.1915. AWM 41 Box 6 File 6/65

66   Letter of 27 July 1915 *Statement* by Babtie DC p 165

67   Diary entry 18 May 1915 Pte E Silas MSS.1840 ML

68   14 August 1915 War diary of the No 2 ASH AWM 4 26/71

69   Letter from Keble to Keogh Mudros 26 May 1915 AWM 41 Butler Collection (unmarked box) File 370.2

70   See DC Question Nos 28791 28809 to Colonel C Ryan

71   (Not to be confused with Major AJ Aspinall AAMC) AWM 27 371.5

72   Major AC Purchas NZAMC DC Question No 31145

73   DC Question No 31239

74   F Bowerbank *A Doctor's Story* Wingfield Press Wellington 1958 p 101

75   AWM 25 Written Records of the 1914–1918 War Item 367/40 'Medical Aspects of Gallipoli Operations — Extracts from War Office Documents Feb–Dec 1915'

76   JW Barrett and PE Deane *The Australian Army Medical Corps in Egypt* HK Lewis & Co London 1918 p 38

77   Cable from High Commissioner's Office London 16 April 1915 AWM 32 2DRL 2[10] Tait Files — Mobilisation of AAMC Units

78   Letter of Col JB McLean (OC No 1 AGH Cairo) to Butler, dated 20 April 1923 AWM 41 3/10.8

79   ML MSS 1006

80   Letter to Hamilton from Field Marshall Lord Methuen, Governor of Malta dated 14 May 1915 AWM 27 370.2 [17]

81   Recollections of Col BJ Newmarch 1st AFA AWM 41 3/11.5

82   AWM 27 370.2[17]

83   Recollections of Lt Col Muirhead (attached to the 1st LHFA on the *Arcadian* in May) AWM 41 3/10.24

84   JW Barrett and PE Deane op cit p 35

85   Diary of Miss C McNaughton No 2 AGH (Loaned to the author by Mrs P Barnes Werribee Australia)

86   OP Kenny 3rd AFA AWM 41 3/9.10

87   Letter of 31 July 1915 from the Governor of Malta to Vice-Admiral Limpus. Limpus Papers Ms 75/139 A NMM. The procedure was that once a hospital ship was full, Keble or his staff at Mudros would advise the DQG General Winters whose duty it was to despatch them and notify Egypt by cable. DC Question No Keble 30081. But in practice this procedure was not always adhered to.

88   AWM 27 [370]

89   Letter of 22 September 1915 from Major-General EA Altham to Sir Alfred Keogh AWM 27 370.2 [15]

90   DC Question No 29271 Egypt

91   OP Kenny 3rd AFA op cit

92   AWM 27 Item 370.5[13]

CHAPTER 5

1   *OHAAMS* Vol 1 p 341

2   JW Springthorpe diary entry for 25 January 1915 op cit The relationship between these two doctors was always an uneasy one.

3   Entry for 25 August 1915. War diary for the 1st ACCS op cit

4   Letter of November (no day given) 1915, by Surgeon-General Bedford to Sir Alfred Keogh AWM 27 370 [11]

5   *On the Anzac Trail* by 'Anzac' William Heinemann London 1916 p 156

6   AWM Tait Files DRL 1200 (2/) Misc. — Sanitation at Anzac

7   Recollections of Cpl Kitson 4th AFA op cit

8   Entry for 29 July 1915 War diary of the 2nd AFA AWM 4 26/45

9   Narrative of Sgt E Clark AWM 41 Item 1/5.9

10 F Waite op cit p 161. See also Bean op cit Vol 11 p 383n for the importance of sea-bathing despite casualties.

11 Entry for 1 August 1915. War diary of the DMS MEF op cit

12 23 May 1915 War diary of the 1st AFA op cit

13 HW Bryant op cit p 262

14 A Hurst *Medical Diseases of the War* Edward Arnold London 1945 3rd Ed p 213

15 Letter from De Robeck to Vice-Admiral Limpus dated 29 June 1915 Lord Nelson Limpus Papers Ms. 75/139 A. NMM

16 A Hurst op cit p 200

17 Personal narrative of Col J Purves-Stewart, Consulting Physician to the Forces AWM 41 Butler Papers (Box 4) File No. 4/62

18 Letter by Hamilton dated 1 October 1915 Hamilton papers 17/7/29/2 LHC

19 Letter of Sister BE Henson dated 23 November 1915 at Lemnos AWM 3 DRL 4063

20 C Midwinter *Memoirs of the 32nd Field Ambulance (1st Irish Division)* Foulgar London 1933 p 33

21 Bean, op cit Vol 11 p 369

22 3 July 1915 War diary of the 1st AFA op cit

23 A Hurst op cit p 256

24 3 November 1915 War diary of the 7th AFA AWM 4 26/50

25 28 November 1915 Diary of J McPhee 4th AFA op cit

26 Butler n.d. personal diary op cit

27 Lt Col RM Bowman acting RMO 9 Btn at Gallipoli AWM 41 Butler Papers Item 1/4.12

28 'Inoculated second time for cholera.' Entry for 25 August 1915 Diary of FH Smith 2nd LHFA ML MSS 2742

29 AWM 25 Written Records of the 1914–1918 War Item 367/40 'Medical Aspects of Gallipoli Operations — Extracts from War Office Documents Feb–Dec 1915'

30 Entry for 5 July 1915 War diary of the DMS MEF (Birrell) op cit

31 Letter to his mother dated 18 July 1915 by Cpl R Gardiner Clerk ADMS 1st Australian Division op cit

32 Entry for 16 July 1915 Diary of the ADMS (Howse) ANZAC Corps AWM 2DRL 1351 File No. 184/16

33 F Waite op cit p 259

34 War diary of the 4th AFA op cit

35 3 October 1915 War diary of the 1st LHFA AWM 4 26/39

36 23 October 1915 War diary of the 6th AFA op cit

37 War diary of the 5th AFA op cit

38 War diary of the 3rd AFA op cit

39 12 December 1915 War diary of the 7th AFA op cit

40 Entry for 18 June 1915 Sister A Kitchen on H. S. *Gascon*, off Gaba Tepe op cit

41 29 September 1915 Private Diary of Captain (later Major) ASD Barton 1st ACCS AWM 27 1/4.6

42 Aspinall-Oglander op cit Vol II p 98

43 R East (ed.) *The Gallipoli Diaries of Sergeant Lawrence* MUP Melbourne 1981 p 84

44 Diary of Pte VO Worland entry for 5 September 1915 AWM 3DRL 3904

45 General Notes for September 1915 War diary of the 2nd AFA AWM 4 26/45

46 *The Gallipoli Diaries of Sergeant Lawrence* op cit p 84

47 Diary entry for 15 August 1915 Sgt GS Tefler 4th LHR MS 9604 MSB 422. SL

48 *OHAAMS* Vol I p 343

49 FM Cutlack op cit p 67

50 Sister NF Selwyn Smith at Lemnos. Letter to Butler n.d. Butler Papers AWM 41 Box 5 'Nurses recollections'

51 Entry for 11 September 1915 Sgt DJ Partridge op cit

52 CEW Bean op cit Vol 11 p 387

53 Entry for 13 June 1915 War diary No 2 ASH op cit

54 Letter dated 20 September 1915 Sarpi Camp West Mudros in FM Cutlack op cit p 68

55 Letter of Sister E Davies from Lemnos dated 12 November 1915 AWM 3DRL 3398

56 W Summons *Med J Aust* 20 November 1915 op cit p 482

CHAPTER 6

1 *OHAAMS* Vol III pp 79–80

2 J Masefield *Gallipoli* Heinemann London 1917 p 97

3 14 May 1915 AWM 25 367/26

4 DC Question No 28857 Lt Col J Gordon

5 Letter from De Robeck to Limpus dated 15 May 1915 at Gallipoli Limpus Papers MS 75/139 A. NMM

6 Letter to his wife by Major SJ Richards of the 1st ACCS dated 17 June 1915 ML MSS. 2908

7 HJ Stewart op cit pp 393–394

8 Letter home from TW Liddell 23rd Btn on Gallipoli dated 1 November 1915 Ms 11568 Box 1674/10–13 SL

9 14 September 1915 War diary of the 5th AFA

10 Diary of HP Moloney 5th Btn entry for 16 July 1915 MS 10984 MSB 359 SL

11 Letter 4 July 1915 to his family by Pte J Brotchie 14th Btn op cit

12 Diary entry 14 June 1915 of VR Laidlaw 2nd AFA op cit

13 Letter to the writer, from Mr L Lambert a member of the 6th AFA during the Gallipoli campaign

14 Report by Birrell Hamilton Papers 17/3/1/89 LHC

15 Bean Vol 11 op cit p 386n. (Derived from Fenwick's (NZMC) diary entry for 7 June 1915 AWM 41 2/7.3)

16 Diary of Pte G Gower stretcher bearer with the 15th Btn (AAMC) dated 30 June 1915 op cit

17 J Vassal *Uncensored Letters from the Dardanelles Written to his English Wife by a French Medical Officer of Le Corps Expeditionaire d'Orient* W Heinemann London 1916 p 92

18 Statement to the Dardanelles Commission dated 17 March 1917 p 6

19 HW Nevinson op cit pp 192–3

20 Diary entry for 6 September 1915 JG Burgess op cit

21 Letter to his wife dated 17 June 1915 by Major SJ Richards (1st ACCS) op cit

22 Cable of 27 August 1915 AWM 25 Written Records of the 1914–1918 War Item 367/40 'Medical Aspects of Gallipoli Operations — Extracts from War Office Documents Feb–Dec 1915'

23 SH Bowden (ed.) *The History of the Australian Comforts Fund* Scotow and Presswell Sydney nd p 234

24 Diary entry for 23 August 1915 VR Laidlaw 2nd AFA op cit

25 Royal Navy Signals, signal of 13 August 1915 from Anzac Admin Staff to 1st Aust Division AWM 25 3 67/26

26 Entry for 20 August 1915 Sir Ian Hamilton Vol II op. cit pp 123–4

27 ibid pp 123–4

28 Diary entry for 21 June 1915 MSS 2742 ML

29 F. Waite op cit p 162

30 Diary entry for 11 September 1915 VR Laidlaw 2nd AFA op cit

31 Letter to the DA & QMS ANZAC from Howse dated 16 September 1915 copy in the War diary of the DDMS ANZAC Corps AWM 4 26/14

32 DC Question No 12375 (Woodward)

33 DC Question Nos 15600–15603.

34 Cablegram from DGMS to Department of Defence Melbourne dated 25 October 1915. Fetherston Collection AWM 12/11/3479

35 Letter from General JG Legge to the Governor-General, dated 5 October 1915 from Gallipoli [re troops at Cape Helles] Novar Papers Ms 696/3604 National Library of Australia

36 M Tilton *The Grey Battalion* 2nd Ed Angus & Robertson Sydney 1934 p 20

37 Bean Vol 11 op cit p 381

38 *OHAAMS*, Vol I p 80

39 Entry for 24 June 1915 War Diary of the DMS MEF AWM 4 26/3

40 Letter from Babtie (en route for Cape Helles) to Sir Alfred Keogh dated 30 June 1915 AWM 27 370.2[14]

41 Copy of a letter from Howse to DA & QMG dated 29 June 1915 War diary ADMS 1st Australian Division AWM 4 26/18

42 HW Bryant 'Some Notes Taken Whilst on Active Service with the No. 1 Australian Stationary Hospital' in *Med J Aust* Vol 1 3rd Year 25 March 1916 p 262

43 Letter from Butler to his wife dated 12 July 1915 AWM 3 DRL 7100

44 11 September 1915 War diary of the 3rd AFA op cit

45 Diary entry for 15 June 1915 Col JW Springthorpe (Senior Physician of No 2 AGH in Egypt) op cit

46 Entry for 3 July 1915 War diary of the 1st AFA op cit

47 *OHAAMS* Vol III p 448

48 Col AL Buchanan, 3rd AFA AWM 41 Item No 1/4.18

49 Narrative of Major G Douglas AWM 3DRL 3275

50 Lt Colonel Begg (NZAMC) quoted by *Br Med J* 4.12.1915 and reproduced as part of a letter to the *Aust J Dent* Vol XX 31 January 1916 p 14

51 J Corbin op cit p 113

52 Diary of Pte AD Gordon 1st AFA op cit

53 Personal diary of Col JL Beeston 4th AFA op cit

54 JL Beeston *Five Months at Anzac* Angus & Robertson Sydney 1916 p 19

55 RR James op cit p 226

56 Letter dated 2 December 1915 G Walsh AASC ML A2660 Vol II 'Letters Written On Active Service'

57 AWM 41 Butler Papers (Box 9) File 9/7

58 Keogh DC Question No 19478

59 War diary of the 5th AFA entry of 4 September 1915 op cit

60 KF Gordon 'Days at An Advanced Dressing Station' in Supplement to *Med J Aust* 3 December 1927 p 466

61 Col Sir Courtauld-Thomson Chief Commissioner of the British Red Cross Society and the Order of St John DC Question No 31045

62 The *British Red Cross and Order of St John Annual Report* London May 1915–February 1916. AWM 41 Butler Papers (Box 28) File No 1/10

63 DC Question Nos 29152–4 to Colonel Begg CO of the NZFA

64 *Report* of 18 September 1915 of the British Red Cross and the Order of St John prepared by Lt Col Sir Courtauld-Thomson, Chief Commissioner Hamilton papers 17/7/29/4 LHC

65 *Report by the Joint War Committee and Joint War Finance Committee of the British Red Cross Society and the Order of St. John in England*, HMSO London 1921 Part XXI p 426

66 J North *Gallipoli: The Fading Vision* Faber & Faber London 1936 p 75

67 CE Fayle op cit p 174

68 Letter from Maurice Hankey to Asquith dated 5 August 1915 MPA. Hankey op cit Vol I p 387

69 Letter from Maurice Hankey to Asquith dated 5 August 1915 MPA Hankey op cit p 386

70   Interview with Surgeon-General CS Ryan on 14 March 1919 AWM 27 370.5[1]

71   Sister LE Young No 3 ASH at Mudros. Letter written to Col Butler dated 19 July 1915 AWM 41 Box 5

72   From a report to Howse from Col Sutton (AAMC) ADMS War diary of the DDMS ANZAC no date but probably September 1915

73   Letter of 5 October 1915 by Bedford to Keogh DGMS AWM 27 370[11]

74   op cit letter of 28 October 1915

75   Diary entry for October A Taylor MS12286 Box 1829/6 SL

76   Lt Col Springthorpe's address to the Australian Red Cross op cit

77   Entry for 18 August 1915 War diary ADMS 1st Australian Division op cit

78   Letter written from Lemnos, 20 September 1915 by Lt TW Garling [attached to a Field Artillery unit] 'Letters Written on Active Service' ML A.2660

79   Carbery op cit pp 107–8

80   Memorandum from Col Howse a/DDMS ANZAC to DA & QMG dated 23 September 1915 AWM 4 26/14

81   Letter of 28 May 1915 to his wife by Major SJ Richards of the 1st ACCS op cit

82   Signal to 1st Inf Bde from Lt Col AJ Bennett CO 4th Bn AWM 25 367/26

83   'Shell shock was not known then.' Mr L Lambert late of the 6th AFA, and who served at Anzac Letter to the author. Butler also noted that the Gallipoli campaign belonged to a stage of the war when the idea of a psychiatric problem 'had simply not entered into the minds of the medical service' OHAAMS Vol III p 77

84   CS Myers Shell Shock in France 1914–18 CUP Cambridge 1940 pp 25–26

85   MD Eder War Shock W Heinemann London 1917 p 4

86   J Laffin op cit p 220

87   OHAAMS Vol III p 100

88   WE Jones 'A Case of Shell Shock' Med J Aust 4 March 1916 p 203

89   M Tilton op cit p 15

90   AW Campbell 'Remarks on Some Neuroses and Psychoses in War' Med J Aust Vol I 3rd Year 15 April 1916 p 323. B White states that 100 days of intermittent battle/combat is the average length of tolerance before non-effective behaviour becomes frequent. In 'Combat Stress Reaction' Defence Force Journal No 55 1985 p 26

91   War diary of the 5th AFA (op cit) Entry for 11 December 1915

92   Diary entry 10 November 1915 of Sgt (later Lt) HHV Woods 4th AFA op cit

93   W Moore The Thin Yellow Line Cooper Ltd London 1974 p 72

94   16 June 1915 War diary of the No 1 ASH op cit

95   General Notes for November 1915 War diary of the 2nd AFA AWM 4 26/45

96 Letter to his wife from Sir James Porter dated 19 August1915 Porter papers PTR/8/1(5) NMM

97 *OHAAMS* Vol I p 249

98 Letter to Butler from Major Fullerton dated 9 January 1926 AWM 41 2/716

99 Notes for November 1915 War Diary of the 2nd LHFA op cit

100 Diary of VR Laidlaw 2nd AFA while on Lemnos entry for 28 September 1915 op cit

101 War diary 2nd LHFA op cit

102 Letter to the author from Mr Lou Lambert 10 March 1988

103 Diary entry of 13 May 1915 PTE JO Maddox 1st AFA MS 2877 ML

104 Diary entry for 4 May 1915 of Pte P Hall No 2 ASH op cit

105 Letter of 20 November 1914 from GG Allardyee (4th AFA) to his father op cit

106 Diary entry of 8 October 1914 Pte J McKenzie No 2 AGH ML MSS 1985

107 Diary entry (n.d. but probably August 1914) of Pte AD Gordon 1st AFA op cit

108 Diary entry for September 1914 by Pte E Silas op cit

109 Letter of 3 May 1915 to AAG GHQ from Lt Col HW Bryant AWM 4 26.70

110 Letter of Sister GM Wilson No 3 AGH dated 6 August 1915 op cit

111 Melbourne *Age* 21 June 1915

112 *University Council Minutes* 5 July 1915 '10. Medical Course and War' University of Melbourne Archives p 243

113 KF Russell *The Melbourne Medical School 1862–1962* MUP Melbourne 1977 p 121

114 *Melbourne University Record of Service* Government Printer Melbourne 1926

115 A. Aspinall, op cit p 122

116 Diary entry of 16 Dec 1914 Col JW Springthorpe ML MSS 1709

117 Notes by Major-General RW Ford sent to General MacPherson (the Imperial Medical History Collator) AWM No. 27 [370]

118 *OHAAMS* Vol I pp 37–38

119 CL Chapman Diary entry for 30 March 1915 op cit

120 War diary of No 1 ASH AWM 4 26/70

121 Personal Narrative of Cpl Kitson AWM 41 3/9.14

122 E Scott *Australia During the War* Angus & Robertson Sydney 1936 p 701

123 Diary of Major LO Betts op cit

124 War diary 2nd LHFA 16 December 1915 op cit

125 Miss Grace Wilson, Principal Matron and acting Matron-in-Chief First AIF quoted in *OHAAMS* Vol III p 535

126 For details on nurses' activities in this theatre, see J Bassett *Guns and Brooches* 1992 OUP Melbourne

127 AM Mitchell *Medical Women and the Medical Services of the First World War* 1978 Limited Edition Sydney p 5

128 DC Question No 31215 Major AC Purchas NZAMC

129 LHC Hamilton Papers 5/5 and 'Press Cuttings' LHC Hamilton Papers 33/2

130 PRO ADM 1/8427/205

131 J Robertson *Anzac and Empire* Hamlyn Melbourne 1990 p 201

132 MP 367 Item 430/2/702 Australian Archives (Victoria)

133 Both Schuler and Ashmead-Bartlett went on to write books of their experiences

134 The *Age* 18.10.1915

135 The *Sydney Morning Herald* 17.5.1915

136 7 July 1915 Statement by Mr HJ Tennant Under-Secretary to the War Office in the House of Commons

137 Report on Army Medical Services, Australian Imperial Force on Active Service, by the Acting Director-General of Medical Services (AIF) Colonel Fetherston AWM 32 2DRL 1200 p 46

138 op cit p 60

139 Letter of 22.10.15 from Bedford to Keogh AWM 27 370 [11]

140 Letter of 6.10.15 from Bedford to Keogh op cit

141 Fisher Papers Ms 2919/9/55 Series 9 National Library of Australia

142 C Pugsley op cit p 349

143 Extract from Supplementary Report by the Hon Sir Thomas Mackenzie, DC Final Report p 95

144 *Med J Aust* 18 December 1915 p 585

CHAPTER 7

1 Neville Howse DC Question No 27675 AWM 51 No 103

2 M Hankey *Government Control in War* Vol II CUP Cambridge 1945 p 524. Hankey cites his diary entry for 29 July 1915

3 J Robertson *Anzac and Empire* op cit p 224

4 Final Report of the Dardanelles Commission Part II p 93

5 Lt Col Beardon AQMG (under General Winter DQMG) DC Question Nos 13844–13853

6 DC p 2 of a statement made by Birrell in response to allegations made by Howse

7 DC pp 8–9 of a statement made by Birrell in response to allegations made by Lt Col J Gordon AAMC

8 Brig Gen EM Woodward DAG MEF DC Question No 12308

9 Sir Ian Hamilton letter of 15 August 1917 Hamilton Papers 17/4/3/36 LHC

10 Brig General EM Woodward DC Question No 12312

11 De Robeck letter to Admiral Limpus 3 June 1915 Limpus Papers Ms 75/139 NMM

12 Letter from De Robeck to Limpus dated 31 August 1915 Limpus Papers Ms 75/139 NMM

13 Letter from Vice-Admiral Wemyss to Admiral Limpus dated 17 May 1915 Limpus Papers Ms 75/139 NMM

14 DC Evidence of Lt Col Thom DADMS to DDMS (Col Maher) Question No 17522

15 Archer quoted in DC Question No 9193

16 Lt Col J Corbin DC Question No 28641

17 DC Question No 28641 and Corbin Question No 28552

18 DC Question No 28552 and Corbin Question No 28573

19 War diary of the 1st ACCS Feb 1915–Dec 1915 Entries for 15 and 23 August AWM 4 26/62 and Fetherston Report AWM 51 DRL 1200 and DC Question No 29448

20 Memo dated 21 August 1915 Lt Gen Altham [Inspector-General of Communications] AWM 370.5[14]

21 Confidential Papers dealing with the appointment of PHTO and arrangements in connection with hospital ships unsigned but probably by Keogh AWM 27 370.2 [19]

22 ibid

23 Submission from the 2nd Sea Lord 21 June 1915 ADM 1/8424/166 PRO

24 Admiralty Nomination List 115 14 June 1915 ADM 1/8424/166 PRO

25 Letter of appointment of 28 June 1915 from the Admiralty PTR/8/1(5) NNM

26 Cipher 5816 WO to GHQ MEF 28 June 1915 Hamilton Papers 17/4/1/51 LHC

27 Cipher No 1073 Hamilton to WO 29 June 1915 Hamilton Papers 17/4/1/51 LHC

28 Staff Surgeon AV Elder (Porter's staff officer) undated memo to Porter probably 1919 PTR/8/1(5) NNM

29 Cable (No. 402) 3 July 1915 Telegram from GHQ MEF to WO Hamilton Papers 17/4/1/52. LHC

30 *OHAAMS* Vol I p 287

31 ibid pp 326–27

32 Cable 29 July 1915 Telegram from GHQ MEF to War Office Porter Papers PTR/8/1/(5) NMM

33 Cable from Brigadier-General Winter GHQ MEF to War Office 29 July 1915 Hamilton Papers 17/4/1/53 LHC

34 Cable 30 July 1915 from GHQ MEF to War Office Hamilton Papers 17/4/1/53 LHC The Regulations referred to by Hamilton were Field Service Regulations Part 2 Chapter 11 Section 90 Paragraph 13

35 PTR/8/1(5) NMM

36 Porter Papers PTR/8/1/(5) NMM

37 Limpus Papers Ms75/139 NMM

38 Letter dated 1 October 1915 AWM 25 Written Records of the 1914–1918 War Item 367/40 'Medical Aspects of Gallipoli Operations — Extracts from War Office Documents Feb–Dec 1915'

39   Letter from Vice-Admiral Expedition Mediterranean to Second Sea
      Lord, marked 'Personal and Private' and dated 3 October 1915 ADM
      1/8424/156 PRO

40   Cipher No 8556 5 October 1915 Hamilton Papers 17/4/1/54 LHC

41   Evidence of Col Thom DC Question No 17619

42   Admiralty Minute 6 October 1915 ADM 1/8424/166 PRO

43   Letter from Sir Arthur May to Limpus 27 October 1915 Limpus
      Papers Ms75/139 NMM

44   Letter to the Admiralty Secretary from the Secretary War Office 19
      November 1915 ADM 1/8424/166 PRO

45   Letter from the Secretary of War to the Secretary of the Admiralty 2
      October 1915 ADM 1/8424/166 PRO

46   Letter from Wemyss to Limpus dated 17 May 1915 Limpus Papers Ms
      75/139 NMM

47   Letter from Porter to Limpus Mudros 17 October 1915 Limpus Papers
      Ms 75/13 NMM

48   Letter from the CO 3rd AFA dated 30 July 1915 Colonel RM Downes
      AWM 3DRL/518

49   Letter dated 18 September 1915 Cairo White supported Howse as
      DDMS of the AIF. AWM 3DRL 251 Bundle 1 Item 8

50   Fetherston Papers Confidential Report to the Secretary of Defence 8
      January 1916 AWM 41 2/7.7 DRL1200

51   Bean op cit Vol II pp 399–400

52   31 May 1915 AWM 4/26/3

53   JL Beeston *Med J Aust* op cit p 24

54   J Hargrave (of 32nd Field Ambulance (UK)) *At Suvla Bay* Constable
      & Co Ltd London 1916 p 155

55   Diary of Sister Florence Elisabeth McMillan Letter from No 3 AGH
      Mudros 9 November 1915 op cit

56   JG Burgess 6th ALH 31 July 1915 op cit

57   Confidential Memo from Capt FP Dunlop DAGMG to DQMG dated
      1 July 1915 Control of Hospital Ships and Transports/...*Galeka*
      Correspondence AWM 41 371.5

58   Diary of HP Moloney 5th Btn AIF op cit Entry for 8 September 1915

59   Extract from a letter written by a wounded officer to his family in
      Australia *Med J Aust* 17 July 1915 p 60

60   War diary of No I ASH Entry for 4 June 1915

61   Narrative of HF Nelson, who was wounded at Gallipoli on 19 May
      1915 AWM 41 3/11.2

62   Interview with Surgeon-General CS Ryan 14 March 1919 re
      evacuation from Gallipoli p 5 AWM DRL 27.370.5 [1]

63   'Narrative of experiences' AWM 41 Butler Papers

64   War diary of the 3rd LHFA op cit

65   Charles Clark quoted in C Pugsley op cit p 307

66   Lt Col VO Stacey of No 2 ASH AWM 41 Item 4/12.5

67   Lt Col JR Muirhead op cit

68   Fetherston Papers Confidential Report 1916 AWM 41

69   Sgt OP Kenny 3rd AFA op cit

70   DC Question Nos 28683 and 28685

71   DC Question No 27686

72   3DRL Fetherston Papers File No 12/11/3470 Bundle I Item 3 Letter of 3 December 1915 from Howse (now DDMS ANZAC) in Cairo to the DGMS Australia [Fetherston]

73   Letter of 17 September 1915 Hamilton Papers 15/10/59 LHC

74   Babtie to Sir A Keogh 29 June 1915 AWM 27 370.2[14] See also Hamilton Papers 15/10/59 LHC

75   Cable to GOC in C 30 August 1915 PTR/8/1/(5) NMM

76   Diary of Dr H Clough, Surgeon Diary entry undated from the R.M.S. *Carmania* off Anzac p 2 P 15 IWM

77   *Med J Aust* 18 September 1915 p 282

78   Confidential Report by Fetherston to the Secretary, Department of Defence 8 January 1916 AWM 41 DRL 1200 Fetherston Papers

79   ibid

80   19 May 1915 (Lt Col HW Bryant OC) 1st ASH Lemnos War Diary op cit

81   Confidential Report by Fetherston to the Secretary [Australian] Dept of Defence op cit (8 January 1916)

82   Novar Papers Ms 696 Item 3578 National Library of Australia

83   Personal Recollections of Dr TEV Hurley op cit

84   Diary entry for 24 July 1915 by Col Springthorpe of the No 2 AGH op cit

85   Letter from Babtie to Keogh dated 25 October 1915 AWM 27 370.2 [14]

86   Confidential Report by Fetherston to the Secretary [Australian] Department of Defence op cit 8 January 1916

87   Letter to Babtie 1917 Hamilton Papers 17/3/2/31 LHC

88   Hamilton Papers 17/4/3/20 LHC Letter from Hamilton to Sir Grimwade Mears the Secretary of the Dardanelles Commission dated 27 July 1917

89   DC Statement by Col Keble p 3

90   War diary of No 1 ASH op cit

91   Fetherston Papers Report AWM 41 2/7.6

92   DC Birrell's Statement p 3 Reply to Howse's allegations

93   Memorandum from Birrell to Hamilton undated but possibly 1917 Hamilton Papers 17/3/2/56 LHC

94   Dated 30 May 1915 Government House Melbourne Novar Papers Ms696 Item 21 National Library of Australia

95   AWM 27 370.2[14]

96   AWM 3DRL/518

97   Fetherston Papers AWM 41 DRL 1200

98   Dr TEV Hurley writing of September 1915 op cit

99   Munro–Ferguson to Maxwell 27 September 1915 Ms 696/3595 Novar Papers Australian National Library

100   Letter from the Australian Governor-General Munro-Ferguson, to Bonar-Law dated 4 October 1915 M.1123. Bonar-Law Papers National Library of Australia

101   Letter dated 18 September 1915 AWM 3 DRL 251 Bundle 1 Item 8

102   Letter dated 31 October 1915 Ms 696 Box 4 Item Nos 3377–3386 Novar Papers, National Library of Australia

103   War diary of No 2 ASH op cit

104   Letter from the CO 3rd AFA dated 30 July 1915 Col RM Downes AWM 3DRL/518

105   Letter to Col Fetherston from Capt TEV Hurley 2nd AFA Anzac Cove 5 June 1915 AWM DRL1200 Fetherston Papers 12/11/3479. Bean op cit Vol II pp 408ff also alludes to the internecine fighting within the AAMC in Egypt

106   Letter from Babtie to Keogh dated 5 October 1915 AWM 27 370.2 [14]

107   Letter to Keogh dated 5 October 1915 op cit

108   Fetherston Papers op cit

109   Letter to Colonel Fetherston from Lt Col RM Downes OC 3rd LHFA acting as a Stationary Hospital at Lemnos 9 July 1915 Fetherston Papers AWM 12/11/3479

110   War diary DDMS AWM 4 26/14

111   Letter dated 28 January 1916 AWM 41 Fetherston Papers Box 1411 Bundle 1 Item No 3

112   Maxwell to Sir Ronald Munro-Ferguson (the Australian Governor-General) 31 October 1915 Ms.696/3589 Novar Papers National Library of Australia

113   Letter to the Secretary of State for the Colonies dated 7 June 1916 op cit

114   Letter to HM King George V dated 30 May 1915 Government House Melbourne Bonar-Law Papers M 1123 National Library of Australia

115   Dated 23 August 1916 Bonar-Law Papers op cit

116   Keble DC Question No 29951 re activities of 7 August evacuations by Major Corbin (evacuation officer)

117   Dr C Checchi to author 23 February 1988

CHAPTER 8

1   Peter Hall of the No 2 ASH in a letter to his mother dated 2 May 1915 op cit

2   Med J Aust 30 December 1930 pp 395–6

3   AWM 41 Butler Papers last (unnamed) Box 'Letters Vol 1929 Bean etc' Letter dated 19 May 1930

4   PFE Schuler Australia in Arms T Fisher Unwin London 1916 Appendices I and II pp 293ff

5   P Liddle Men of Gallipoli Allen Lane London 1976 p 98

6   AWM 41 Butler Collection — Personal Narratives [Box 5] Folder 5/25 General Sir CBB White
7   *Gallipoli As I Saw It* William Kimber London 1965 p 91 [5 June 1915]
8   Bundle 1 Item 8 AWM 3DRL 251
9   J Corbin op cit p 113

APPENDICES

*   *OHAAMS* Vol I p 812
1   JH Plumridge *Hospital Ships and Ambulance Trains* op cit p 169
2   War diary dated 13 December 1915 Col N Howse DDMS op cit
3   *Royal Army Medical Corps Training* p 321
4   Extracts from *Manual of Elementary Military Hygiene* op cit pp 58–61
5   ibid pp 62–63
6   New Zealand figures exclude death from disease, and are derived from TJ Mitchell & GM Smith, *The Official History of the Great War — Casualties and Medical Statistics* HMSO London 1932
7   C Pugsley op cit p 346

ABBREVIATIONS USED IN NOTES

AWM: Australian War Memorial, Canberra
DC: Dardanelles Commission: Proceedings
IWM: Imperial War Museum, London
LHC: Liddell Hart Centre for Military Archives, King's College, University of London
ML: Mitchell Library, Sydney
NMM: National Maritime Museum, Greenwich, London
OHAAMS: *Official History of the Australian Army Medical Services* (A.G. Butler, 3 Volumes)
PRO: Public Records Office, Kew, London
SL: State Library of Victoria (La Trobe Collection)

Index